Missionaries Go Home?

MISSIONARIES GO HOME?

A Sociological Interpretation of an African Response to Christian Missions

A Study in Sociology of Knowledge

by

E. M. Uka

PETER LANG

Berne · Frankfurt am Main · New York · Paris

CIP-Titelaufnahme der Deutschen Bibliothek

Uka, E. M.:
Missionaries go home?: a sociolog. interpretation
of an African response to christian missions; a study
in sociology of knowledge / by E. M. Uka.–
Berne; Frankfurt am Main; New York; Paris: Lang, 1989
ISBN 3-261-03874-8

Printed by Weihert-Druck GmbH, Darmstadt

DEDICATION

This book is dedicated to the European and African Missionaries who served, suffered and died in honest endeavour to lay the foundations of the Christian Gospel in Africa.

They serve as beacons of light and as land-marks in the history of Christianity in Africa.

TABLE OF CONTENTS

5

LIST OF TABLES

ACKNOWLEDGMENT

I owe a great debt of gratitude to many people and organizations who have supported and guided me along the way.

First of all, I thank the Presbyterian Church in Canada for their suport and encouragements throughout my Doctoral program out of which, this book has emerged. My thanks also go to the Program Agency of the Presbyterian Church in the United States who awarded me a one-year full scholar-ship at Princeton Theological Seminary. The Trustees and Director of the Overseas Ministeries Study Center did me a world of good by providing a most comfortable and convenient base (in both housing and library facilities) to carry out my research and writings.

I am also highly indebted to the distinguished members of my dissertation committee - Dr. Gerald H. Anderson, co-editor of Mission Tends, Professor Graybeal and Dr. Karen Brown both of the Graduate School, Drew University. Their suggestions, comments and corrections were most helpful.

I wish to express my indebtedness to the libraries which made it possible for me to make a thankful use of their services. Don Vorp of Drew University library, John Dickenson of Speer Library, Princeton Theological Seminary, Mrs. Margaret Bronkema of the Missionary Research Library, Ventnor, New Jersey and Mrs. Barbara Griffs of Union Theological Seminary, New York, were particularly helpful to me.

I wish also to place on record my thanks to Fred Bronkema of I.D.O.C. Participation Project, Eugene L. Stockwell, Secretary of the Division of Overseas Ministeries of the National Council of Churches, U.S.A., Professor Charles W. Forman of Yale University and Professor Ogbu U. Kalu of the University of Nigeria, Nsukka for the useful articles they sent to me.

My gratitude to my wife is incalculable as it is to my three sons Nnamdi, Chidiebere and Kelechi whose interruptions reminded me that I had responsibilitiès towards them as a father.

Finally, I wish to thank Mrs. Ruth Wise and Mrs. Linda Lancaster for typing the scripts.

PREFACE

This work is a sociological perspective on Afro-Euro en-counter in the context of missions. It was a doctoral dissertation submitted to the Graduate School of Drew University in Madison, New Jersey, U.S.A. Its original title was: Moratorium: Ideology or Utopia? A Sociological Interpretation of an African Response to Christian Mission.

Now, the dissertation has been reworked for publication under the title: Missionaries Go Home? A Sociological Interpreta-tion of An African Response to Western Christian Mission.

Technical terms in the work have been removed and in some cases simplified for easy comprehension by both students and scholars.

In becoming a Christian through missionary instruction and family upbringing, I looked forward to a church such as envis-aged by Bonhoeffer when he said:

> The church is the church only when it exists [i.e., is there] for others. To make a start, it should give away all its property to those in need. The clergy must live solely on the free-will offerings of their congregations, or possibly engage in some secular calling. The church must share in the secular problems of ordinary human life, not dominating, but helping and serving. It must tell men of every calling what it means to live in Christ, to live for others.[1]

Also I looked forward to a world in which production would be organized for the benefit of people rather than the extraction of profits; a world where there would be no balance of payments problems; a world where goods could move freely to where they are needed most and where they would be put to the best possible use; a world in which all kinds of useful labour would be equally valued and where each person would be recompensed equally for a day's work. My dream was one of a world in which the

---

[1] Dietrich Bonhoeffer, **Letters and Papers from Prison**, enlarged ed. (New York: Macmillan Co., 1972), pp. 382-383. It has to be remembered that Bonhoeffer wrote in a situation in which the church in Germany received direct financial help from the state.

division of labour among individuals, regions and continents would be such that it would promote the overall well-being of mankind and not threaten or jeopardize world peace, prosperity or progress.

I thought Christianity and Western civilization would offer and foster such a world since missionaries portrayed Western civilization as resulting from "ideas derived from the gospel of the kingdom; the brotherhood of man and the fatherhood of God; ... the promise of human progress; the rights of man; the removal of oppression; the reign of justice and love displacing the reign of force."[2]

My hopes are being dashed as I behold the twentieth century socio-economic and historical realities, particularly the activities of Western "Christian" powers in Third World affairs and the tendency of some missionaries to acquiesce in national conduct which directly contravenes the very Gospel they proclaim and propagate.

My response (typical of other African Christians as well) to the incongruities of Western "Christian" civilization is that of confusion and protests. These protests do not reflect despair and disappointment but rather prompt African Christians into activist roles in history since these Christians seek to translate their hopes in Christianity into actuality. Although some responses reflect certain kinds of protest, this study is not a protest per se but an explanation of a protest.

Essentially, this work is a radical study of African missions since it questions some of the underlying socio-cultural and economic assumptions which underlie the thinking of missionaries and the missionized. It is the argument of this study that the impact of the sociological factors acting on missionary agents and on mission converts is so great that to ignore them in any missiological treaties will amount to a great dis-service to missiology. Therefore, the focus of the study is on the socio-political and economic environment of "missionary senders" and "missionary receivers" and the impact of such a milieu on the thinking of either group, both before and after their enforced contact.

[2] Robert Handy, **A Christian America: Protestant Hopes and Historical Realities** (New York: Oxford University Press, 1971), p. 110.

FOREWORD

Practically everywhere, our social institutions, if not the ideas that form their foundation, like life in general, are in a crisis. The crisis has drawn critics from many quarters and all ages. But the greatest need of our age is for understanding and action rather than fear. The reason is simple enough. The human crisis is always a crisis of understanding, of knowledge and action.

No where is the crisis of our age more manifest and the critics of our time, more militant than in the post-colonial societies. The peoples of these new states, whether in South America, Afica or Asia, are animated by two powerful, almost independent, and often opposed motives -- the desire to control their individual destinies and the desire to participate as equal partners in setting world agenda. Paradoxically, they are forced to carry the cultural load of their departing imperial masters, both temporal and spiritual, just as they must, at least initially, work with the institutional infrastructure created by colonial rule.

The institutional infrastructures left by colonialism are under attack. At the political level, post-colonial societies are working out policies and strategies that might help them to sustain self-reliant development. Leaders of organized religions, which by definition are rooted in colonialism, are beginning to question the traditional structures which link their institutions with the Metropolitan Church; and particularly resented are those features of the institutions that are demonstrably neo-colonialist.

Missionaries Go Home? is an interpretation of a rebellion by the post-colonial church against forms of institutional structures which still govern missionary enterprises in the Third World. The study is not in the tradition of protest literature on missology. It is an intellectual exploration of the reaction of the post-colonial Church against continuing "colonizing evangelization" and the confusion of transplanted Western culture with the transplanted Christian Gospel.

The problem discussed by the Revd. Dr. E.M. Uka in this path-breaking work was thrown up by history - the recent encounter between the Western World and its institutions and the rest of the world. History creates a framework within which great thinkers and artists do their work; and works that ultimately change or challenge the accepted "world view" of a given age owe much to the history of their time. If every age in history has its own pre-occupation, the post-colonial society is certain-

11

ly preoccupied with the problem of inequality -- inequality among nations and within nations. This study deals with institutional inequality within the Christian Church, particularly the problem of unequal access in the process of the evangelical enterprise by nations united by the same faith in Christ.

Our understanding of social phenomena is sometimes limited by what Susanne Langer calls "generative ideas or a **grande idee** -- the wealth of formulative notions with which the mind meets experiences".[1] The generative idea that inspired this study is the call for a Moratorium in the ways Christian evangelical enterprises are conducted. The Revd. John Gatu states the case for a moratorium most graphically when he asserts that:

> We cannot build the church in Africa on alms given by overseas churches, nor are we serving the cause of the kingdom by turning all bishops, general secretaries, moderators, presidents, superintendents, into good enthusiastic beggars, by always swinging the tune of poverty in the churches of the Third World. Let the mission be the mission of God in the world, but not of the West to the Third World (page 195 of this book).

The central problem, therefore, is the dominant role which the West and its institutions play in the lives, institutions and in the cultures of the Third World. This problem is some how paradoxical. It has surfaced at a critical period in world history when cultural interdependence among the nations of the world is almost leading to cultural convergence in the field of organized religions. It is precisely becauce of this development that the loss or apparent loss of cultural and institutional autonomy is viewed as an unacceptable political price to pay in the name of cultural-religious convergence.

Religion has long been recognized as an integral part of European nationalism. The Reformation would have run an entrely different course were it completely apolitical. In the Third World, an understanding of the political environment within which the moratorium question was posed is essential to a comprehension of this question. The author called attention to this factor and many others. He has provided his readers some in-

---

[1] Langer, S., **Philosophy in a New Key** (New York: Mentor Books,1962), p. 19.

sights into the political economy of organized religion. Within this framework of political economy, the author's interest has been essentially interpretative. He can be portrayed as a pilgrim in search of understanding of a social phenomenon: the differing interpretations given to the moratorium question by the two parties concerned. The parties are united in Christ but divided by their worlds.

According to Plato, truth or knowledge presents itself in basically four shapes. Imagination is the first gateway to knowledge, another is action, a third is through science, and a fourth through dialectic. If we accept the Hegelian thesis that "The truth is the whole", we are likely to conclude that each of the four Platonian epistemological ladder must be experienced, each for its own sake and for the partial perspective it yields. For a rounded knowledge, we would need not one but all the four perspectives. There is an alternative interpretation. "Each rung of the (epistemological) ladder, each segment of the divided line, ... is a vantage point on truth. "Each is in itself partial, but each is nonetheless accurate and in some distinctive way essential to the achievement of knowledge. Truth, which is not reducable to any one prospective on reality is grasped only through the totality of those perspectives, by holding them all together all at once".[2]

Dr. Uka's theoretical approach is not Platonic, at least not in its formal sense. It is macrosociological in places but its dominant theme is constructionist. The Sociology of knowledge which informs the study is rooted on the promise that every category of understanding, every social structure of meaning, is a creation of human mind arising from social interaction. In short, that social reality is constructed. Without ignoring other contributors, Dr. Uka draws heavily from Karl Mannheim, whose theoretical insights he improves upon (pp. 29-47; 251-255). Applying Karl Mannheim's categories -- Ideology and Utopia - to the moratorium debate, the author attributes to the dominant European group an **ideological** orientation and to the dominated Africans, a **utopian** orientation. He sees the interaction between the two groups as producing a dialectical reaction and also a programme of action, of which the moratorium is the end product. In his words "... the encounter between the African conservative ideology and the European expansionist ideology produced

---

[2]Allan, G., **The Importances of the Past** (A Mediation on the authority of tradition) (State University of New York Press, 1986), p. x.

an African revolutionary mentality ... The thinking of the dominant class is ideological (and) unconsciously tend to maintain,
protect and defend the status quo. The African group with its
utopian mentality is critical of the existing patterns of relationship (which) it considers inadequate, faulty and outdated" (p.
248).

From a sociological point of view an idelogy may be
defined as a form of world view (explicit or implicit), which
inspires a programme of action for organizing the resources,
institutions, purposes and power relations of society. History
is the real test of ideology because history provides the actual
battle ground of the human values which ideology represents.[3]
Ideology is both the distortion of thought by interest - public
or private, consciously known or not. It is also the study of
such distortion.[4] The author, true to his stated objective of
not pursuing the sociological theory of knowledge, is not interested in the process by which social reality is distorted. He
simply takes them for granted.

There is no question but that the Euro-American missionaries represent a priviledged group, a **status quo,** and African
church leaders, a deprived class, in the mission enterprise. Whether by extension the former is ideological in orientation and
the later utopian will probably be debated. What does not call
for a debate is the impressive scholarship of this study whose
thesis is logically and convincingly argued.

Victor C. Uchendu
Professor of Sociology and Anthropology
University of Calabar
Calabar, Nigeria

---

[3] Auerbach, M.M., **The Conservative Illusion,** (Columbia University
Press, 1959) pp. 6; 251.

[4] Macrae, D., **Ideology and Society,** (London, Heinemann, 1961),p.64.

INTRODUCTION

The Subject of this book is on the call on Western missionaries in the early 1970's by African, Asian and Latin American church leaders to go home. This call, particularly by the All African Conference of Churches during its meeting in Lusaka, must be understood in the context of the world missionary situation and the world capitalist system.

Missionary thinking has been dominated by theological categories. The call has been interpreted in theological categories as well. This study attempts an alternative analysis in primarily sociological categories. It analyzes the socio-economic and political conditions under which the call was made, and the social location, temporal orientation and collective aspiration of the group from which the call emanates. It argues that the call was partially a consequence of the socio-economic and political conditions under which the advocates "lived and moved and had their being". It attempts to grapple with the hidden tensions underlying the call and tries to expose those tensions.

The conceptual tool for the analysis is the Sociology of Knowledge with its method of a systematic investigation and analysis of the social and historical contexts out of which ideas and beliefs develop.

This analysis deals with the contemporary missionary ideas of John Gatu and Burgess Carr from Africa, Emerito Nacpil from the Philippines and Jose Miguez-Bonino from Latin America in relation to the call.

The study employs Karl Mannheim's sociology of knowledge which is concerned with social determination of ideas and the identification of ideas with the mind-set of particular groups of people. Mannheim's method provides "ideal type" constructs-"ideology" and "utopia"--for categorizing and organizing different perspectives through which experiences may be interpreted and towards which divergent groups respectively gravitate. Ideological thinking relates to a social perspective concerned with preserving the existing social and political arrangements, and in so doing becomes blind to the disruptive and negative factors within it. Utopian mentality seeks to destroy the existing social order in order to usher in a new and better one. It does not see any valid or useful aspects inherent in the existing social order.

With Mannheim's method and categories, the study proceeds to determine how Africans and Europeans think by analyzing their socio-historical conditions before and after their enforced contact. Their encounter produced a dominant European

15

group whose mentality has ideological tendencies and a dominated and dependent African group whose thinking protrays utopian characteristics.

This analysis concludes that the call is "utopian". It arises from a dominated group perspective. It is born out of disatisfaction with the then existing injustices and inequities in the socio-economic and missionary world order. Hence it is critical of the situation and seeks to change it. It is sensitive to new possibilities which offer alternatives to the present order of things. Though it is destructive in terms of denouncing present injustices, it is constructive in the sense of proposing a better order free from the extant injustices of domination. In effect, the call, when interpreted as having utopian characteristics, tends to become a useful instrument for critical social thought.

By interpreting the call sociologically, this study attempts to dramatize the socio-economic and political issues which must no longer be ignored in missiology. Finally, the study portrays the conflict generated by the call, which manifests a tension between "social context" and "social vision", as constructive and functional to the missionary endeavor since it offers opportunities for a more realistic appraisal of the issues of power relations in Afro-European missionary organization.

The format of the whole study goes like this:

Chapter I refers to the paradox of Western Christian presence in Africa.

Chapter II describes the essential features of sociology of knowledge. It isolates Karl Mannheim's formulation as the theoretical framework for the analysis of moratorium. This chapter draws attention to Mannheim's categories (Ideology and utopia), his research method, and the three essential elements of his system. It also comments on the application of Mannheim's conclusions to the moratorium question

Chapter III and **IV** examine the socio-historic base of each party connected with the moratorium, noting their ideological way of thinking before their encounter.

Chapter V deals with the encounter and its consequences which inaugurated a dominant-dependent relationship between missionary-sending churches in Europe and the missionary-receiving churches in Africa. This dominant/dependent relationship later developed into ideological/utopian patterns of thinking in the cross-cultural missionary movement between Europe and Africa.

Chapter VI presents the contemporary socio-economic and missionary contexts which the moratorium reacts to.

Chapter VII reviews the moratorium discussion in World Missionary Conferences and establishes its utopian tendencies. The chapter concludes with an assessment of the functional contributions of the moratorium debate to the Euro-Afro missionary enterprise and the author's personal remarks on the subject.

Give us a full-rounded chance. The sea of difference between you and us should be no more. The sea of our failure to bring any contribution to the Kingdom of God shall be no more. You white folks may bring your gold, your great banks and your big buildings, your sanitation and other marvellous achievements to the manger, but that will not be enough. Let the Chinese and the Japanese and the Indians bring their frankincense of ceremony, but that will not be enough. We black people must step in with our myrrh of child-like faith . . . then the gifts will be complete.

. . . God grant that you who have heard this plea from Africa will trust us . . . and will give us a chance to make that contribution to the world which is in the design of God.

Dr. James E. K. Aggrey of Ghana (International Missionary Council, Lake Mohonk, New York, 1921), quoted by Byang Kato, **Theological Pitfalls in Africa** (Kenya: Evangel Publishing House, 1975), p. 133.

The churches of the Third World must be allowed to find their own identity. The continuation of the present missionary movement is a hindrance to this selfhood of the church. . . . Let mission be the mission of God in the world, but not of the West to the Third World. . . . By discontinuance of missionaries and money in the churches of the Third World, we shall have provided for a definite transformation, not only of a new relationship but of new images of the church. . . . The Gospel will then have a deeper and a more far reaching effect than our mission Christianity has provided so far.

John Gatu, Presbyterian Executive, Kenya (now Chairman of the AACC), in 1972, cited by Paul R. Gregory (General Secretary, Mission Division, United Church Board of World Mission, USA) in "Towards a UCBWM Stance on 'Moratorium,'" a personal statement.

CHAPTER I

THE PARADOX OF WESTERN CHRISTIAN MISSIONARIES' PRESENCE IN AFRICA

Robert Rotberg writes in his book, **Christian Missionaries and the Creation of Northern Rhodesia (1880-1924):**

The activities of Christian missionaries are of outstanding importance in the emergence of modern tropical Africa. The missionaries purvey the ideas of the West and are responsible both for the earliest articulation of these new concepts and for their careful introduction into indigenous circles. They necessarily became agents of many types of social, economic, and political change. As such, the missionaries exercised, individually and collectively, a powerful influence, both directly and indirectly, over scattered villages and, in time, whole tribes. They prepared young Africans to appreciate the advantages of Western life and encouraged them to benefit from the temporal and spiritual concepts that were part of its foundation. The stations subsequently became the training grounds of indigenous leadership and, at the same time, the centers of anti-European disaffection.[1]

Elements of this anti-European disaffection have been building up since the 1900's with the conquest, colonization and Christianization of tropical Africa. It hat erupted in the call for a moratorium on Western missionaries and funds in the 1970's. The call manifests the desire on the part of Africans to give a place to indigenous leadership, to be self-reliant and to abolish the colonial relationship which persists in the missionary enterprise. The call reflects a desire for liberation from the oppressive paternalism of some Western missionaries. In a sense, the call for a moratorium poses for Africans the vision of a new order of relationships free from the injustices and incongruities of foreign institutions and domination.

This study, therefore, inquires into the compeling socio-economic and political circumstances in Africa and the West under which the missionary enterprise was conducted and the consequences arising therefrom.

---

[1] Robert I. Rotberg, **Christian Missionaries and the Creation of Northern Rhodesia (1880-1924)** (Princeton, N.J.: Princeton University Press, 1965), p. vii.

One of such consequences has been the call by Africans for missionaries to go home. Our concern in this study is not whether the call is right or wrong, needed or not needed. [2] Instead we shall focus on why the call was made and what was its character and content.

The major premise for the inquiry is Mannheim's sociology of knowledge which argues that a people's social group, their temporal orientation and collective aspiration rather than their inherent nature significantly determine the way they think and act. Mannheim says the task of sociology of knowledge is "to comprehend thought in the concrete setting of an historical social situation out of which . . . thought only very gradually emerges." [3]

From the outset, we have to recognize that European missionaries deserve credit for introducing Christianity into Africa about four centuries ago. Their task was not an easy nor an enviable one. They encountered problems of health, persecution, language, culture, transport and communication and even death. Some had no salaries and they had to trade to earn a living while they preached the Gospel. Africa owes the foundation of its modern western education, its industrial economy, its medical, scientific and vernacular literature developments to these missionaries.

But this is only one side of the coin. The other side of the coin which concerns us in this study deals with the bane that accompanied the blessings of the Western missionary enterprise and the reaction arising from it.

----

[2] Analysis of the Call as right or wrong or for what type is needed has been done by a host of authors and Ecumenical ad-hoc Committees. Some of the authors include: Pius Wakatama, **Independence for the Third World Church** (Downers Grove, Illinois: Inter-Varsity Press, 1976); Howard J. Habegger, **The Mennonite,** Decembre 2, 1975, pp. 684-685; Peter Wagner, "Colour the Moratorium Grey, "**International Review of Mission** April 1975): 165-176; Gerhard Mey, "Theological Education in a Post Moratorium World, "**International Review of Mission** (April 1975); 187-192.

[3] Karl Mannheim, **Ideology an Utopia: An Introduction of the Sociology of Knowledge,** trans. Louis Writh and Edward Shils (New York: Harcourt, Brace, 1954), p. 3. It should be noted that Mannheim was not dealing with a missionary problem, at least not directly. But his sociology of knowledge helps us to delineate a framework for the analysis and categorization of the mentalities of those involved in the moratorium debate in a clearer light than the missiologists have done.

The missionaries were part of a larger program of European colonization of Africa. Their activities cannot be properly appraised unless seen in the light of their connection with the European trader, diplomat and settler. The Christianity they brought appeared in many denominational forms throughout the continent: Roman Catholics, Anglicans, Methodists, Lutherans, Presbyterians, Baptists, and so forth. They operated as rival factions and became divisive rather than unitive. The new religion was foreign to the Africans and hovered on the periphery of their hearts. It introduced an element of ambivalence intheir religious mentality. The Africans sensed and resented, from the outset of their encounter with Western missionaries in the nineteenth century, what appeared to be pretense and hypocrisy on the part of the missionaries. They noted an apparent lack of congruence between the missionaries' utterances and their actions. They observed that some of the missionaries did not seem to be involved in the vital issues of Christian concern, such as relationships in which the African was despised, enslaved and exploited by his European colonizers. They were not clearly and openly against imperialism and their voices were not forcefully heard on issues of colonial abuse and misuse of the Africans in their own land. The missionaries did not, in most cases, affirm Christian commitment to justice for the weak and the Christian obligation to protest against injustice and exploitation. They tended to repress the Biblical view of justice and politics. Often the missionaries joined their other European tribesmen to use the slogan of "communist menace" as the real cause of political problems in Africa and as the key to the interpretation of such problems. Within political turbulence of this century, the Third World Christians expect missionaries, indeed all Christians, to be bold and thoughtful, risking in prayer and faith, the preaching and practice of the great Biblical principles at stake in world affairs. This posture may place them in opposition to big business and against the foreign policies of great capitalist nations.

Yet some Western missionaries are caught between a desire to be faithful to the gospel--to keep it from being too strongly identified with European political and business interests-- and a desire to build support from their home church members who often find it difficult to understand the political and economic complexities of Western capitalism in Africa, Asia or Latin America. Although missionaries sometimes desire to be faithful to the nationals struggling for liberation from indigenous and foreign structures of economic and political injustice, they do not want to lose the support of their home churches. This dilem-

21

ma calls for recognition as we attempt to place the call for a moratorium on missionaries and mission funds in its proper socio-political and historical context. So our concern is to investigate and account for the social factors which led to the call for moratorium.

We shall consider the moratorium call from the All Africa Conference of Churches which met in May 1974 at Lusaka, Zambia. It was during this conference that the assembly declared inter alia:

> To enable the African Church to achieve the power of becoming a true instrument of liberating and reconciling the African people, as well as finding solutions to economic and social dependency, our option as a matter of policy has to be a Moratorium on all external assistance in money and personnel. . . . We recommend this option as the only potent means of becoming truly and authentically ourselves while remaining a respected and responsible part of the Universal Church. . . . .[4]

This option for the churches in Africa constitutes the heart of the moratorium question that became a central issue in almost every ecumenical conversation in the early seventies. The Lusaka declaration was the climax of a series of developments which was sparked by John Gatu, an African church leader from Kenya, who proposed the moratorium call, in October 1971 during his speech at a Milwaukee Mission Festival of the Reformed Church in America. He proposed a moratorium on all Western missionaries and mission funds for at least five years.

Since then, moratorium in missionary theory has become a term used to suggest a period of time in which all Western mission agencies should stop sending missionary personnel and money to churches in Africa. It also means the departure of missionaries now serving in Africa, a halt to the sending of new mission workers, and the termination of all financial aid to mission-related churches in Africa. In sum, the moratorium is a call for the dismantling of the traditional methods of doing mission. It is a search for new patterns, new relationships, new paradigms. It is an attempt at self-affirmation, self-identity and a rejection of a dominant-dependent relationship within the world missionary movement.

---

[4] Ecumenical Press Service, June 20, 1974, p.11

The moratorium proposal seems to arouse the consternation of Western missionary agencies who, for over a century, have been sending missionaries and money to churches in Africa. For example, a former President of the American Society of Missiologists, Louis J. Luzbetak, said:

> Let met express my personal view about a popular subject, which we cannot leave out in any discussion . . . the so called "moratorium," a strategy of self reliance by means of a temporary withdrawal of all foreign funding and personnel as expressly requested by a particular church. No matter how radical the idea may seem, too many highly respected individuals support the idea. . . . Nevertheless, somehow I wish that a moratorium would be declared on the moratorium. . . . I am suggesting that missiologists grapple with the real issue. As I see it, the real issue is not the moratorium itself but how to achieve international and mutual enrichment. The word "moratorium" is misleading and confusing.[5]

Commenting on the moratorium call, Johannes Verkuyl, a renowned Dutch missiologist, said:

> The focus of attention should not be a moratorium but on the task which still remains to be done. . . . Hundreds of millions of people stand either wholly or in part outside the range of gospel communication. This is no time to while away precious moments and waste reams of paper in endless debates about moratorium.[6]

---

[5] Louis J. Luzbetak, "Two Centuries of Cultural Adaptation in American Church Action: Praise, Censure or Challenge?" in **American Missions in Bicentennial Perspective**, R. Pierce Beaver, ed. (Pasadena, Cal.: William Carey Library, 1977), pp. 348-349.

[6] J. Verkuyl, **Contemporary Missiology: An Introduction**, trans. and ed. Dale Cooper (Grand Rapids, Mich.: Eerdmans Publishing Co., 1978, p. 339.

Other responses from the West to the moratorium call were not very favourable at the outset.[7] Concerning Western responses in general, Emilio Castro, editor of the **International Review of Mission,** said: "We seem to have organized ourselves in Mission in such a way that we cannot stop. It is almost as if we were a great business enterprise with its own rhythm of production which cannot be interrupted without causing great calamity."[8] The debate that has ensued between the advocates of moratorium and their opponents has, according to Castro, "led us (i.e. Westerners) to caricature our neighbour, accusing him of being an 'enemy of mission' or a neo-colonialist."[9]

One of the central arguments of this study is that the call for moratorium on Western missionaries and funds has been largely misunderstood in the West. This misunderstanding is reflected in a host of questions raised by the West such as:

What is the reason for the moratorium call?

Does it call into question the purpose of mission?

Is the call realistic?

Is the foreign missionary a sign of the universality of the church?

Would the absence of foreign missionaries increase the isolation of your church?

Does the call reveal a lack of gratitude on the part of receiving churches?[10]

---

[7] Howard J. Habegger, "Responses to Moratorium," **The Mennonite,** November 25, 1975; cf. Robert McFee Brown, **Theology in a New Key** (Philadelphia: Westminster Press, 1987), pp. 102-129.

[8] Emilio Castro, "Moratorium," **IRM** (April 1975): 120.

[9] Ibid.

[10] "The Moratorium Debate: Responses to a Questionnaire," **IRM** (April 1975): 148-164. Canon Burgess Carr, former general secretary of the All Africa Conference of Churches (AACC), tried to answer some of these questions in his address to the Executive Committee of the Division of Overseas Ministries of the National Council of Churches of Christ in the USA. See Burgess Carr, "The Mission of the Moratorium," **Occasional Bulletin of the Missionary Research** Library (March/April 1975): 1-9; Harvie Conn raised further ques-

These questions have arisen because at the outset, some Western missionaries and missiologists interpreted the call to mean either a rejection of, or a retreat from mission.[11] Some interpret it to be an act of ingratitude[12] on the part of the Africans who for over a century have enjoyed the free services of the missionaries. Others consider it to be a sign of the retreat of Christianity, or the advance of Communism in Africa;[13] yet some interpret it as contrary to the universality of the Christian church, or as having isolationist implications for churches in Africa.[14] In sum, most of the Western critics consider the call as both unrealistic and irresponsible.[15]

The fact that the moratorium call has been made and that it has been opposed in principle suggests that there now exist

tions arising from Western responses. See Conn, "The Moratorium Massage to Evangelicals," **Issues: Briefs from Westminster Theological Seminary** (January 1977): 1-3.

[11] Arthur P. Johnston, "The WCC's Impact on the Future of Missions, **"Evangelical Missions Quarterly** 12 (1976): 78; W. Bryant Hicks, "Why We Still Need More Missionaries," **Review and Expositor: The Impact of the Third World on Missions, A Baptist Theological Journal** 74 (Spring 1977): 210-228. At the International Congress on World Evangelization, held at Lausanne in July 1974, Billy Graham in his opening address rejected the idea of a moratorium on sending missionaries. See J. D. Douglas, ed., **Let the Earth Hear His Voice** (Minneapolis, Minn.: World Wide Publications, 1975.

[12] "The Moratorium Debate: Responses to a Questionnaire," **IRM**, p. 159; see also Wade T. Coggins, "What's Behind the Idea of a Missionary Moratorium?," **Christianity Today,** November 22, 1972, pp. 172-173.

[13] Johnston, pp. 78, 85.

[14] Gerald H. Anderson, "A Moratorium on Missionaries?," **IDOC No. 9-- The Future of the Missionary Enterprise** (May 1974: 83-86. Anderson claims, "We also wish to affirm the validity of the missionary presence as essential to our understanding of the universality of the church." ". . . The moratorium . . . would limit us to mission where we are, an altogether unbiblical concept."

[15] Habegger, "Responses to the Moratorium." This article is the second in the series of Habegger's three articles on the moratorium. See first article: "Moratorium: What's Behind the Call?," **The Mennonite,** November 18, 1975, pp. 650-651; and third article: "Moratorium and the Future of Mennonite World Mission," **The Mennonite,** December 2, 1975, pp. 684-685.

competing views on cross-cultural mission between the West and Africa, i.e., between traditional senders of missionaries and traditional receivers of missionaries. The situation has the potential for creating distrust between the parties involved. And within the context of distrust, no one any longer inquires into the content of beliefs and assertions to determine whether they are valid or not, nor does one confront an assertion with relevant evidence. Rather, an entirely new question is introduced: Why has there emerged a rival African point of view that challenges the traditional view? At this stage, the competing views become functionalized and interpreted in terms of their psychological, economic, social or racial sources and functions. In General, this functionalizing of views occurs when the intention of statements is doubted or considered biased. At this level one no longer examines the evidence for or against the statement but only the grounds for its being made. Such alien statements, says Robert Merton, [16] are explained by or imputed to special interests, distorted perspectives and social positions. In folk thought, this could involve reciprocal attacks on the integrity of opponents. In systematic thought, it leads to ideological argumentation, that is, arguments in which systems of ideas of a social group function, at the same time, to affirm, disguise and advance its sectional interest. This is the point where Mannheim's sociology of knowledge and its connection with Marx's theory of ideology become relevant for our study.

---

[16] Robert Merton, **Social Theory and Social Structure** (Glencoe, Ill.: The Free Press, 1951), pp. 218-219.

CHAPTER II

THE SOCIOLOGY OF KNOWLEDGE

The sociology of knowledge invites us to discover how thought is shaped or determined by socio-historic factors. Its basic contention is that beliefs and ideas are influenced by the social and historical circumstances of the persons or group of people who hold them. As a discipline, the sociology of knowledge is a systematic investigation and analysis of the social and historical contexts from which ideas and beliefs develop. It is concerned both with the way in which systems of thought are conditioned by social factors and with the relationship between systems of thought and their social milieu. As a branch of learning, its first aim is to understand the socio-historical origin of ideas. It excludes unprovable ontological or metaphysical questions. Hence it constitutes a method of explaining ideas in the light of their social situation. The discipline is not concerned with the theory of knowledge. It does not deal with the problem of the validity of ideas, or attempt to find out if they are real or illusory. With regard to this distinction, the sociology of knowledge strives to be non-evaluative, and makes every effort to avoid passing value judgments as to the intrinsic superiority of science over mythology or the "higher" truth of religion as compared to the "mere" experimental truth of science. Knowledge in the context of sociology of knowledge is a non-evaluative term and carries with it no implication as to the truth or falsity of that knowledge.

At all stages of sociology of knowledge we are concerned only with establishing a relationship between ideas and people and not between statements and reality (material truth) or between statements and other statements on a strictly logical level (formal truth). That is, we are not conerned with establishing the material or formal validity of ideas and thought systems with which we deal as our subject matter, but only in discovering their subjective meaning for the human agents involved, and in relating the acts of judgment through which these subjective meanings arise, to certain more pervasive currents of thought, and the social situations which condition them.

The sociologist of knowledge is interested in how the problems that knowledge attempts to solve reflect the problems with which a social group is faced. He may describe how the structure of people's societies influences the structure of their thought. He may show how certain parts of people's experiences become more vital to them at some times rather than others. And he may even attempt to demonstrate that certain of their thought structures have lost their utility for purposes of certain practical adjustments, or that they operate to inhibit the most efficient solution of specific problems. But even in this last case the sociologist of knowledge is relating ideas to people, and not ideas to the objects to which they may refer. The epistemological implications that may be found in these observations may be of concern to the philosopher, but not of immediate concern to sociologists. The most that sociology of knowledge may contribute to the general theory of knowledge is to demonstrate the sociological limits within which a conceptual position can hope to attain acceptance. That is, it may demonstrate within a sociological frame of reference, and in terms of the human agents who do the thinking, who are limited by their social heritage and the structure of the society in which they exist, why specific ideas are not likely to attain complete acceptability by all people at all times and under all conditions, and why no particular individual can possibly attain a total picture of reality which would include all possible human points of view. In a common adage this insight is expressed thus: "A man is a product of his times."

The sociological theory of knowledge, as contrasted with the sociology of knowledge, is an epistemological position which attempts to infer from the findings of sociology of knowledge certain hypotheses concerning the relationship between propositions and that which the propositions are about. Of such a nature are the statements of Emile Durkheim about the social locus of the referents of the categories of time, space, causality and the like. If this position is pressed too far, it results in a kind of social idealism which posits that the "world" is not the "idea" of any specific individual, but a kind of "collective idea" and exists only in the "collective consciousness." When Durkheim makes this kind of statement, he is no longer speaking about sociology but about epistemology. Such epistemological statements must be carefully distinguished from the preliminary analysis of sociology of knowledge which Durkheim makes about social factors, such as religious festivals, kinship and clan groups, the spatial arrangements of villages and the like, and their influence on the primitive conceptions of the categories of time, space, causality, relation, being and so forth.[1]

---

[1] Emile Durkheim, **Elementary Forms of Religious Life** (New York: The Free Press, 1915), pp. 1–33, 235–267, 337–455.

In this study we shall bear in mind this distinction between the sociological theory of knowledge and the sociology of knowledge, and the exclusive reference of sociology of knowledge propositions to the relationship between **thought and thinkers,** and **not thoughts and facts.** Our emphasis will be on the people's social existence which significantly determines their consciousness or their orientation to other social groups. By limiting ourselves to this aspect of the sociology of knowledge, we are delimiting our application of Mannheim to exclude his sociological theory of knowledge. Being more of a philosopher than a sociologist, Mannheim tended to fuse and confuse the two approaches to the study of knowledge. This confusion has exposed his system to sharp criticisms.[2]

Having limited the method of sociology of knowledge per se, let us briefly consider the nature of sociology of knowledge research, the focus of interest from which it approaches its data, the conceptual tools which it may find useful and the aspect of ideas with which it is primarily concerned.

As in all sociological inquiry on the interpretative level, sociology of knowledge must make some basic analytical distinctions in approaching its problems. There are first the social facts to be explained. For sociology of knowledge these facts are to be found in the thoughts or ideas that are explicit or implicit in communication between individuals or groups. Although we are primarily concerned with the thoughts and ideas that play a role in the communicative process, we nevertheless have to approach these ideas indirectly, that is, through their concrete manifestations in language or some other symbolism. Furthermore, sociology of knowledge is not concerned with thought of a theoretically isolated individual, existing in a social vacuum, "but with knowledge of concrete persons who are members of social groups and who orient their thinking to other persons by attempting to communicate or express their ideas in some overt manner, either by

---

[2]For a critique and evaluation of Mannheim's sociology of knowledge see: Jacques J. Maquet, **The Sociology of Knowledge: Its Structure and Its Relation to the Philosophy of Knowledge—A Critical Analysis of the Systems of Karl Mannheim and Pitirim A. Sorokin** (Boston: The Beacon Press, 1951), pp. 49-69; Frank E. Hartung, "Problems of Sociology of Knowledge" in **The Sociology of Knowledge, A Reader,** ed. James E. Curtis and John W. Petras (New York and Washington: Praeger Publishers, 1970), pp. 686-705; Robert Merton, **Social Theory and Social Structures** (Glencoe, Illinois: The Free Press, 1951), pp. 258-264.

embodying them in language or expressing them in gestures, ritual or art."[3] The sociologist of knowledge is not merely concerned with understanding the meaningful elements of knowledge; he must also, as a sociologist, attempt to relate these meaningful complexes to the socio-historical conditions within which they occur. For example, it is not enough to say that the call of moratorium is the product of a deeply rooted resentment which the advocates have for Western missionaries. We must go further than that to discover the genesis of this resentment within the system of socio-ecclesiastical organization which confronts the advocates and within which they function.

· All these elements are necessary to arrive at an adequate sociological explanation: the social actions which provide us with our data, the interpretation of the social actions in order to make them understandable and meaningful, and the causal, functional and structural investigation of the socio-historical situations in which social actions occur and from which individual subjective orientations arise.

Robert Merton has constructed a paradigm[4] in which the major elements in the sociology of knowledge are stated in a compressed and coherent form. In the paradigm, he identifies the existential basis of thought or mental productions as both social and cultural. The social basis includes such items as social position, group-structures, historical situations, ethnic affiliation, power structure and the like. The cultural basis consists of such things as values, culture mentality,"Weltanschauungen"and the like. He locates the mental production to be analyzed in moral beliefs, ideologies, religious beliefs, social norms and the like. These are related to their existential bases either by causal or functional relations. The nature of resulting relationshipas is expressed in such terms as determination, correspondence, conditioning, functional interdependence and dependence. Merton's paradigm articulates the general agreement among sociologists of knowledge. He shows that the sociology of knowledge lends itself to classification chiefly in terms of locating the existential bases of ideas, identifying the ideas themselves and their relationship to social and cultural situations. These elements, however, are characteris-

---

[3]Gerard De Gre, "The Sociology of Knowledge and the Problem of Truth," in **The Sociology of Knowledge, A Reader**, ed. Curtis and Petras, p. 662.

[4]Merton, pp. 221-222.

tic of all sociological interpretations that attempt to do justice to both the causal and the meaningful aspects of social action. They do not apply only to the sociology of knowledge. So let us turn to the consideration of their application to the problems that are of particular concern to the sociology of knowledge.

There is first the problem of why in certain social situations specific aspects of experience are stressed more than others. For example we may ask: How did the socio-historical situation of the Middle Ages condition the widespread preoccupation with the problems of the Kingdom of God and the slavation of the soul?[5] Second, the sociology of knowledge seeks to discover the social roots of the manner in which experience is interpreted. It inquires into the concrete ideas that give insight into the ultimate values, sentiments, interests, beliefs and attitudes that influence the perspective or meangingful orientation of persons to their experience. These factors are related to the sociological factors existing in the historical situations in which they are found.

Karl Mannheim's discussion of "ideological" and "utopian" mentalities illustrate this focus of inquiry. The constructs are ideal types, heuristically designed generalizations not restricted to any particular socio-historical situation. Since they fit our objective, we shall apply them to our study. By an "ideological" mentality Manheim means a social perspective that is so much concerned with preserving the existing social and political arrangements that it is blind to any factors that might tend to disrupt or invalidate them. In contrast, the "utopian" mentality is so obsessed with the idea of destroying the existing social order that it cannot see any of the valid or useful aspects that are inherent in it.[6] These two constructs represent two differing perspectives through which experience may be interpreted and towards which divergent social groups may respectively gravitate. Mannheim's sociology of knowledge concerns itself both with the social conditions that influence groups to gravitate towards one or the other of these mentalities and with how particular concrete thoughts may be a function of these more general perspectives.

Since these two concepts in Mannheim's sociology of knowledge will be central to our study of the moratorium call, we shall elaborate on them later. Meanwhile, let us briefly com-

---

[5] Paul Tillich, **Systematic Theology**, vol. 1 (Chicago: University of Chicago Press, 1973), Introduction and Chapter One.

[6] Karl Mannheim, **Ideology and Utopia: An Introduction to the Sociology of Knowledge** (New York: Harcourt, Brace and Company, 1936), p. 31.

ment on our choice of Mannheim's model rather than that of other sociologists of knowledge such as Peter Berger and Thomas Luckman.[7] Berger and Luckman focus on the question of how whatever is accepted as knowledge in a society comes to be accepted as such. For them, sociology of knowledge is concerned with the analysis of the social construction of reality. Berger describes the process as **"Externalization"**...the ongoing outpouring of human being into the world, both in the physical and mental activity of men. **"Objectivation",** the attainment by the product of this activity of a reality that confronts its original producers as a facticity external to and other than themselves. **"Internalization",** the reappropriation by persons of this same reality."[8] This approach leans towards functionalism. Its emphasis tends to be on the production of one uniform "group or national spirit" within any particular society. They make no provision for discovering the reciprocal influence of socio-historical conditions on ideas nor of the construction of diverse and sometimes opposed "total ideologies" within one society or nation. Even if they argue that each group constructs its own reality, they have provided no intellectual bridge or any form of reciprocal interrelationship between different "realities," such as we find in Mannheim's categories of "ideology and utopia." Berger and Luckman's sociology of knowledge could be termed the "passivist theory of knowledge." They do not give indication of "knowledge" or ideas being an instrument of action, which is one of the strong points that Mannheim sought to demonstrate, nor do their system have any revolutionary dimension which Mannheim identified in the clash of conservative ideological mentality and expansionist ideological orientation.

For a fuller understanding of Mannheim's sociology of knowledge, let us examine his intellectual background, his concepts of "ideology" and "utopia" and their relevance for our study.

---

[7] Peter Berger and Thomas Luckman, **Social Construction of Reality** (New York: Doubleday Anchor Book, 1967), p. 3

[8] Peter Berger, **The Sacred Canopy: Elements of a Sociological Theory of Religion** (New York: Doubleday Co., 1967), p. 4.

Mannheim's Background

Karl Mannheim (1893-1947)[9] was born of a Hungarian father and a German mother. He studied at Budapest, Freiburg, Paris and Heidelberg. His first interest was the philosophy of knowledge. He was also interested in the social sciences and is numbered among the representatives of **Wissenssoziologie.** His formulation of the sociology of knowledge was considered to be the most advanced of his age. It was a discipline to which he devoted a large part of his intellectual career. In 1929, he was appointed a professor of sociology and economics at the University of Frankfurt. He was there till 1933, when he was forced out by the Hitler regime. He then moved to England where he spent the rest of his life. He served as a lecturer in sociology at the London School of Economics, then as a professor of education at the University of London. Just before his death in 1947, he was appointed director of the United Nations Educational, Scientific an Cultural Organization (UNESCO). During the course of his career, his academic interests shifted from philosophy to sociology and economics, and later while in England, to social planning and education.

The intellectual constellation which preside over the birth of his **Wissenssoziologie** in Germany included Marxism (particularly in Karl Marx and Georg Lukaes) and Neo-Kantianism (since he was influenced by Max Scheler and was a student of Edmund Hussel). Of these influences, that of Marx, and through him, Hegel, was preponderant; so much so that we may say that Mannheim's sociology of knowledge is principally an elaborated formulation of Karl Marx's theory of ideology. He presents the sociology of knowledge in this perspective.

The essentials of his sociology of knowledge are found in his book, **Ideology and Utopia,** published in Bonn 1929. The book was translated into English and published in New York in 1936. Other books by Mannheim include: **Man and Society in an Age of Reconstruction** (1920); **Diagonses of Our Times** (1943) and **Freedom, Power and Democratic Planning** (published posthumously in 1950). There are also several volumes of collected essays which

---

[9]Kurt Wolff, ed., **From Karl Mannheim** (New York: Oxford University Press, 1971), Introduction; and Lewis Coser, **Masters of Sociological Thought** (New York. Harcourt Brace Jovanovich, 1971), pp. 441-449.

[10]Ibid.

include: **Essays on Sociology of Knowledge** edited by Paul Kecskemeti (1952), **Essays on the Sociology of Culture** edited by Ernest Mannheim and Paul Kecskemeti (1956) and **Essays on Sociology and Social Psychology** edited by Paul Kecskemeti (1953); **From Karl Mannheim,** edited by Kurt H. Wolff (1971). Of all these works, we shall concentrate chiefly on his **Ideology and Utopia** and **Essays on Sociology of Knowledge.**

The leading theorist of the nineteenth-century German intellectual tradition who exercised great influence on Mannheim was the philosopher, George Hegel. Hegel held that each historical period should be studied as a whole and any aspect of a culture must be understood in relationship to the entire culture and its stage of development. Hegel stands at the origin of both Marxism and historicism. His resolute historicization of philosophical ideas, his stress on the historical conditioning of the human spirit and the dialectical relationship between historical phenomena and the process of thought, all these elements are part of Mannheim's inellectual equipment. In effect, it is difficult to think of Mannheim without reference to Hegel. Hegel's thoughts were further developed by German historicists such as Wilhelm Dilthey,[12] who argued that the thought of any period of history should be analyzed from its own point of view--its total context--rather than from the external point of view of a different era. Ideas, beliefs and vlues were thus seen as grounded in a particular historical configuration. The dominant theme here was an overwhelming sense of the relativity of all perspectives on human events, that is of the inevitable historicity of human thought. The historicist insistence that no situation could be understood except in its own terms could readily be translated into an emphasis on the social situation of thought. Certain historicist concepts such as "situational determination" and "position in life" (**Sitz im Leben**) could be directly translated as referring to the "social location" of thought.

Building on the German historicists, Karl Marx[13] contended that not only are belief systems part of a socio-cultural

---

[11] Sidney Hook, **From Hegel to Marx** (Ann Arbor: University of Michigan Press, 1962), Introduction and Chapter One.

[12] See Berger and Luckman, p. 7-9.

[13] Karl Marx, **A Contribution to the Critique of Political Economy,** trans. from N. I. Stone (1897) (New York: International Library Publishing Co., 1904), pp. 1-12.

context, but they are merely a surface manifestation of the underlying economic structure. Therefore, Marx argued that systems
of belief are ideologies that can be properly understood only as
reflections (and sometimes logical justifications) of the class position of those who hold them. By this thesis, Marx gave an
important impetus to the development of the sociology of knowledge as a search for the social conditions that underlie systems
of thought. Mannheim depended heavily on Marx's theory of
ideology. We shall elaborate on this later.

Max Scheler[14] also belongs to the German tradition of
the socioogy of knowledge. He sought to preserve some notion
of universal truth against the threat of relativism engendered by
the emphasis on the social foundations of knowledge. For this
purpose he distinguished between the "real world" and "ideal essences." The latter consists of unchanging values and truths, the
nature of which is not affected by external conditions. However,
the social conditions that constitute part of the real world shape
the form in which these essences appear and the extent to which
they are manifesed in different times and places. Scheler's distinction between the real and ideal did not become part of the
mainstream of the sociology of knowledge, but his analysis of the
manner in which social conditions determine the forms of knowledge had a marked effect. He argued that society determined the
presence (**Dasein**) but not the nature (**Sosein**) of ideas. He emphasized that human knowledge is given in society as an apriori to
individual experience, providing the latter with its order of meaning. This order, although it is relative to a particular socio-
historical situation, appears to the individual as the natural way
of looking at the world. Scheler called this the "relative-natural
world view."

Following Scheler's formulation of the sociology of knowledge as the procedure by which the socio-historical selection of
ideational contents is to be studied (it being understood that the
contents themselves are independent of socio-historical causation
and thus inaccessible to sociological analysis), there arose an
extensive debate in Germany concerning the validity, scope and
applicability of Scheler's theory. Out of these debates emerged
Mannheim's conception of the sociology of knowledge,[15] in which

---

[14]Max Scheler, "The Sociology of Knowledge: Formal Problems" in
Sociology of Knowledge, ed. Curtis and Petras, pp. 143-170.

[15]Mannheim, **Ideology and Utopia,** pp. 1-47.

he argued that knowledge is socially determined. He therefore rejected Scheler's distinction between real and ideal knowledge. In spite of this, Mannheim still gave Scheler credit for being the first to elaborate a comprehensive plan for the sociology of knowledge, and for his ability to distinguish between thought from within, in terms of its logical structures, and from without, in terms of its social functioning and conditioning. Mannheim's sociology of knowledge therefore differs from Scheler's in its rejection of neo-platonic ideas in favor of an activist conception of the role of ideas. He did not share Scheler's ontological assumptions. He coined the term "relationism" (in contra-distinction to relativism) to denote the epistemological perspective of his sociology of knowledge. This aspect of Mannheim's study, however, is not our concern; rather we shall consider his theory of ideology which is central to his sociology of knowledge. This theory of ideology is expressed in his **Essays.**

Mannheim's Essays on Sociology of Knowledge

We begin by a quick review of the relevant issues in Mannheim's **Essays on Sociology of Knowledge**[16] which preceded his final **magnum opus--Ideology and Utopia.** Mannheim's doctoral dissertation--"Structural Analysis of Epistemology" (published in 1922)[17] --sets the stage for an understanding of his method. As the title of his dissertation indicates, his study dealt with a philosophical analysis of knowledge. However, in his works on sociology of knowledge, his emphasis shifted from philosophical to sociological analysis of ideas. He applied his "structural" method of

---

[16] In this particular book--**Essays on the Sociology of Knowledge,** ed. Paul Kecskemeti (London: Routledge and Kegan Paul Limited, 1952)--Mannheim treats such topics as: the theory of Weltanschauung; Historicism (Geistesgeschichte); The Problem of a Sociology of Knowledge; Competition as a Cultural Phenomenon; The Sociology of Education and the Problem of Generations. These six essays were written by Mannheim during the early part of his academic career in Germany. They particularly indicate the trend and texture of his thought wich eventually led to his major work on Sociology of Knowledge: **Ideology and Utopia.**

[17] See Karl Mannheim, **Essays on Sociology and Social Psychology,** ed. Paul Kecskemeti (New York: Oxford University Press, 1953), Chapter One and Introduction.

analysis to his sociology of knowledge. According to him, the consideration of an idea from a structural point of view means explaining it, not as an isolated, self-contained unit, but as part of a wider structure or frame of reference.[18] To express his viewpoint, he says that it is not enough to say **twice two is four because this gives no clue as to when, where and by whom the assertion was formulated.**

Mannheim applied this principle to his essay on "Interpretation of Weltanschauung" (1923).[19] Here, he argues that to interpret a cultural phenomenon such as works of art, religion, music or philosophy, one must presuppose and grasp some totality, some system of which meaningful elements are parts. Thus, the knowledge or ideas conveyed by cultural phenomena were "historical knowledge," and this was best understood within a historical context.[20]

This brings us to Mannheim's "Essay on Historicism."[21] For German historicists, history was a metaphysical reality; it was an absolute having a normative value. But Mannheim transformed the philosophical theory of historicism to mean, not the need for some communion with the Absolute, but an attempt to rescue creeds (political or religious) from dogmatic shallowness. This, he argued, could be achieved through defining creeds, ideas or beliefs in the context of the constellation of socio-historical factors which impinge on them.

In response to his position which implied some elements of relativism, anti-relativists protested against having all knowledge be a mere reflection of a passing historical constellation. Mannheim countered this protest by asserting that historic knowledge must fit the known facts and be able to account for them. Hence he rejected the application of static truth criteria to historic knowledge.[22]

---

18 Mannheim, **Essays on the Sociology of Knowledge**, p. 76.

19 Ibid., pp. 33-83.

20 Ibid., p. 61.

21 Ibid., pp. 84-133.

22 Ibid., p. 85.

Another important essay by Mannheim was "German Conservative Thought in the Early Nineteenth Century."[23] This was an essay he submitted prior to his appointment as a lecturer in the University of Heidelberg. In it Mannheim came out boldly in favour of Formulations of sociology of knowledge in non-abstract terms. He persuasively argued that the function of sociology of knowledge is to demonstrate how specific styles of thought are associated with specific concrete groups of people. Hence the development of ideas, of art or religion, according to Mannheim, cannot be fully understood apart from the mind-set to which they belong and apart from the socio-political changes taking place in that group. His study of the German political scene between 1800-1830 revealed that it was made out of two influential groups: the landed nobility and the bureaucratic personnel of centralized monarchic administration. Besides these landed aristocracy and the absolutist bureaucracy, there was the rising class of bourgeoisie who emerged to challenge those in power. This challenge led to the formulation of "conservative"[24] platforms by which the landed aristocracy defended their power and entrenched class interests which were being threatened. They warned against the danger of discarding everything on the basis of a few self-evident truths.

The proletarian group accepted the changes introduced by industrial civilization created by capitalism. They wanted it for their own advantage, but were also opposed by the landed aristocracy who considered their protests a negative force, a threat to the stable organic life patterns on which order and culture were secure.

---

[23] A modified version of this essay appeared in **Archif für Sozial-wissenschaft und Sozial-politik**, vol. 57 (1927). I am indebted to Paul Kecskemeti for my insight into this essay on "German Conservative Thought." See his Introduction to Karl Mannheim, **Essays on the Sociology of Knowledge,** pp. 20-22.

[24] Conservatism, according to Mannheim, does not refer to the traditional sense of the meaning, marked by an instinctive clinging to familiar habitual ways of thought and action. Rather it is a fully self-conscious position worked out in response to a poser challenge. In nineteenth century Germany, conservatism was the product of the threat of social transformation.

Mannheim later in his book, **Ideology and Utopia**, described conservative thought as essentially "ideological," and
proletarian thought as essentially "utopian." Conservative thought,
he contended, concentrates upon the past insofar as the past lives
on in the present; and proletarian thought tries to grasp elements
of the future which also exist in the present, by concentrating
on those present factors in which the germs of a future society
can be seen.

In another essay, "Competition as a Cultural Phenomenon,"[25] a paper he delivered to the Sixth Congress of German
Sociologists (published in 1929), Mannheim reviewed the main
categories of his sociology of knowledge. Sociological analysis,
he contended, is to deal with existentially determined thinking
as contrasted with the abstract, neutral type of thinking encountered in the natural sciences. This existentially determined thinking, according to Mannheim, reflected collective social aspiration,
and portrayed theories about society, history and man which had
a volitional, practical and political basis.[26]

Different modes of thinking, said Mannheim, express different power positions in terms of those in power and those not
in power and in terms of the rich and the poor. Each group has
its own interpretation of the world and seeks to make it univer-
sally accepted. Thus, theoretical discussion of each group's ideas
or world views in society may be conceived as incidents in the
general struggle for power.[27] As Mannheim described it, when
social power is monopolized by one group, then one mode of interpretation reigns supreme. However, when rival theories and interpretations begin to compete with the dominant view, monopolies
of power inevitably break down, and no class or group view is considered to exhaust the complete meaning of world process.[28]

In sum, we would say that Mannheim's sociology of knowledge seeks to discover typical relationships between ideas and
social situation, and to provide an outline or a method for studying ideas as a function of social involvement.

---

[25]Mannheim, **Essays on the Sociology of Knowledge**, pp. 191-229.

[26]Ibid., p. 212.

[27]Ibid., p. 198.

[28]Ibid., p. 142.

In his final work on this subject, **Ideology and Utopia**, Mannheim concerned himself with a study of how people think. He attempted to work out a suitable method for describing and analyzing thought and the changes and problems associated with it. His principal thesis on sociology of knowledge was that there are modes of thought which cannot be adequately understood as long as their social origins were obscured.

The starting point of Mannheim's sociology of knowledge is not from single individuals, but from a social group. Because of this, his sociology of knowledge seeks to comprehend thought in a historical situation out of which thought very gradually emerges. Hence his method does not sever concretely existing modes of thought from the context of collective action. The significant element in his sociology of knowledge is the discovery that political life (i.e., the relationship between the ruling class and the ruled, the rich and the poor) is integrally related to social life, not to a philosophical dogma nor to any ontological credo. Therefore, sociology of knowledge for Mannheim examines thought or ideas, not in isolation but within its socio-political context.

In view of the preceding argument, Mannheim contends that sociology of knowledge is an attempt at a systematic analysis of the relationship between thought and existence. As a theory it is an investigation through description and structural analysis of the ways in which social relationships influence thought.

In light of the preceding statement on Mannheim, we find that there are at least three major factors present in his sociology of knowledge: **the social factor, the social situation** (or location of a group in society), and **the historic situation.**

The social factor plays the role of an independent variable. It is the group. More explicitly, it is, on the one hand, the situation of a group in society and in history and, on the other hand, it repesents the objectives and necessities of its collective action. For our purpose, the social factor is represented by both the African and the European groups.

Mannheim, as we have shown, defines the situation or location of a group in society mainly in terms of power--both political (as rulers or the ruled) and economic (as rich or poor). For example, he describes the utopian thinking of the anabaptists as corresponding to their lack of political and economic power.[29] We shall likewise analyze Euro-Afro relations in terms of a power relationship, a relationship between the powerful and the powerless.

---

[29]Mannheim, **Ideology and Utopia**, p. 205.

The "historic" situation of a group, as we have already shown, refers to its creeds or beliefs in the context of its historic dynamism.[30] This is to say that for Mannheim ideas or bliefs are grounded in socio-historical reality. They do not stemm from any philosophical dogma or are they formulated in abstract terms; rather they are associated with specific groups of people. For our study, this implies that we shall consider the call for moratorium within the general framework of Euro-Afro relationships and in the specific context of the missionary enterprise in which the Europeans were the dominant and powerful group and the Africans were the subordinate and powerless group.

Mannheim describes the mentality of a dominant group as "ideological" and that of a subjected group as "utopian." By the ideological concept Mannheim means:

> . . . the one discovery which emerged from political conflict, namely, that ruling groups can in their thinking become so intensively interest-bound to a situation that they are simply no longer able to see certain facts which would undermine their sense of domination. There is implicit in the word "ideology" [therefore] the insight that in certain situations the collective unconscious of dominant groups obscures the real condition of society both to itself and to others . . .

and by the utopian concept he means:

> . . . the opposite discovery of the political struggle, namely that certain oppressed groups are intellectually so strongly interested in the destruction and transformation of a given condition of society that they unwittingly see only those elements in the situation which tend to negate it. . . . In their thinking they seek to change the situation that exists. Their thought is never a rational diagnosis of the situation; it can be used only as a direction for action. In the utopian mentality, the collective unconscious, guided by wishful representation and the will to action, hides certain aspects of reality. It turns

---

[30]Cf. Karl Mannheim, "Das Konservative Denken" (i.e., German Conservative Thinking) in his **Essays on the Sociology of Knowledge**, pp. 20-22. See also **Ideology and Utopia**, p. 245

its back on everything which would shake its belief or paralyse its desire to change things. [31]

Given the provisions of Mannheim's sociology of knowledge, therefore, we shall conduct a descriptive investigation and structural analysis of the ways in which social relationships and social changes within the Euro-Afro missionary encounter influence the thinking of both the Africans and the Europeans. To facilitate the analysis we will employ Mannheim's concepts of ideology and utopia in our subsequent discussion to describe the pattern of thinking and of relationship between the "ruling and powerful" European group and the "powerless and poor" African group.

Mannheim's sociology of knowledge also helps to focus our attention on the cultural-historical context in which the Christian faith has been shaped and nurtured both in the West and in Africa. A study of this context will show that for Africans, their Christian faith was nurtured during a period of rapid Westernization. Hence they were trying to find the meaning of the gospel between two conflicting cultures--European and African. Furthermore, while the African tries to discover the price of his Christian witness in a situation of oppression and subjection, the West enjoyed Christian faith in a situation of relative freedom from tyranny and oppression. Also, while the African seeks the meaning of Christian faith in the insecurity of chaotic social conditions caused by conquest and colonization, the West practiced Christian faith in a society in which law and order prevails. Hence they tend to consider a situation of lack of law and order as "anti-Christian." In addition to this, while the African is forced to recognize the severe limitations of poverty and powerlessness, the Western Christian enjoys a sense of abundance in power and resources. Consequently, the Western Christian tends to identify the Christian Gospel with technological advance and Europeanization. Thus, all non-Europeans and non-technologically advanced people are viewed as objects of sympathy and even as anti-Christians.

The preceding observation is part of what we shall be considering as the context and consequences of Euro-Afro Christianization. It will enhance our application of Mannheim's concepts of "ideology" and "utopia" to the missionary enterprise. It will help us to establish the European-African relationship in terms of power--both political and econimic, as Mannheim has

----

[31] Mannheim, **Ideology and Utopia**, p. 36.

42

theorized. After examining the political aspect of the relationship as mirrored through colonization, we shall also in Chapter VI examine the economic aspect of the relationship as portrayed by trade and investment relations. Given the socio-political and economic context from which European missions are carried out, we will argue that they manifest ideological tendencies, while the African responses reflect utopian characteristics. Within this broad ideology-utopian spectrum, we shall later account for some of the anomalies and exceptions to Mannheim's theory of the social determination of ideas. In the interim let us highlight some of the important points in Mannheim's concepts of ideology and utopia and comment on their relevance to our discussion.

Mannheims's Theory of Ideology

Mannheim's understanding of the sociology of knowledge is significantly related to Marx's theory of ideology. In order to inquire into Mannheim's use of Marx's concept of ideology, we need to further elaborate on the theory of ideology as formulated by Marx. One vital source for such information is **German Ideology,** where Marx attacks the classical definition of ideology as the attempt of those in power to justify the status quo.

Marx and Engels, in **German Ideology** (1846),[32] were among the first to give the term "Ideology" its sociological meaning. They proposed that philosophies, ideals, laws, social knowledge, must be seen as intimately linked to the material conditions of those who produce such knowledge. Ideology reflects class interests and is characterized by its function of helping to maintain an existing class structure. Thus Marx and Engels systematically elaborated the relationship of political, religious, intellectual and legal knowledge to social structure.

Marxist ideological analysis was used as a polemical weapon against the dominant group. Dominant-group ideas or ideologies were considered distortions of reality because they disguise group interests. Unmasking these hidden interests by showing their relationship to certain intellectual conceptions was the

---

[32]Karl Marx and Friedrich Engels, **The German Ideology** (New York: International Publishers, 1939); also for statements on Marx's views on ideology see: T. B. Bottomore and Maximilien Rusel, **Karl Marx** (Middlesex, England: Pelican, 1963), pp. 21, 169-174.

goal of Marxist ideological analysis. In this method of analysis, one understands an idea by laying bare the interest it conceals. This method was contrary to the epistemological method where controversy remained principally upon the plane of ideas.

Mannheim borrowed this idea of unmasking of hidden interests and applied it to his sociology of knowledge to unmask the "collective unconscious" of any group of people. He also derived his idea of social causation (i.e., the relation of an idea to its social class) from Marxism. He observed that in political discussion of modern democracies, ideas were clearly representative of certain groups. Hence, the social and existential determination of thought were easily visible.

According to Mannheim, people in their political struggles become aware of the unconscious motivations that always guide their thought. Political struggle is from the outset more than a theoretical argumentation; it is the "tearing off of disguises," "the unmasking of those unconscious motives which bind the group existence to its cultural aspiration and its theoretical arguments."[33] As the unmasking proceeds, it penetrates the social roots of thought. Therefore, the discovery of the social situational roots of thought takes the form of unmasking. Hence ideological analysis for Mannheim takes the form of unmasking ideas, beliefs or symbols which are unconsciously generated by any social group to protect itself against others, to legitimate its powers, and to defend its privileges.

Mannheim systematically refined and expandes Marx and Engels' notion of ideology. He argued that ideological thinking was not limited to the ruling class, but that all classes had a particular existence, a particular social perspective and a set of interests. Hence the ideas produced by all classes would have to be ideological in nature. Mannheim, therefore, argued for a ·distinction between two categories of thought: ideologies, ideas that functioned to maintain the existing social order; and utopian ideas, which contained visions of a different social order and implied a critique of the existing one. It is the special significance of these concepts--ideology and utopia--that led him to chose them as the title of his book.[34]

Mannheim expanded the concept of ideology from a particular to a total context. The particular conception of ideology differs in three fundamental respects from the total conception

---

[33] Mannheim, **Ideology and Utopia**, p. 35.

[34] Ibid., p. 36.

44

of ideology.[35] Whereas the particular conception of ideology des-
ignates only a part of the opponent's assertion (and this only with
reference to its content), the total conception of ideology calls
into question the opponent's entire system of thought, his total
Weltanschauung, and attempts to understand these concepts as an
outgrowth of the collective life of which he partakes.

Second, the particular conception of "ideology" makes
its analysis of ideas on a purely psychological level. It claims
that since both parties share a common criterion of validity, it
is possible to refute lies and eradicate sources of error by
referring to accepted criteria of objective validity common to
both parties. By contrast, the total conception is concerned with
the noological level, i.e., the level of logical structures of thought,
where the form, content and conceptual framework of a "mode
of thought" is conceived to be unavoidably bound with life situation.[36]

Finally, and as a corollary, this particular conception
of ideology operates primarily with a "psychology of interests"
whereas the total conception seeks only to establish a "correspondence" between the social setting and the system of thought. Thus,
the latter conception does not require the imputation of motives
but rests with the indication of understandable correspondences
between modes of thought and the concrete situation.[37]

Since Mannheim's emphasis is more on the total conception of ideology, a summary of what this means is appropriate
at this point. The total conception of ideology is a person's entire
system of thought, his total **Weltanschauung,** which arises from
the collective life in which he participates. It embodies the form,
content and conceptual framework of his mode of thought which
is bound up with his life situation. Working from the total conception of ideology, the analyst seeks to establish "correspondences" between the social milieu and the system of thought. This
approach reveals the integrated system of thought of a group
which is implicit in the judgments of its members.

Having analyzed Mannheim's concept of ideology, let us
now examine his concept of utopia. We may call utopian the
striving for unrealizable goals; or we may consider a state of
mind utopian when it is incongruous with the state of reality

---

[35] Ibid., pp. 49-53.

[36] Ibid., pp. 50-51.

[37] Ibid., p. 62.

within which it occurs. This incongruence is always evident in the fact that such a state of mind in experience, in thought and in practice is oriented towards objects which do not exist in actual situation.

Mannheim, however, contends that we should not regard as utopian every state of mind which is incongruous with and transcends the immediate situation. "Only those orientations transcending reality will be regarded as utopian which when they press over into conduct tend to shatter, either partially or wholly the order of things prevailing at the time."[38] Mannheim limits the meaning of the term "utopia" "to that type of orientation which transcends reality and which at the same time breaks the bonds of the existing order; a distinction is set up between the utopian and the ideological states of mind."[39] Every period in history, according to Mannheim, contains ideas which transcend the existing order, but these ideas do not function as utopian. They are rather appropriate ideologies to that stage of existence as long as they are "organically" and harmoniously integrated into the world-view characteristic of the period. In other words, such ideas are not utopian if they do not offer any revolutionary possibilities.[40] For example, when a clerically and feudally organized medieval order locates its paradise outside of society, in some other-worldly sphere which transcends history and dulls its revolutionary edge, this paradise is still an integral part of medieval society and not utopian.

In order to determine how his theory of "ideology and utopia" works out in practice, Mannheim conducted socio-historical research to establish the connection between concrete modes of thought and the composition of the group and strata which expressed themselves in that manner. Hence he chose four types, the Anabaptist-Chiliastic, the Liberal-humanitarian, the Conservative, and the Socialist-Communist, and related their "ideologies" or "utopian mentalities" (i.e., their ideas, symbols) to their particular social location and to the collective purpose of their protagonists.

Mannheim showed that the Anabaptist-Chiliastic group emanated from the poverty-stricken classes of peasants who were poorly educated but still maintained a medieval mentality. Their

---

[38]Ibid., p. 103.

[39]Ibid., p. 173.

[40]Ibid., p. 174.

poverty demanded a complete, rapid change of condition; their religious faith made them look towards the beyond.[41]

Liberal utopia emanated from the bourgeoning middle classes who were climbing slowly but steadily up the social hierarchy. They optimistically conceived of time as perpetual progress. The extremely rational character of the Liberal ideal may be related to its secular and rationalist education and the fact that Liberals had been kept from power for a long time. There was no brush with political reality to limit their rationalist tendencies.[42]

The conservatives did not need a utopia because they were in power. The present state of affairs seemed to them to be a natural part of the order of the world and did not raise any theoretical problems. The attacks of the liberals, however, led them to reflect on their position and to create a utopia of defense. They turned towards the past, "to the **Volksgeist,**" which gave them the impression that the State belonged to those whose ancestors had been the leaders of the people--that is to say, to themselves. Thus, for the conservatives, history became an evolution plunging into the past. The present is justiefied because it is the "flowering" of the past.[43]

Finally, the socialist-communist conceptions differentiated historical time in a more complex manner, distinguishing between the immediate and remote future while emphasizing that the concrete present embraced not only the past but also the latent tendencies of the future. "Communism for us (according to Marx and Lenin) is not a condition that is to be established nor an ideal to which reality must adjust itself. We call communism the

---

[41]Mannheim, **Ideology and Utopia**, p. 117, 125. The anabaptist-chiliastic experienceis characteristic of the lowest strata of society. Underlying them is a mental structure peculiar to oppressed peasants (p. 204). Their extreme need for theory is the expression of a class society...Their irrationality goes with revolution (p. 117). Theirs is the ideology of a "putschist" group (a protest group) (p. 125). The ethics of the earliest Christian communities is primarily intelligible in terms of the resentment of oppressed strata (p. 40). The liberal conception of freedom was that of a group which sought to overthrow . . . the social order. The conservative ideas of "freedom" was that of a stratum which did not wish to see any radical revolutionary changes (p. 245).

[42]Ibid., pp. 108-110, 197-206.

[43]Ibid., pp. 106-108, 206-215.

actual movement which abolishes present conditions."[44] By for-
mulating these connections between social location, collective
aspirations and temporal orientation, Mannheim has shown that
a people's social location affects and conditions their collective
aspiration.

The Relevance of Mannheim's Categories: Ideology and Utopia

It is important to reiterate the main points in Mannheim's concepts of ideology and utopia. Ideology as we know it
in ordinary parlance is a systematized theory of social organization which provides a basis for the political, economic and cultural life of a nation or community.[45] In a sense it is an attempt
to descirbe systematically how people live together in an orderly
way. Mannheim refers to ideology as dealing with sociology, not
with ultimate realities. Ideology for Mannheim is not essentially
a philosophy or a theology, though it could include both as part
of its system.

Karl Marx considered ideology to be attempts by those
in power to justify the status quo (i.e., they attempt to explain
the facts of their domination in a rational, consistent way). In
this way ideology attempts to build structures of ideas which look
convincing and error free. Marx thinks that an ideology which
is used to defend one's or a group's position produces false consciousness and is misleading. Mannheim, on the other hand, sees
ideology as a system of ideas, symbols or beliefs which flows out
of a particular perspective, i.e., out of a particular view of the
world.

Mannheim considers ideologies within the context of a
social frame of reference. He sees ideology as subjective in that
it is formulated by a group (or the individual) to serve its (his/
her) interests. It controls a group's (or individual's) social frame
of reference through the consciousness possessed by that individual
or group. For example, a white middle class American is most
likely to believe in the status quo. He/she can justify it in terms
of his upbringing which parades before him the negative charac-

---

[44]Ibid., pp. 112, 125, 225.

[45]Arne Sovik, "The Church and Current Ideologies," **Missiology: An
International Review** 2 (1974): 237.

teristics of blacks who are in the minority and are held in low esteem.[46] He will not like to occupy an inferior or minority status, and hence he/she is likely to seek ways necessary to preserve the system. In this way an ideology controls a group's or individual's activities because they are determined by social relations and the mental constructs based on them.

Ideology may as well function in dissimilar ways for non-middle class, non-white American citizens who live in the same society. In this case, ideology as a world view may have an other-worldly function in which a person influenced by its vision of a new order sees him/herself as free from subjection or from minority status. When ideology functions in this visionary way, it denies the extant historical reality, and becomes a "utopia" according to Mannheim. That is to say, utopians have a vision of what the world and their own community might be like if the relations of economic and political power were altered to effect a closer approximation of their understanding of social justice. Their vision of human possibility when confronted with human actuality prompts them to an activist role in human history, and inspires them to struggle for a more just society in spite of their disadvantages. As we have already mentioned, Mannheim claims that the term "utopia" specifies "only those orientations transcending reality, . . . which when they pass over into reality, tend to shatter, either partially or wholly, the order of things prevailing at the time."[47] Mannheim insists that orientations which do not break the bonds of the existing order while transcending reality are ideologies which serve the interest of the ruling or dominant group. As we have already indicated, Mannheim's research portrayed the utopian vision and mentality as emerging from the context of an oppressed or dominated group (like the Anabaptist-Chiliastic group) and it served as the goal or horizon towards which they struggled. As a mental orientation identified with an oppressed group, utopia engages in a constant dialectic with the dominant group and seeks to change or transform the old order of relationships (that keeps them in a subordinate and disadvantageous position) into a new order in which the injustices of the old order will be abolished.

---

[46] Charles W. Forman and Gregory Baum, "Is There a Missionary Message?," **Mission Trends**, no. 1, ed. Gerald H. Anderson and Thomas F. Stransky (New York: Paulist Press, 1974), pp. 78-86.

[47] Mannheim, **Ideology and Utopia**, p. 192.

Given a situation of tension or conflict between two social groups, such as the European and African groups, Mannheim's approach seeks to establish how each group thinks within the complexity of the social organization that holds them together. We should remember that Mannheim intended this utopia-ideology system to affirm the existence of a certain relationship between mental production and social factors. He did not deny the possibility of other kinds of conditioning of mental production. For him the sociology of knowledge was a systematic attempt to clarify the relationship of ideas to society. This did not imply in any way that an effort to bring to light an inverse relationship [48] was invalid or would be unsuccessful. Mannheim did not establish a strict determination of ideas by social factors, but merely a correspondence. A correspondence between social circumstances and an idea indicates that these circumstances constituted at least one of the factors which explain the origin of the idea. The explanatory value of Mannheim's system may be characterized as not being complete (in the sense that it does not totally account for the origin of the idea), but it brings to light one of the social elements which, joined to other factors (psychological, immanent), gives a genetic explanation of the idea.[49] Hence a sociological interpretation of moratorium does not totally account for but brings to light its socio-historical dimension.

Mannheim believed that there were three possible interpretations of ideas: sociological, psychological and immanent. The first two sought to establish the genesis of an idea through social scientific interpretation. The immanent interpretation was confined to the plane of ideas whereby the origin of mental production was sought in another mental production. Thus something like Thomism was explained as a synthesis of Aristotelianism and traditional Christian thought.

Mannheim's point of departure on the question of "social determination of ideas" began with theories that knowledge did not develop solely in accordance with immanent laws. Rather, its emergence was influenced at numerous crucial points by extra-theoretical factors of a social nature, and the influence of these factors was more than peripheral. "They are relevant not only to the genesis of ideas, but penetrate into their forms and content and . . . furthermore, they decisively determine the scope

---

[48] Maquet, pp. 53-54.

[49] Mannheim, **Ideology and Utopia**, pp. 257-260.

50

and intensity of our experience and observation."[50] This results in knowledge being linked to a particular perspective. When a person thinks, he thinks from the point of view of the interests and aspirations of his group. He thinks ideologically according to Marx; his ideas flow from a particular view of the world. In this context it is odd to talk of absolute or valid knowledge in a world or society stratified along class, race, and sex lines. If this is true, what validity can partial knowledge have? This means that a perspective really appears to be synonymous with distortion of reality. An application of this problem is the proverbial elephant that was described differently by six blind men depending on what part of the elephant they touched.

The argument about perspective leads to the problem of "Relativism,"[51] that is, what can knowledge, produced by a point of view, teach about reality? How can a perspective on thought have an undistorted knowledge of reality? Remembering the distinction between the sociological theory of knowledge and the sociology of knowledge, and realizing that this problem could well furnish a topic for a separate dissertation, we must conclude that for the purposes of this study, it must suffice merely to have raised the question. Our concern now is to proceed to explore the collective ssocio-historical and intellectual settings of both Africa and Europe within the context of the call for moratorium in missions in the 1970's.

Since Mannheim's sociology of knowledge attempts to work out a suitable method for describing and analysing thought, its changes and problems in relation to its context, we shall use Mannheim in analysing the mode of thinking of Europeans and Aricans, both before and after their encounter. We shall turn in the next chapter to consider the socio-cultural conditions of the Africans and their mode of thinking before their contact with the West.

---

[50] Ibid., p. 240.

[51] Ibid., pp. 252-256.

CHAPTER III

TRADITIONAL AFRICAN SOCIETY

From the preceding discussion of Karl Mannheim's sociology of knowledge, we see that knowledge, beliefs and ideas
emerge from a people. To understand the origin of these ideas
one must study the people's socio-cultural history. This is also
true for Africans and their mode of thought and action. In order
to understand them, it is necessary to inquire into the nature
and characteristics of their traditional society and culture. This
culture is conservative in the sense that it clings to familiar and
habitual ways of thought and action.

This chapter will describe the general nature and characteristics of traditional folk or pre-literate societies and their
culture[1] using the insights of Robert Redfield's research on "The
Folk Society." Redfield's examples are ideal types, conceptual
models useful for analyzing a variety of folk societies such as
those in Africa. His assumption is that folk societies have certain
common features which enable anthropologists to think of them
as types. We shall apply these basic characteristics to the African
milieu in order to highlight its main features as a folk or traditional society before its contact with the West.

According to Redfield, folk and traditional societies are
homogeneous and their members have a strong sense of solidarity.
A folk society is relatively small and isolated; therefore the
people know one another well. There are no strangers. A high
proportion of social relationships in the folk community are
primary, long lasting and intimate, having an intrinsic significance,
and are valued as ends. The family and extended kinship network
are central to life's experience. These relationships are characterized by devotion, love and sacrifice. Kinship relationships

---

[1]See works on pre-literate societies: Kingsley Davis, "Primary
Groups," in **Life in Society: Introductory Readings in Sociology**, ed. Thomas
E. Lasswell, John H. Vurma and Sidney H. Aronson (Chicago: Scott, Foresman
and Company, 1965), pp. 171-177; Ferdinand Tonnies, **Community and Society**,
trans. and ed. C. P. Loomis (Ann Arbor: University of Michigan Press, n.d.),
pp. 12-18; Robert Redfield, "The Folk Society," in **Life and Society**, ed. Lasswell et al., pp. 320-332; Emile Durkheim, **Division of Labour in Society**,
trans. George Simpson (New York: Macmillan Co., 1933), pp. 200-229.

dictate an all-embracing participation in which members need, seek, sacrfice for and love one another.[2]

In a folk society, behaviour is largely regulated by custom rather than formal law. As William G. Sumner states, "where mores as well as informal norms exercise a strong hold upon behaviour, there is little need for formal law. Law we might say is part of the tradition: it is not modified or rationalized; not enacted or dictated; but, emerges from the cumulative experience of the society, it is incorporated in the customs known and accepted by members."[3]

In folk society there is a simple division of labor. Sex roles and age roles are most important because of the social, econmic and religious functions of males and females. By virtue of one's sex and age, a person's behaviour, status, and function are determined. Besides this simple functional division, there are few other divisions of labour in these technologically simple societies.

Folk societies' limited size and relative isolation tend to make them socially homogeneous, stable and resistant to change. Thus, they are usually not motivated towards innovation, experimentation or reflection. Consequently they are slow to respond to change. There are few specialized associations and few specialized mechanisms for social control.

Having described the ideal type of folk society, we can now examine its culture. The distinction between a society and its culture needs to be posited. One way to make this distinction is to say that society refers to the people per se while culture refers to their ways of life. With this basic difference between society and culture in mind we can employ the discipline of the sociology of knowledge to inquire into ideas, customs, and knowledge of a society. Therefore, we do not assume that a people's culture exists as an a priori, conceptual or metaphysical norm. Culture is a human product and therefore is subject to analytic study.

People produce and have culture. E.B. Tylor defines culture as "that complex whole which includes knowledge, beliefs, and morals, law, custom and any other capabilities and habits

---

[2]Redfield, pp.320-321, 323.

[3]William Graham Sumner, "Folkways and Mores," in **Life and Society,** ed. Thomas E. Lasswell et al., pp. 47-48.

acquired by man as a member of society."[4] Thus culture consists not only of art and music, but also of the values and norms people live by, their language, and religion. It is a learned complex. Each individual is born into a group which already possesses culture. This culture is transmitted to the individual through a learning process referred to as socialization.

Culture is not only learned, it is also shared. Culture is an attribute of a group rather than an individual. According to Clyde Kluckhohn:

> A culture is learned by individuals as the result of belonging to some particular group, and it constitutes that part of learned behaviour which is shared by others. It is one of the most important factors which permit us to live together in an organized society, giving us ready-made solutions to our problems, helping us to predict the behaviour of others, and permitting others to know what to expect from us.[5]

Culture is a people's total "life way," their "design for living," their way of thinking, believing, and feeling.[6] Culture includes the group's knowledge stored in its memories, myths, proverbs, songs, objects and books. People's culture, their way of life, regulates their life whether they are conscious of it or not.

Some aspects of culture are material. Material culture consists of the objects people produce and use while the non-material aspects of culture are such intangibles as values, norms and beliefs. Although these constitutive elements are discernible, nevertheless the full significance of any element in a culture can be accurately viewed only in the context of that culture as whole. Every group's way of life is a unified structure rather than a haphazard collection of patterns of belief and action. A culture is an interdependent system. This is true for African culture as well.

In sum, a culture is the distinctive way of life that is handed down as a social heritage. With this view of culture in mind, we can now turn to culture theory to organize the complex

---

[4] E. B. Tylor, **Primitive Culture** (London: J. Murray, 1871), p. 1.

[5] Clyde Kluckhohn, **Mirror for Man** (New York: McGraw-Hill, 1949), pp. 32-33, 26.

[6] Ibid.

54

mass of data related to traditional African culture. African culture is like other cultures in that it emphasizes certain values which determine the way of life of its people. We shall inquire into the values which determine traditional African ways of life by surveying some common aspects of the traditional society and culture of the peoples of Tropical Africa.

Before its contact with the West, Africa south of the Sahara was made up of about 800 tribal societies ofvarious sizes, scattered throughout the continent. Guy Hunter in his book, **The New Societies of Tropical Africa,** [7] asserts that in spite of the differences in culture among the societies in Africa, certain basic characteristics are common to all of them. Hunter identifies four which include: a simple level of technology, a clan-based political organization, pervasive belief in the spirit, and a subsistence economy. To elucidate Hunter's thesis in greater detail, we shall analyze each point in turn.

First, the folk societies of Tropical Africa had an extremely simple technology at the handicraft stage. However, this sometimes includes the working of iron, tin, copper or bronze for tools, weapons and ornaments. [8] In these societies the African lived in partnership with his environment rather than as an exploiter of it. Second, African social and political organization was built almost invariably on the extended family, lineage or clan system, although this basic structure was sometimes cross-cut horizontally by organizations of age-grades. [9] The existence of a chief did not necessarily imply simple tyranny. Third, African societies were dominated by an intense and pervasive blief in the spirit. There was often a belief in a supreme being, often conceived in very lofty terms. There were also lesser and more capricious spirits who needed worship and propitiation and the personal spirits of the individual person. [10] Fourth, "the underlying basis of the economies of Tropical Africa was the rural subsistence economy." [11] Hunter observes that their subsistence economy

---

[7] Guy Hunter, **The New Societies of Tropical Africa** (New York: Frederick A. Praeger, 1962), p. 11.

[8] Ibid.

[9] Philip O. Nsugbe, **Ohaffia: A Matrilineal People** (Oxford: The Clarendon Press, 1974), p. 58.

[10] Hunter, p. 13.

[11] Ibid., p. 14.

involved an alternation between plenty and starvation. Thus Africans feasted or starved without great surprise or complaint. However, this situation caused an intense life-long passion for land (the only security). Land was valued. Not only was the portion undercultivaton valued, but also the surrounding areas were reserved as a reservoir of wild food, game, and as a place for recreation. This subsistence economy produced an intense cohesion for the community, since land and community were inseparable.

Given the preceding general characteristics of folk societies and their cultures, and bearing in mind the four features Hunter suggests as distinctive in informing the whole of life in Tropical Africa,let us now examine a specific and fairly typical example within the broad spectrum of cultures in Tropical Africa: the Igbo people of Nigeria. Our inquiry shows that the generalities about folk societies and the peoples of Tropical Africa are also true for the Igbo. Their culture is a system in which the parts --social, economic, political and religious--are so inter-related and informed by the same set of values that one cannot isolate parts of it without jeopardizing the integrity of the system.

A traditional African society is in Mannheim's terms "ideological," since its goal is to maintain an existing order and harmony between the realm of the spirit and natural and social worlds. We shall examine the structures by which the Igbo ideologically ensures social stability and continuity. In order to do this a descriptive analysis of their spirit world (God, spirit, ancestors), their **Omenala** (the traditional customs of the people and their socialization process), their kinship system, their prohibitions, and their political and economic arrangements is necessary. If we understand the functioning and inter-relatedness of these features of Igbo traditional society and culture, then we can see that their mode of thinking, acting and feeling is chiefly geared towards preserving existing order. Since they wish to preserve traditional order, the Igbo's desire to be independent of external controls or threats alien to their culture and ethos is central. This desire tends to erupt when their culture is invaded beyond tolerable limits. Later we shall see how this tendency is borne out in the history of the relationship between Africans and their European missionary (and political) colonizers. First, however, let us examine traditional Igbo society and its culture beginning with an inquiry into its religion.

Traditional Igbo* Society: Analysis of Its Religion

The Igbo Traditional religion has an inherited way of doing things, of feeling about life, of thinking about or relating to the supreme God, surrounding spirits, ancestors, or to the people and world of nature. Ibo religion exerts great influence upon the thought and life styles of its people. Their religion evolved gradually without a founder. It has no sacred scriptures. Its beliefs and teachings are enshrined in ceremonies, rituals, symbols, myths, and proverbs. It has a wealth of beliefe about God, spirits, man and the world of things (plants, animals and the physical universe). Religious leaders include **village and family elders** (recognized and respected due to their age and store of knowledge about tradition), **priests** (male and female) of the various local deities, **diviners** (interpreters of the will of the deities or means to consult deities), **medicine-men and sacral rulers.** These officials serve as interpreters of the tradition and as guardians of social solidarity and religious stability. Since religion mingles with festivals, with work and the various incidents of life. Ibos hardly distinguish between the sacred and the secular or between what is spiritual and what is material. Their world is a single whole, which is constantly animated by religion. Religion is not merely a system, with a creed, a moral code and a liturgy, but. an institution in which one has one's whole life.[12]

Religion permeates the social, economic, and political life of the Ibos. It also embodies and symbolizes their sense of community. It helps them to interpret their values, dreams, symbols and deep wishes. Ibo religious beliefs are not formulated in a systematic set of dogmas which a person is expected to memorize. Their beliefs and practices are transmitted and engraved in people's mind through the process of living. Everybody is a religious carrier and thus specialized missionaries and proselytisers are unnecessary in Ibo religion.

Among the Ibos, religion is not primarily for the individual but for the community of which he is a part. Indigenous Ibo society does not contain non-religious people because for the Ibos being human implies participating in the beliefs, ceremonies, rituals, and festivals of the community. A person cannot detach himself form his religion and still be considered human. There-

---

*Igbo and Ibo mean the same thing and are used interchangebly.

[12] R. Laroche, "Some Traditional African Religions and Christianity," in **Christianity in Tropical Africa,** ed. C. Baeta (Oxford: Oxford University Press, 1968), p. 295.

fore, to be without religion is to be severed from one's roots, foundation, security, kinship and that group which makes a person aware of his own existence. The Ibos, therefore, do not know how to exist without religion. They are instinctively religious. Religion is one with their life. What Idowu says for all of Africa applies to the Ibos: "They are in all things . . . religious."[13]

For a deeper inquiry into the nature and function of religion in Ibo society[14] we shall consider the peoples' idea of God, spirits, ancestors and the kinship system. We shall also examine the religion's socialization processes and mechanisms of social control. The fact that all these processes work together to ensure harmony at home and in the community, to protect the vital bases of the economic life of the community, to prevent the disturbance of what is accepted as the normal rhythm of nature and to ensure proper reverence for the ancestors and the community of the spirit world, indicates the ideological orientation of this African traditional religion.

Belief in a supreme God[15] is central to Ibo traditional religion. This supreme God is worshipped most often through other divinities, who are ministers and intermediaries between him and his people. The Ibo name for the supreme God is **Chi-Ukwu,** that is, the great God. He is also referred to as **Chineke,** the God that creates all things visible and invisible. The divinities and all other categories of spirits are created by the great God. They are his offspring and agents and cannot exist or function without him. For the Ibo, **Chi-Ukwu** or **Chineke** is real. He is not an abstraction, but a personal God who deals with this world. He is not a mythical or a withdrawn God. He is believed to be an ever-present, living God. He is not only seen as the great and creator God; he is also believed to sustain, maintain and govern both the material and spirit worlds. His creative and sustaining power is manifest in human and animal procreation, in the produc-

---

[13] E.B. Idowu, **Olodumare: God in Yoruba Belief** (New York: Frederick A. Praeger, 1963), p. 1.

[14] E. O. Iwuagwu, "Chukwu: Towards a Definition of Ibo Traditional Religion," **West African Religion** 16 (1975). For works in traditional religon of other African societies, see E. E. Evans Pritchard, **Nuer Religion** (Oxford: The Clarendon Press, 1961); S. F. Nadel, **Nupe-Religion** (London: Routledge and Kegan Paul, 1954); Michael Gelfand, **An African's Religion: The Spirit of Nyajena (Case History of a Karanga People)** (Cape Town: Juba and Co., 1966).

[15] Iwuagwu, pp. 30-31. See Edmund Ilogu, **Christianity and Ibo Culture** (Leiden: E. J. Brill, 1974), pp. 17-20.

tion of food and other necessities. Rain and sunshine are seen as tokens of his providence. God is believed to ordain the order and destiny of everything.

There is a strong element of determinism in Igbo traditional religious thought. Consequently, any natural or social disaster is associated with God who is believed to order the course of creation. Disorders such as drought, epidemics and death which are beyond human control are attributed to God's anger. He is not blamed for such calamities, but rather brought into the picture primarily in an attempt to explain what challenges human comprehension. Such explanations serve to comfort the victims of such calamities and they also compel them to seek to appease God through the appropriate divinity or divinities. God is also thought of as a judge. This accounts for the association of justice, punishment and retribution with God. This notion of God as a judge strengthens Ibo traditional ethical sancitons, and this in turn upholds community solidarity. Ibo people believe that God punishes what is wrong and rewards what is right. Therefore, the breaking of social norms incurs God's punishment while respect for the social custom (**Omenala**) ensures prosperity.

Omenala[16] is a complex concept embodying the traditional world view, customs, practices, morals and the traditional way of life of the Ibo people. Essentially it is the moral order. It is supported and protected by the Earth Deity (**Ala**) and the ancestors, who punish all those who violate **Omenala.** The survival and welfare of the community which presupposes the survival of the individual depends on upholding **Omenala.** Violations of **Omenala** are believed to bring automatic punishment from **Ala** and the ancestors; hence the **Omenala** is respected. If violations occur, appropriate sacrifices (propitiatory and cleansing) are offered to restore order. In this way, **Omenala** ensures and promotes conformity to the existing socio-cultural order.

In addition to the great God there are the smaller god (spirits or divinities) who express His immanence in the world. These divinities[17] which the Ibo people recognize include **Ala,** "the mother earth," "the divine-female principle." As we have seen, she is the guardian and supervisor of morality. She is in charge of productivity and fertility. Elaborate sacrifices are offered to **Ala** for appeasement, especially during the festivals, when people need special favour, or when they break **Chukwu's**

---

[16] Ilogu, pp. 22-24.

[17] Iwuagwu, pp. 31-34.

59

taboo. It is also an obligation to thank **Ala** for her bounties during an important holiday, the New Yam Festival.

Agriculture is important in Ibo-land and therefore **Ajoku**, the "patron divinity of the farmer," is placated. It is believed that yam leaves may turn yellow and wither during the growing season and may result in a bad harvest if the farmer commits a crime on his farmland. The farmer must do all in his power to avoid breaking any of the rules of the farmland and of **Ajoku**, his patron divinity. He should not steal or change his farm's boundary. This provides an important insight into communal nature of the ethic--an offense committed by one farmer can ruin the harvest of other farmers around him.

Ibo men treasure **good** health. So there is a special divinity responsible for herbalism and for traditional medicine. This is **Agwu**, the patron divinity of the medicine man. **Agwu** grants the power of healing. He knows the herbs and all the antidotes against illnesses and "bad medicine." **Agwu** can choose the votary on whom he invests the power of performing wonderful healings. Such healers do not charge much money for their cures for fear that **Agwu** in annoyance could withdraw his healing power. In addition, there is **Ikenga**, the divinity responsible for protection. He grants the necessary immunity against all forms of witchcraft, charm, talisman and dangeours medicine. **Kamalu** or **Amadioha**, the thunder divinity, represents the righteous wrath of **Chukwu**. When crimes appear to escape the notice of other guardians of morality, **Chukwu** may roar from heaven through his thunder. When lightning kills, it is often believed that it is the result of **Chukwu**'s retributive justice.

The cults of the divinities are important for a number of reasons. The divinities are mediators, servants of **Chukwu**. They must be appeased if their favour is to be gained. Particular divinities are believed to be in charge of certain needs. In order to solve problems, relevant divinities must be consulted. For this reason, sacrifices are offered to **Chukwu** through them.

The Ibos strongly believe that their ancestors[18] are alive and still part of the family. They have lived an exemplary life on earth and thus occupy a glorious position in the order of beings, in the spirit world. This position, it is believed, gives them a unique priviledge of watching over and interceding for their children. In order to keep them happy and guarantee their con-

---

[18] Ibid.

tinued support for the living, the Ibo are obligated to give them their share of the family food and drink.

As we have already noted, the belief in **Chukwu,** the great God, or **Chineke,** the creator god, is central. Belief in the divinities is important but secondary. The Ibo man's faith in the power of the divinities and ancestors is not as immutable as it appears at first sight. For instance, in order to satisfy material needs and cure physical ailments, there is the tendency to go from one divinity to another until help is received or the pain or suffering is terminated by death. Traditional religion does not teach resignation to the will of God. The Ibo's religion is a practical one and he seeks for practical solutions for the problems of life. Therefore, if he fails in one direction, he still hopes that success wil come in another. Now and then he is tempted to despair. However, he is quickly encouraged because there is usually no end to the number of divinities to whom he can appeal. The disappointments encountered by some of the traditional religion worshippers, even at the hands of supposedly powerful divinities, gave rise to such proverbs as **"Aja achu onwu"**--sacrifices do not prevent death.

In sum, the principles of Ibo religion give custom, order, discipline and cohesion to the traditional society. These principles create in the people the concept of solidarity in life and of mutual and corporate responsibility in socio-economic matters. Religious practices express a deep spiritual dimension of culture which serves the traditional society in various ways. Ibo religion gives people an insight into the unknown; and it enables them to gain more knowledge of the mysteries about this life and about their relationship to the invisible world. It equips them with spiritual power to deal with some of the baffling, socio-religious problems around them. Moreover, the practices of religion and its world-view give guidance to the people as to what to expect in the future. Therefore, their religion provides a basic cosmology where in they live and carry on their cultural, economic, social and political activities. It is a religion of strong conservative tendencies that seeks to maintain the social equilibrium that preserves the system. It also enables the people to know who they are, where they belong and how they are related to the gods and to one another. In order to inquire further into the nature of the Ibo social relationships, let us examine the kinship system.[19]

---

[19] Ilogu, p. 11; cf. J. S. Mbiti, **African Religion and Philosophy** (London: Heinemann, 1967), pp. 104-109.

The Ibo kinship system is like a vast network of relationships, which embrace everybody in a given local group. It involves the extension of relationships outward from the nuclear family, embracing father, mother, son, daughter, brother and sister, to grandparents, uncle, aunt, nephew and grandchild. Consequently, everybody comes to be related to everybody else. For the Ibo, this relationship extends not only to the living people but also to the members of the family who have died and to those who are yet to be born.[20] A kinship system among the Ibo is either matrilineal or patrilineal.[21] It is matrilineal when it traces its descent in one line through females exclusively to a common ancestress as an entitlement to membership in a discrete group. It is patrilineal when the same procedure applies to the male line of descent. In some societies, both groups exist, so that an individual is at once a member of his father's patrilineal group and his mother's matrilineal group.[22] For the Ibo, communities are either matrilineal like the Ohaffia people or patrilineal like the Awka-Onitsha communities.[23]

As a system, the kinship relationships imply a relationship of interdependence between the component parts, i.e., the social categories and their associated rights and duties.[24] This interdenpendence governs an regulates matters related to descent, succession, inheritance, marriage, extra-marital sexual relations and residence. It also helps to group, recognize, and classify genealogical and affinial relationships for social purposes and provides customs by which the behaviour, thinking and outlook of the individual is conditioned to conform to the ethos of the community to which he/she belongs in so doing. the kinship system acts as a vehicle for mediating the various rights and obligations of its members. It also has various and complex relations with the other social institutions (economic, political, and religious) which make up the total social system.[25]

---

[20] Mbiti, p. 105. Mbiti's remarks are applicable to the Ibos.

[21] Leslie A. White, "Kinship System," in **A Dictionary of Social Sciences**, ed. Julius Gould and William L. Kolb (New York: Free Press, 1964), pp. 366-368.

[22] Nsugbe, **Ohaffia: A Matrilineal Ibo People.**

[23] Ilogu, p. 11.

[24] Fred Eggan, "Kinship," in **International Encyclopedia of Social Sciences**, vol. 8, ed. David Sills (New York: Free Press, 1968), pp. 355-390.

[25] Ibid.

In sum, the system functions to maintain group solidarity and cohesion and orients individual members to the social maze-way. It seeks to preserve itself from disintegration and abuse by punishing acts of violation which endanger or threaten its stability, integrity or continuity. In so doing, the kinship system re-affirms, re-establishes and re-vitalizes its communal solidarity and its values, beliefs and practices. It strengthens its cohesion and renews its beliefs and practices through the celebration of periodic and collective rites, feasts and ceremonies. These features and the various functions of the Igbo kinship system enhance its enduring character and suggest that it provides a foundation for a strong social structure which maintains and manifests ideological tendencies.

Other practices that encourage the maintenance of the existing order are enshrined in prohibitions,[26] or mechanisms of social control. These operate at a subconscious level of socialization and consist of prohibitions designed to preserve domestic life, regulate sexual urges, protect economic life, preserve the normal rhythm of nature and ensure proper reverence for the ancestors and the community of the spirit world. Those designed to regulate domestic life and ensure harmony in the home include the prohibitions against adults deliberately inflicting harm on their parents, a wife throwing her husband to the ground in a fight, or a husband stripping his wife naked in a fight, and so forth. Prohibitions which regulate or control powerful sex urges in people include those against adultery (either by husband or by wife), homosexuality by menfolk, incest, and any form of sexual relation with an animal. Prohibitions designed to protect economic life include prohibitions against the theft of yams, domestic animals or any valuable belongings of another person; alteration of land boundaries in secret; arson and any act betraying the community's

---

[26]Michael Olisa, "Taboos in Ibo Religion and Society," **West African Religion,** no. 11 (January 1972), pp. 4-10. Taboos, according to Olisa, involve those acts regarded as offensive to **Ala,** the Earth goddess, and to the Ancestors. But E. O. Iwuagwu, pp. 30-32, gives the impression that the taboos are "laws." He analyses them in terms of moral laws, social laws, ritual laws and customary laws. This seems to suggest that the traditional society was legalistic. This view is modified by the "shame-guilt" categories, which considers guilt feelings as arising from knowledge of a prohibition transgressed, and of shame-feeling as response to a goal not reached; see F. B. Welbourn, "Some Problems of African Christianity: Guilt and Shame," in **Christianity in Tropical Africa,** ed. Baeta, p. 184.

secrets to an enemy. Prohibitions which are designed to prevent the disturbance of the normal rhythm of nature include a woman climbing a palm tree, acts of deliberate or accidental homicide, a woman giving birth to more than one baby at a time, and a baby coming out feet first at birth, or developing the upper teeth first before the lower ones. Prohibitions instituted to ensure proper reverence of ancestors and the community of the spirit world are made against the killing and eating of totem animals, the disclosure of the identity of a masquerader or the breaking of mourning customs. The existence of this system of prohibitions is further indication that Ibo traditional society is conservative in nature and ideological in orientation.

Given the importance of these socio-religious beliefs, practices and prohibitions to the Ibo individual and community, grave damage, dislocation and discontent were caused when missionaries unwittingly but unsparingly condemned and banned these rites and religious beliefs. However, before we consider the consequences of this ban we shall examine Ibo traditional economy and government.

Traditional Economy

The Ibo's modes of economic production and distribution are the products and consequences of this same conservative ideological orientation. Concerning the traditional economy, Ilogu aptly states:

> Ibo traditional society knows only of subsistence economy and trade by barter. Self supportive family units do farm work on land sometimes commonly owned. . . . They alternate this farmwork with the making of crafts of household necessities . . . land, food, crops, communal work, pure craftsmanship and attention to the gods of economic life are the main factors of such economy.[27]

In short, it is neither a money economy nor a wage-earning form of production system. The aim of agriculture is to provide food for the family and for festive occasions as required by custom. Livestock (cows, chickens, goats, pigs) is reared to meet mainly

---

[27]Ilogu, p. 20.

domestic and ceremonial needs. Communal farmwork is practised to strengthen the existing extended family ties. In addition, this extended family structure provides for the care and maintenance of the aged, the infirm, or handicapped. Wealth is measured for the adult male in terms of the number of his wives and children, the type of titles he acquires and the number of yams he owns. Since yam production is more for prestige than for trade or consumption, the goal is to have a barn full of yams in order to earn a yam title.[28] These items of wealth are more or less perishable commodities, since, there are no adequate storage facilities or perservation techniques for such farm products. Besides, they yield no "monetary interest" when they are stored as in a money economy. There is a distinction here which must be clearly understood. For the Ibo the importance of wealth lay in its social significance rather than in the wealth itself. Thus the person earning a yam title (**"igwa nnu"**) with a thousand or more yams shares them with all the members of his community. He is expected to support the needy members of his family and extended family. By contrast a wealthy man in an industrial capitalist society would be more apt to use his wealth to create further wealth rather than spend it or share it.[29]

On the level of material culture, Ibo techniques are in the handicraft stage. Occupations are mainly manual and range from wood-carving, pottery, cloth weaving, blacksmithing, fishing, hunting, farmwork and sculpture.

There are other occupations which are not subsistence oriented, but these are mostly oriented to religious expressions. As Ilogu observes: "Almost all sculpture in Ibo land are devoted to religious uses and therefore are not regarded as economic activity at all."[30] Art in general does not earn income for the artist. Prestige is not determined purely on economic pursuits, for the artist is frequently honored for his work. At the same time, for the artist, as well as every other member of society, there are clearly defined norms of acceptability. Hence the whole arrangement is aimed at maintaining things as they are. Change is not welcome and the urge for experimentation, innovation and research in art or technology is minimal.

---

[28] Victor C. Uchendu, **The Igbo of Southeast Nigeria** (New York: Holt, Rinehart and Winston, 1965), p. 26.

[29] E. M. Uka, "Elements of Protestant Ethic in African Traditional Culture" (term paper, Graduate School, Drew University, 1978).

[30] Ilogu, p. 22.

Traditional Government

No society can live without a governing body to make decisions, pass judgments, allocate power and resources and initiate courses of action calculated for the preservation of law and order within the society. Thus, for Ibo society, as for every other society, it is necessary to invest power in the hands of an individual or in a group of selected people.

In his book, **Ohaffia: A Matrilineal Ibo People,**[31] Philip Nsugbe succinctly describes the traditional political system of the Ibo people of Ohaffia in Nigeria. He points out that government is vested in age-grades, the number and limits of which are fixed by custom. One has to attain a certain age before qualifying for certain positions in the traditional governmental system. This shows that the people recognize authority in age as well as in traditional office. Among the Ohaffia people (according to Nsugbe), the regulation of political relations in the village is the responsibility of age-based association of males. The structure of the system is pyramidal with a broad base which derives directly from a system of age-grade organization. It is based on the formal recognition of the 36-45 age-grade, the **Akpan.** Above this are two other age grades based on selected members of 46-55 years of age, the **Umuaka,** then finally by survival is the age grade of the elders of 56 years and older, the **ndi Ichin.**[32]

The function of the **Akpan** age-grade is to enforce the laws of the land, and announce and implement the edict of **Umuaka,** the most powerful governmental body in the village. The **Akpan** members are also required to keep watch over the village farms and over the village itself.

The **Umuaka,** the ruling class, is recruited by the retiring elders from the **Akpan** age-grade on the basis of character and achievement. One such worthy person would be a man who maintains full stacks of yam and holds the title of "Ike oba." To understand the meaning of this title one has to underscore the place and significance of "yam" in Ibo society.

Yam is the staple food crop of the Ibo. All other crops are subsidiary. Much of the social and religious life of the people center around the cultivation of yam--so there

---

[31] Nsugbe, **Ohaffia: A Matrilineal Ibo People** (Oxford: Clarendon Press, 1974).

[32] Ibid., p. 59.

are yam festivals, yam deities, and yam titles. Among the Ibos a man's social prestige depends to a great extent on the number of yams he is able to display. **Ike oba** is a yam title in Ohaffia which a father is expected to obtain for his son. A candidate for a political office is expected to have acquired this minimum but important yam title. The highest yam title in Ohaffia is **Igwa-Nnuu.** It is accorded to a man who has over a thousand yams of a particularly prized type ("ezi ji"--the best yam) in his barn.[33]

The candidate for the **Umuaka** membership must also be one who is acknowledged in the village to have lived a life that is above reproach. He must not have been a thief, given to deceit, bad debts, loose living, lying or intemperance. As an association, **Umuaka** is not graded within itself. It has no orders and no hierarchy of office holders, although it has its officials who perform specific duties.

The elders, **Ndi Ichin,** are those who because of their age have retired from active participation in the running of the affairs of the village. They are referred to as "elder statesmen" (i.e., Elders of **Umuaka**). Although they are no longer members of the ruling body, they are sometimes invited to its meetings for advice when serious matters are to be discussed. The prestige and influence of the elders derive from the fact that among the Ibos, wisdom and knowledge of local traditions are generally associated with age. When there are disputes over land, "the elders" are the ones to be consulted. Their views can strengthen or weaken any course of action that **Umuaka** might take. Their role is essentially advisory.

The village assembly (**Ama Ala**) is the fourth body which is generally an ad hoc village assembly of men convened only when issues of moment affecting the whole village develop, such as untraced murder, an external threat, or a proclamation of a change in custom is made. All these issues arouse public interest or indignation and are generally outside the scope and authority of **Umuaka.** The village assembly is the one body in Ohaffia which can stand in the path of **Umuaka** and reverse any unpopular course of action set in motion by **Umuaka.** The village assembly meeting is open to any category of age-groups who may not only attend but have the right of hearing and can contribute to the discus-

---

[33]Ibid., p. 62.

sion freely. Concerning this village assembly meeting, a British administrative official in Ohaffia had this to say:

> Every male person had the right to attend a meeting . . . and to speak when he so desired. This was an indisputable privilege bestowed on each individual and handed down to posterity and such was the conservative mind of the people that any suggested modification or diversion from this rule of government would have been regarded as bordering on the ridiculous. The members of the village council only began to operate administratively when the subject matter of the meeting had already been discussed.[34]

In sum, we find that the political organization is built on age-grades and is rooted in the people's tradition. It combines a rigid framework of support, elements of grass-roots democracy and a system of checks and balances to avoid an undue concentration of power in one age-grade. For those parts of Ibo land where chiefs existed, there was not necessarily, as the Europeans are apt to think, a single concentration of power. Chieftaincy did not imply an autocracy.

The people's political orientation is also aimed at maintaining the social equilibrium. The political structure frowns at people and developments that tend to upset the existing system. Being a part of the cultural system of the traditional society, the political structure is guided in its activities by previously established, comprehensive and interdependent conventional understandings. It is therefore conservative in nature and "ideological" in its tendencies. This condition notwithstanding, George Murdock contends that traditional culture changes. As he puts it, "it is fundamental characteristic of culture, that despite its essentially conservative nature, it does change over time and from place to place."[35] Meyer Fortes states the idea of culture change more forcefully when he said:

---

[34] Ibid., pp. 66–67.

[35] George Murdock, "How Culture Changes, "in **Man, Culture and Society,** ed. Harry L. Shapiro (Oxford: Oxford University Press, 1956), p. 250.

Social structure is not to be thought of as static, but as a condition of equilibrium that only persists by being continually renewed, like the chemical-physiological homostasis of a living organism. Events occur which disturb the equilibrium in some way, and a social reaction follows which tends to restore it.[36]

The important point here is that all cultures involve some elements of change, and some elements of stability. Ibo culture, though strongly conservative, was not, because it could not be, totally moribund. There was change, growth, and development within the traditional structures. These slow changes notwithstanding, we can say from the preceding analysis that traditional societies of Tropical Africa are not very responsive to external change agents. Their culture remains conservative, and hence their mental orientation manifests ideological tendencies.

Socialization Processes

The socialization process is one of the most powerful methods of ensuring the continuity of the preceding social, cultural and religious beliefs and practices of a society. Two important socialization processes are traditional education and rites-of-passage.[37] Traditional education not only teaches a child

---

[36] Meyer Fortes and E. E. Evans Pritchard, **African Political Systems** (Oxford: oxford University Press, 1970), p. XXII.

[37] The rites-of-passage (Obon and Akang) described here are those the writer has taken part in. For classic references on the subject, see Arnold Van Gennep, **The Rites of Passage** (Chicago: University of Chicago Press, 1960). The basic stages of Separation, Transition, and Incorporation identified by Van Gennep are important. Y. A. Cohen, **Transition from Childhood to Adolescence: Cross Cultural Studies of Initiation Ceremeonies, Legal Systems and Incest Taboos** (Chicago: Aldine Publishing Co., 1965). Besides rites-of-passage, which mark the individual's transition through various social and psychological statuses from birth to death, there are others. Rites, as rituals in action, are also performed in the traditional society, "installation rites" of a chief or a priest; there are "travel rites" performed before any lengthy and possibly hazardous journey is undertaken; rites are performed in laying the foundation of a house and before the new house is occupied. There are "curing rites," that is, ritual activities related

the language, beliefs, customs, taboos and genealogies, it also includes the learning of a trade or business for purposes of earning a living. It acquaints a child with the culture of the clan. This begins at the family level, in the home where the child is born. He is taught the language of the clan. This is important, as language equips the child with the tools for self-expression, for social interaction and for cultural identity. The child learns the customs and etiquette needed to be effective in the community. This learning process is not necessarily achieved in a conscious or calculated manner. A child learns (for example) how to respect the elderly through the examples of others or through the kinds of stories he is told, and so forth. Socialization equips him for social integration, guarantees his self-identity and ensures that the individual is better equipped to bear and transmit his secular or religious culture.

The initiation rite serves as a good example of one of the methods of direct or deliberate socialization. By it, a male youth is ritually introduced to the art of communal living. Until then, he is considered an **"Ikpo,"** a fearful weakling who must have to grow out of childhood and enter into adulthood physically, socially and religiously. In this rite he undergoes a change from passive to active membership in the community. To achieve this new status, he has to go through a period of withdrawal from his family and the society, during which time he is instructed and introduced into the ideals, accomplishments, and magical power of the community. He is also exposed to various tests of skill, strength and endurance. The occasion often marks the beginning of acquiring knowledge which is otherwise not accessible to those who have not been initiated. It is a period of learning to endure hardship and to live with other members of the community who are not immediate brothers. The initiation rite also provides the occasion for the initiates to learn the secrets, mysteries, activities and language of the new "secret" society

---

to curing diseases, purification, and exorcism. Traditional medical beliefs and concepts rest on the assumption that disease and sickness result from supernatural attacks by ancestors or malevolent spirits. See also B. M. Eliade, **Birth and Rebirth: The Religious Meanings of Initiation in Human Culture** (New York: Harper & Brothers, 1958), p. 2. He distinguishes three categories of initiations: 1. the collective rituals whose function is to effect the transition from childhood or adolescence to adulthood, 2. those which mark entry into a fraternity or secret society; and 3. the rites involved in assuming a mystical vocation.

they join. In many Ibo clans such as in Afikpo in Imo State of Nigeria, the manhood initiation rite, "Egbela," is a complete system of education which lasts for seven years.[38]

Let us consider concrete examples of initiation rites of the Ohaffia people, an Ibo clan to which the writer belongs. One of such initiation rites is **Obon.** It is for boys between the ages of four and seven. Its procedure is as follows: Before puberty, all boys (in some cases girls) have to undergo rites whose aim is to introduce them into the full communal life and membership of the clan. The youth is sponsored by an adult member who takes him by the hand to the place where the initiation is to take place. The **Obon** youth club to which the neophyte seeks admission engages in a lot of drumming, singing, and dancing which is conducted mostly at night under the full moon. At the scene of the merriment and activity is a small shelter covered all over with pieces of cloth. In this cloth-bound house, the guardian of the boy announces his ward's intentions to the officers of the **Obon** youth club who are responsible for initiating new members into the society. A customary admission fee is paid by the neophyte before negotiations between the initiate and initiators are conducted. After this the lad is led into the cloth-bound house and shown the "mysteries" of **Obon** while members give him knocks on the head for being a fearful weakling, **Ikpo.** An oath of utmost secrecy with threats of dire consequences is administered.

The social significance of the initiation ceremony is worthy of note. A child is weaned from his family (nuclear and extended) into a wider social group where he begins to know his age group and peers. He becomes distinguished from females and is socialized into male roles and group activities like bird hunting, fishing, farming, and so on. He acquires the skills and knowledge necessary for survival in his environment. It is considered embarrassing for a boy to be told to stay indoors with females when **Obon** is being played. Other children feel free to ridicule such a boy. He has no rights, so others could call him nicknames such as **"Nwa-Ikpo,"** i.e., "Little ignoramus."

---

[38] Agha U. Agha, "Egbela Initiation in Afikpo" (research paper submitted to Trinity College, Umuahia, Nigeria). Agha is a product of the Egbela initiation ritual. He outlines the training he received to include: swimming, wrestling, climbing trees, archery, setting up traps and fighting with sticks. Training in self-discipline includes a series of prohibitions.

The **Obon** provides a great source of entertainment. Its rich rhythms and exhausting dance style suit energetic young people. Moreover, the temptation to betray secrets is so great that the clubs offer a very impressive training in moral solidarity among these young boys.

As the young Ibo boy grows into a young adult, he might decide to join **Akan.** This society belongs to teenagers, the lads of a higher age-grade than those of **Obon.** An admission fee (higher than that of **Obon**) is charged. The initiation ritual puts the young man through an obstruction or endurance test of his manliness. The location is usually the bush behind the village. The leaders blindfold the candidate in such a way that he can see very hazily. They take him away from the village compound into the bush. His task is to take a specified route through the bush path to the compound hall where **Akang** is being played. Members hide along the route to beat him, make frightening noises or place logs of wood in the candidate's path. The candidate dares not touch the blindfold or take another route. Some unlucky candidates, weakened by the blows, remove the blindfold and run back to the village. Such failures incur worse taunts. Those who suffer through it and are able to get to the hall amidst the blows and obstacles are considered worthy and strong enough to be members of **Akang.** They are initiated and henceforth are admitted into all the privileges and immunities that belong to members of **Akang** society such as the right to marry, to defend the village during inter-tribal wars, and the right to political franchise.

In the days when inter-tribal warfare was rampant, **Akang** was a test of one's ability to work with a group and survive the long, tedious head-hunting campaign. When a raiding band is organized, no consideration is given to a young man who has not joined **Akang.** This means that he would never join a victory parade if the clan won. Peers would tease him as a coward. Girls would avoid accepting his hand in marriage. In the village, people would refer to him as merely " a pair of testicles," but not a man.

From the preceding account of **Obon** and **Akang** initiation rites, we observe that initiation rites are forms of preparation for major changes in the course of a lifetime. The rites announce changes in status for an individual or a group. They are means by which the society reaffirms its values and beliefs. In addition, the social rites-of-passage enhance a person's or group's social identity. The other rites--of birth, marriage, and death--are attended to with a deep religious regularity calculated to ensure equilibrium in the existing order.

Given the preceding description and analysis of the religious, socio-economic and political conditions of traditional Ibo society and culture, we could identify some of the content of its ideas as follows:

It is a communal and caring society, and hence it places higher value on human life than on material wealth. This idea is reflected in sayings such as **"Nwa ka ego,"** i.e., a child is more precious than money.

The society treasures its solidarity and religious stability, and hence it considers change in its customary beliefs and practices not only ill advised but also impious.

The political arrangements provide for a "village assembly" of all males, and hence the wisdom of all males is considered better than the wisdom of one man or even of one age group. The community finds strength in its unity and number, and hence it has such sayings as "Igwe bu ike," i.e., community is strength, which means strength is determined by the population of a community.

The society places higher value on males than on females, and hence it is better to be male than female.

Age is respected and associated with wisdom and godly living, and therefore it is better to be old than young.

A member of a community is seen as normal and entitled to all the rights and privileges in the society if he/she is born the proper way, i.e., in a manner that does not violate the customary beliefs and practices of the society; for instance, a person has to be born head first, not feet first, not as a twin nor as a hermaphrodite.

The religious orientation, both in thinking and in vocabulary, is basically pragmatic and utilitarian rather than spiritual and mystical; hence Ibo religious ideas lack emphasis on missionary presentation and interpretation of "eschatology." The Ibo believe in a future life and in the fact that conduct in this life has some bearing in one's fate in the next. In spite of this, the whole tenor of prayers and sacrifices is directed mainly towards long life here on earth, concrete protection from specific ills, prosperity, and so forth.[39]

---

[39] The staple diet of Christian missionary preaching was "Eschatology"--the doctrine of the last things. It was presented in such a way to direct the attention of African converts to the next world--where they will

Having considered the factors that shape the thinking of Igbo and the product of such thinking, we shall now turn in the next chapter to the corresponding nature of the British mentality and the consequences of the encounter between British and African mentalities which transformed the African mentality from a conservative ideological orientation to revolutionary utopian tendencies.

---

inherit and enjoy all the good things which they believe have been denied them in the present world. Missionaries presented the doctrine of Eschatology as the hope of the Christian for a reward in heaven. This type of futurist eschatology excels in and encourages hunting for signs of imminent end of the world in such events as famine, earthquakes, wars and rumours of wars. In so doing, it tended to produce among African converts a type of mentality which evaded responsibility and involvement in the existential moment of here and now in the Christian life. For a full discussion on the subject in rela-tion to the "Evangelization of Tribal Africa," see John Mbiti, **New Testament Eschatology in African Background** (London: Oxford University Press, 1971).

CHAPTER IV

THE BRITISH VICTORIAN MENTALITY

In order to inquire into the characteristics of British Victorian mentality we need to understand their attitude towards the world, especially the non-Western parts of the world like Africa.

Jean Copans' article, "African Studies: A Periodization," is instructive at this point. [1] He presents a five-period chronological classification of Afro-Euro connections. The first period goes from the beginning of the eighteenth century to 1860. This was for Britain the period of exploration of Africa, and with this early contact the ideological and theoretical confrontation focused on questions about the origins of human society. The literature that furnished the information about Africans during this period was largely travel accounts. The second period (1860-1920) refers to the period of colonial conquest, action which was rationalized by Social Darwinism. This period marks the high water mark of the British missionary enterprise in Africa. The third period (1920-1945) marks the period of development, when Western countries (Britain) felt "self-justified" in developing Africa on their own terms without any critical evaluation of the theoretical and ideological complications of their policy. The period of 1945-1960 marks the period of de-colonization, with the massive entry of Africans into history and science and the consequent questioning of the colonial connection. The fifth period, 1960 onwards, marks the period of Neo-colonialism: the discovery of the illusions of independence and the emergence of radical criticism of the political, economic, religious and cultural connections with Europe. The contemporary call for a moratorium is a product of the era of the seventies, but its roots lie well beyond the sixties (with the emergence of the African independent churches and African independent nations) and could be traced down to Henry Venn (1796-1873) in England and Rufus Anderson (1796-1880) in the United States of America, both of whom developed in the nineteenth century the "three-self" formula of self-governing, self-supporting and self-propagating churches in the mission fields to

---

[1] Jean Copans, "African Studies: A Periodization," in **African Social Studies,** ed. Peter C. W. Gutkind and Peter Waterman (New York: Monthly Review Press, 1977), p. 19.

deal with Western missionary paternalism and imperialism.[2]   In view of the socio-historic context in which the call for a moratorium emerged, we argue that it is not only theological or missiological criteria which can account for the call. We opt for a sociological interpretation of the call in which we contend that historical, economic an political forces also combine to make the call intelligible.

The preceding over-view enables us to locate easily the periods we are chiefly concerned with, that is, the early nine-teenth century (1800-1860) and the secondhalf of the twentieth century which spans from 1960-1970's and after. This means we shall be concerned on the one hand with the nineteenth century issues which tropical Africa posed for Britain since the dawn of the Evangelical revival and the rise of secular liberalism (i.e., the movement that thought man could improve his lot in the world without any special religious revelation mediated through the ecclesiastical establishment), and on the other hand with the questions of Africa's struggle to free itself from overdependence on Europe and North America in the twentieth century. We direct our attention to Britain as the leading European world power in the first period and to the United States as the leading world power in the northern hemisphere in the last period. (The former will be dealt with here and the latter will be the focus of Chapter V. We shall deal with these two polar periods because the nineteenth century British assumptions about itself in relation to Africa, i.e., her sense of moral and material superiority, her idea of having an obligation to enlighten Africans, her sense of the need for reparations, i.e., the working off of "white man's guilt" for harm done to Africans, and the subtle but ever-present tendency to colonize and control Africans, are quite similar to those of the Americans even in this twentieth century.

---

[2]Peter Beyerhaus and Henry Lefever, **The Responsible Church and the Foreign Mission** (Grand Rapids, Mich.: Eerdmans Publishing Co., 1964), pp. 25-32. The issue of selfhood for the "younger churches" has since been discussed in succeeding conferences of the International Missionary Council (IMC) to wit: The Madras Conference (1938), see **The Growing Church,** "The Madras Series," vol. 2 (New York: IMC, 1939), p. 276ff; The Whitby (Ontario) Con-ference (1947), C. W. Ranson, ed., **Renewal and Advance** (London: Edinburgh House Press, 1948), pp. 173ff; The Willingen Conference (1952), IMC, "The Indigenous Church," **The Missionary Obligation of the Church** (London: Edin-burgh House Press, 1953), pp. 8ff; **The Bangkok Assembly 1973** (New York: World Council of Churches, 1973), p. 104.

And with British decline in power, these assumptions seem to manifest themselves on the American scene as well, now that she is a leading power in this century. This makes the moratorium issue a combination of old nineteenth century grievances and new twentieth century concerns.

The issues that Britain dealt with in her relation with Africa in the first period were derived from the ethical implications of the Evangelical movement and the rise of liberalism. The British saw their duty in terms of freeing the African slaves, converting them to Christianity and replacing slave trade with legitimate trade in goods (raw mineral and agricultural products from Africa in exchange for manufactured goods from Britain). The statutes of 1807 had declared the slave trade illegal and throughout the century the churches and anti-slavery societies were to respond. Concern for Africa flowed from some of the most vivid conceptions of Victorian religious and political life. And for this reason the chief African issues for the Victorians were atonement and duty. The chains had to be broken from the African's neck. He must be converted. He must be civilized. One should trade with him. One must open the gates of progress to him. During this period "all that was generally known about Africans consisted of horrible tales of the 'Middle Passage,' fables about noble savages degraded by muskets and gin, and an infant race awaiting the Gospel dawn." [3]

In this chapter we will inquire into the nature of Victorian mentality by examining the intellectual, political and religious climate of the period. We will focus particularly on the difficulty the British had in translating their grand objective or theory into practice, or of crystalizing a principle into a fact. We will examine how this difficulty is to some extent reflected in the British humanitarian movements--the missionary movement and the anti-slavery movement--and in the British colonial policy towards Africa. We will analyze the social, political and religious implications (for Africa) of the British mentality with due attention to the unconscious tendencies engendered in their attitude. Finally, we will examine the structures and modes of operation by whych they carried out their objectives and sought to maintain and preserve their privileged position.

---

[3] Ronald Robinson and John Gallagher with Alice Denny, **Africa and the Victorians, The Climax of Imperialism** (New York: Doubleday Anchor Books, 1968), p. 27.

The Elizabethan-Puritan England which preceded the Victorian era witnessed, according the Louis Wright, "a congenial alliance between religion and trade." [4] This alliance attained a level of maturity and sophistication in the Victorian age when we hear David Livingstone say his mission to Africa was to introduce Christianity, Commerce and Civilization.[5] Though these three factors represent three levels of activity, their representatives--the missionary, the trader, the diplomat and the settler-- share the same world view, the same citizenship, the same religion; their interests were interwoven and they helped each other. For one to think of them as three independent units is to miss the point. The three factors--commerce, civilization and Christianity--constitute the mission of the people of England to the rest of mankind. In fact the seventeenth century English preachers saw no distinction among the tree C's. This same sentiment runs through from the Elizabethan period to the Victorian era.

The other factor at work in the Victorian Briton that reinforced his views about himself vis-à-vis the African was his heritage of the Enlightenment attitude towards the world, "he dared to know." [6] He dared to know about the physical universe, so he studied the physical sciences (physics and chemistry) and learned the nature and composition of matter. He dared to know about the stars and planets, so he learned astronomy; he dared to know about the history of the earth, so he studied geology.[7] These daring endeavors to learn, to properly organize and apply Reason, led the British to discover or rediscover nature beneath the concealing corruptions of religion, social structure, conventions and misleading impressions of sense experience.

---

[4]Louis B. Wright, **Religion and Empire, The Alliance Between Piety and Commerce in English Expansion** (New York: Octagon Books, Inc., 1965), p. v.

[5]William Cecil Northcott, **Cristianity in Africa** (Philadelphia: Westminster Press, 1963), p. 38.

[6]James Livingstone, **Modern Christian Thought: From the Enlightenment to Vatican II** (New York: Macmillan Co., 1971), p. 4.

[7]K. S. Latourette, **A History of the Expansion of Christianity**, vol. 4 (New York: Harper & Brothers, 1941), pp. 10-14.

The inevitable result of the learning endeavour was progress. [8] The enlightened man tended towards a simple view that the agent of progress is the effective application of reason to the control of the physical and cultural environment. Education therefore became one of the major ways in which reason was to do the work of reform. This led to an optimistic, this-worldly belief in human power, of human beings brought up rationally from infancy to achieve steady and unlimited progress towards material comfort and spiritual happiness for all people upon this earth. The standards employed as the touchstone of progress were seen in the control of diseases, the improvement in the methods of farming, in material productivity, in the reduction of back-breaking labor, in the techniques of rapid mass communication and in the spread of literacy.[9]

The Enlightenment mentality, particularly as informed by its idea of reason and progress, contributed to the dawn of the Industrial Revolution when the use of machines driven by inanimate power (steam, water and electricity) and production at all levels (food, clothing, housing, population) multiplied. Invention and innovations grew apace. The factory, railway, steamship and the telegraph, all combined to usher in the dawn of a new era in the nineteenth century. Therefore, with the extension of knowledge and the mastery of physical power, the ability to alleviate man's chronic enemies--hunger, poverty, disease, ignorance, and war--the Victorian Briton felt he was at the apex of civilization, and assumed it was Britain's responsibility to help others climb up the ladder of progress, especially those at the zero point of human society. This sentiment finds expression in such sayings as this:

> Upon the ladder of progress, nations and races seemed to stand higher or lower according to the proven capacity of each for freedom and enterprise: the British at the top, followed a few rungs below by the Americans, and other 'striving-to-go-ahead' Anglo-Saxons. The Latin peoples were thought to come next, though far behind. Much lower still stood the vast Oriental communities of Asia and North Africa. . . . Lowest of all stood the 'aborigines' whom it was thought had never learned

---

[8] Crane Brinton, "Enlightenment," in **Encyclopedia of Philosophy** (New York: The Macmillan Co. and The Free Press, 1967), 1:519-522.

[9] Ibid., p. 520.

enough social disciplines to pass from the family and tribe to themaking of a state.[10]

This optimism on progress was well articulated by influential thinkers like Condorcet.[11] He argued that it was reasonable to expect human species to be capable of indefinite progress. He evaluated progress in moral terms, that is, moral progress was to be instrumental in the abolition of inequality between nations; by it, "the human race will be emancipated from its shackles, released from the empire of fate and from the enemies of progress, advancing with sure step along the path of truth, virtue and happiness." [12]

This belief in progress became universal in the nineteenth century. The expectations of science and technological progress became more specific, fed by the constant triumphs of discovery and invention and their application to daily lives of people. There was also belief in the steady moral advances with the advances in knowledge. These two sides of progress were seen as two facets of an advancing civilization, with people becoming naturally humane once their mind had been emancipated from bondage of ancient superstition and dogma. Evil was seen to be based on ignorance and error; the Platonic doctrine that virtue was knowledge tended to hold sway; and the term Enlightenment covered both.

The nineteenth century, therefore, was a time of intellectual ferment. The Industrial Revolution and the mind-set of the Enlightenment contributed to other revolutions not only in terms of machines but also in terms of ideas. Therefore, the period marked the development and articulation of the doctrines of individualism, laissez-faire economics and capitalism which thrived on free competition. These ideas found their philosophical and scientific rationalization and application in the nineteenth century theory of evolution put forward by Charles Darwin in his book, **Origin of Species** (1859).[13]

---

[10] Robinson et al., pp. 2-3.

[11] Condorcet, **Essquise d'un Tableau Historique de Progres de L'Esprit Humain** (1795) [Sketch for a Historical Picture of the Progress of Human Mind], trans. Jane Barraclough (New York: Noonday Press, 1955), pp. 199-210.

[12] Ibid.

[13] Charles Darwin, **On the Origin of Species,** 1 st ed. (London: John Murray, 1859). See its abridged version in **Darwin and Darwinism,** ed. Harold Y. Vanderpool (London: D. C. Heath and Co., 1973), pp. 43-74.

In it, Darwin argued that evolution by natural selection and not by creation accounts for the origin of life. He provided a systematic theoretical explanation of the biological workings of an evolutionary process from lower to higher species. This evolutionary process was also interpreted in terms of progress.

It was Herbert Spencer who bestowed scientific respectability upon the application of biological evolution to social life. He was among the first to give social response to the evolutionary thought. For him in England and his American disciples, notably William Graham Sumner, the concept of evolution through the struggle for survival became the key that unlocked the secrets behind human social development. He argued that through evolution by natural selection, human society slowly and steadily progressed from hostile, regimented, primitive communities to peaceful, interdependent, complex ones. And the way to assure that further progress occurs is to make sure that the stern, self-operating natural laws of individualism and competition continue to eliminate the unfit and to place the future power and influence in the hands of the most intelligent and talented.

Darwinian theory of evolution by natural selection also legitimized Adam Smith's earlier theory of laissez-faire, best known through his book, **The Wealth of Nations,** published in 1776.[14] In that theory Adam Smith extolled "the natural effort of every individual to better his condition when suffered to exert itself with freedom and security . . . in a civilized country as long as he does not violate the laws of justice."[15] He argued that if security was created by the legislator without unduly restraining spontaneous individual activity, an invisible hand led man to promote socially desirable ends. Smith, therefore, maintained that competition, motivated by private interest, was the key to economic success both on the personal and on the national level. He supported the idea of laissez-faire ("let them do"), a concept of non-intervention by government developed by the eighteenth century French economists in reaction to British mercantilism. Smith, like the French economists, believed that market mechanism in a free enterprise competitive economy tends towards full employment without government intervention. This idea was compatible with the ideals of the Puritan Protestant ethic which

---

[14] Adam Smith, **The Wealth of Nations,** ed. with Introduction Edwin Cannon and Max Lerner (New York: Random House, 1939).

[15] Ibid, bk. 3, chap. 1, pp. 355-356.

made individual competition and economic success both desirable and respectable. The idea of less government control on individual and collective economic pursuits consequently led to the concept of separation of Church and State whereby the church felt free in the nineteenth century to form missionary societies without waiting for the state to grant it a charter to carry out mission overseas.

Besides Adam Smith's works, Herbert Spencer's socio-logical writings [16] also came to be embraced by political and economic and religious leaders of the late nineteenth century England whose interests were thus given the appearance of scientific legitimation. Social dislocation of the time was written off as the inevitable price of progress. What survived out of the struggle was seen as the fittest. Dominant persons, groups or nations began to assert that dominance was justified. Evolution was then seen as a cosmic process not to be resisted. As the theory came to be applied to human history, evolutionary principles supplied the conceptual framework for progress. Hence it was fashionable for the Victorian Englishman to believe in a progression from the cave man to the upper middle class Victorian family, the height of civilization.

With the convergence and combination of all these dynamic forces--intellectual, technological, industrial, commercial-- all within the conceptual framework of Social Darwinism, the Victorian British, as we have observed, ventured beyond their borders in what could be read as a spontaneous expression of an inherently dynamic and prosperous society. The dominant note of the period was one of optimism, confidence and hope spurred by rapidly increasing wealth, new discoveries in the realm of natural sciences, fresh inventions, the expansion of trade and of colonies, the opening and the occupation and development of virgin lands gave them a sense of accomplishment. With the multiplication of physical comforts and luxuries, studies in medi-cine, hygiene and public health, the growth in the number of schools and universities, and the alleviation of disease and poverty and war, society was declared to be on the way to perfection. Thus, there was an outward surge of men and ideas from England sweeping across North and South America, past the Middle East

---

[16] Herbert Spencer, "Society Conditioned by Evolution," in **Darwin and Darwinism,** ed. Vanderpool, p. 190; cf. William R. Catton, "The Development of Sociological Thought," in **Handbook of Modern Sociology,** ed. Robert E. L. Faris (Chicago: Rand McNally Co., 1964), pp. 928-930.

to India, breaking in on the coasts of China, entering the mind of Japan, and on across to Australia and New Zealand. The lands which had not submitted politically had at least been touched by English commerce, and most of them had been modified by the British culture.[17] A consequence of this expansion was the disintegration or transformation of non-European cultures under the impact of British culture.

Even though other nations like France, Spain, Portugal and Germany had emerged during this period, the English-speaking people were the undisputed leaders. They were first to develop the use of machines and to become industrialized. On the sea the British Navy was supreme. They had the lion's share of the commerce of the world. Their empire, according to Latourette, "surpassed any the world had ever known."[18]

The Ambivalence in British Mentality

Given this nineteenth century British mentality and this sense of social, scientific, technological and religious superiority over non-Europeans, we may now examine the social implications of their posture vis-à-vis the Africans whom they considered to be at the zero point of an ascending socio-religious and cultural evolution.

Karl Mannheim as we have noted, examines how people think, given their rank or situation in society, and the unconscious tendencies that are generated from their thinking. He contends that the ruling class thinks ideologically, that is, in a manner in which they become so intensively self-focused that they are no longer able to see certain facts which would undermine their sense of superiority. Likewise, Mannheim points to the opposite direction of utopian thinking, namely that certain oppressed groups in a society become so strongly interested in the destruction and transformation of a given condition of society that they unwittingly see only those elements in the situation which tend to negate it.[19]

---

[17] Latourette, pp. 12-14.

[18] Ibid.

[19] Karl Mannheim, **Ideology and Utopia: An Introduction to the Sociology of Knowledge**, trans Louis Wirth and Edward Shils (New York: Harcourt, Brace, 1954), p. 36.

Applying Mannheim's insight to nineteenth century British mentality vis-à-vis the African, we observe that implicit in the British idea of being at the pinnacle of an ascending human civilization is the notion that there are those like the Africans, at the zero point of human civilization, whom they must help to rise up the ladder of civilization. In principle their objective was grand, but in actual practice, it resulted in the use of a language of "Us" and "Them." This language of division and separation is what Gregory Baum, writing on the implications of Anti-Jewish trends present in Christian preaching, describes as "a rhetoric of exclusion."[20] He contends that such rhetoric, if unchecked, is capable of producing from the dominant group "spontaneous, yet untruthful judgments about others, leading possibly to the creation of institutions that embody such wide-spread contempt."[21] Such feelings on the part of the dominant group could tempt them to feel justified in treating those who differ from them as less than human. This accounts for one of the reasons why the British slaughtered the primitive tribesmen of Australia for their land.[22]

With reference to the British missionary enterprise, some elements of this "rhetoric of exclusion" could be detected in some of the things they said about Africans. The missionaries, as creatures of their age, were convinced of the superiority of their culture which they did not always differentiate from their faith in the superiority of Christianity. They were inclined to think of the African as a heathen, and some aspects of their conception of a heathen are well portrayed by Robert Glover in his book, **The Progress of World Wide Mission.** This book has been revised and enlarged recently by Herbert Kane. Glover's views about the temporal, moral and spiritual condition of the heathen are worthy of note. He describes their temporal condition as marked by "dire poverty, wretched homes, unremitting toil, gross intellectual ignorance, all in a mute and pathetic appeal for help." Their moral condition is described as "reeking with filthy and degrading habits, abominable practices, unmentionable cruelties and crimes."

---

[20] Gregory Baum, "The Jews, Faith and Ideology," **The Ecumenist** (July-August 1972): 71-76.

[21] Ibid., p. 72.

[22] Paul G. Hiebert, "Missions and Anthropology: A Love/Hate Relationship," **Missiology: An International Review** 6 (April 1978): 166-178.

Glover portrays the heathens as "spiritually lost, wicked, willful sinners, without Christ, having no hope, and without God in the world."[23]

This sort of picture of the condition of the "heathen" was, according to Eugene Stock, a British church historian, the main part of the appeals, speeches and sermons of the leaders of the mission societies in Britain.[24]

The Christian stands in contrast to the heathen and is exemplified by the Western man or missionary. He is seen as good, honest, peace-loving, benevolent and high-minded, a philanthropist. Proof of the devotion of the missionaries lies in the large percentage of them who died at their post, with new recruits always arriving to carry on the unfinished task.[25] The schools, hospitals and printing presses which have come into existence through their efforts are considered as distinct milestones of progress. Often the very presence of a missionary, it is said, raises the moral standard of all who come in contact with or even gain a sight of his daily life. He/She was always seen as a spectacle of a holy, self-restrained, chaste, benevolent and laborious person, who astonishes, attracts and gradually brings into subjection the will of the unsophisticated races.[26] The implication of these realities of the "rhetoric of exclusion" accounts at least in part for the inability of Britain to actualize her ethical goals for Africa. She tended to fuse and confuse absolute ethical principles which derive from the Evangelical revival with her relative cultural values. She aimed at converting the heathen to Christ and at the same time to civilize him to become like one of them. A classic example of this fusion of Western civilization with Christianity perhaps is best ilustrated in an article

---

[23] Robert Hall Glover, **The Progress of World Wide Mission**, rev. and enl. H. Herbert Kane (New York: Harper and Brothers, 1960), pp. 4-5.

[24] Eugene Stock, **History of ChurchMissionary Society: Its Environment, Its Men and Its Work** (London: CMS, 1899) 1:130-131.

[25] T. A. Beetham, **Christianity and the New Africa** (New York: Frederick A. Praeger, 1967), p. 11.

[26] Robert N. Cust, **Africa Rediviva** (New York: Union Theological Seminary Library, n.d.), p. 3.

entitled "Influence of Missions on the Temporal Conditions of the Heathen."[27] The author argues that

> . . . the office of the gospel is to bring the heathen nations to be like Christian nations because a true civilization cannot exist apart from Christianity. And the proof of this is attested by the fact that the heathen possess 'no Chambers of Commerce, no insurance companies, no banks, no joint stock association' because the complete development of the tender affections and the institution of those associations by which men express their interests in one another depends almost entirely upon the diffusion of Christianity.[28]

By reasoning in this fashion, the missionary unwittingly shared in some of the basic values of the British culture. So he or she dressed in a certain style, lived monogamously, believed in abstract justice, ate certain foods in certain ways and favoured the specific econimic and political system of his fellow countryman. At the same time missionaries represented a subculture within the British social life, for they emphasized theology and morals more than other people. They were more honest (or were supposed to be) and were more concerned with the minor taboos of drink and verbal prohibitions against obscenity, profanity and blasphemy. As one anthropologist has pointed out, "a missionary is thus a member of his society, characterized by the culture of his society only differing from other members of his society by emphasis in particular aspects of his culture."[29]

In the light of such thinking the missionaries and their supporters believed that both the African institutions and African "character" had to be transformed. Missionary work was "to make these [savages] abodes of ignorance and degradation, as happy, as gladsome, as the happiest and most gladsome village in our

---

[27]"Influence of Missions on the Temporal Conditions of the Heathen," **Baptist Missionary Magazine** 29 (April 1849): 101–105, cited by Robert F. Berkhofer, **Salvation and the Savage** (University of Kentucky Press, 1965), pp. 1–15.

[28]Ibid.

[29]G. Gordon Brown, "Missionaries and Cultural Diffusion," **American Journal of Sociology** (November 1944): 214.

peaceful land." [30] To achieve these goals of character transformation and the introduction of civilized institutions, the "savage"
had to be instructed. The missionaries were to "persuade" the
Africans by every rational motive to the practice of civilization.
And civilization in this respect meant that Christianity and
Protestantism were seen as embracing the highest evolution of
morals. Hence the missionary had only to focus on its superiority
over the savage degradation in order to secure mass conversion,
which was conceived as an instructional problem. These services
and activities tend to induce missionaries largely by unconscious
processes to create illusions of themselves and their vocations.
Thus Philip Curtin wirtes:

> Perhaps the most striking aspect of the British immage
> of Africa . . . was its variance from the African reality.
> . . . Reporters went to Africa knowing the reports of
> their predecessors and the theoretical conclusions already
> drawn from them. They were therefore sensitive to data
> that seemed to confirm their European preconceptions,
> and they were insensitive to contradictory data. . . .
> Data that did not fit the existing image were most often
> simply ignored. As a result, British thought about Africa
> responded very weakly to new data of any kind. . . .
> The image of Africa, in short, was largely created in
> Europe to suit European needs, more often intellectual
> needs. . . .[31]

Ideological projections of this kind, found in all realms
of culture, clearly exist in Euro-Afro cross-cultural mission. Missionary ideology then becomes, in part at least, the bearer of
Western illusions and a screen that cuts the missionaries off from
socio-economic and political realities in their relationship to
Africa. Even when missiologists interpret mission as **missio Dei**
--God's own mission--it could still become for the Western mis-
sionaries a defense of their prejudices, their superstition and their
position of power. Western missionaries tended to operate in
Africa as if they were the sole bearers of the Truth about God.
Hence they apply Truth as an occasion of triumphing over the
Africans; they rejoice that they are right and the Africans are

---

[30] Quoted in Berkhofer, p. 13.

[31] PHILIP D. Curtin, **The Image of Africa: British Ideas and Action
1780-1850** (London: Macmillan & Co., 1965), pp. 479-480.

wrong, or they could say: We are Christians and they are heathens. As a result of this kind of thinking, any attempt to send missionaries from Africa to Britain is dubbed a reverse flow--i.e., "missionary in reverse."

Paul Hiebert considers Britain who, when her missionaries, explorers and anthropologists had come face to face with a bewildering variety of peoples from different races and cultures, wondered whether these other people were fully human in the same sense that the educated people of the West were thought to be human. [32] As we have seen, the missionaries thought in terms of giving the natives the blessing and privileges of Western civilization. The anthropologists, Hiebert says, thought in terms of studying the "natives" in order to understand the ways of helping them. In either case, both anthropologists and missionaries were operating from a common cultural base which saw Britain at the apex of human civilization and were unconsciously committed to uphold her prestige over against the other group.

To this end, the anthropologists studied the non-European cultures as objects in the physical sciences. This scientific methodology was very dehumanizing and took no account of the people's indigenous sciences, their social organization and their religious beliefs. Given their atheistic and deterministic stance, the anthropologists treated the non-European people's religion as irrational superstition. They gave scientific explanation for human beliefs and activities in terms of economic and environmental factors on the one hand and socio-political factors on the other hand. Eventualy, both the anthropologists and missionaries became involved in the colonial process and most of their projects were funded by the British colonial office.[33] It is at this point that their unconscious ambivalent tendencies come to light to demonstrate that early anthropologists and missionaries shared the same basic colonial assumptions as their compatriots. In spite of some of these ambivalent attitudes towards non-Europeans, and the irony implied, Britain still thought of herself as the bearer of the torch of civilization to the rest of the world, the uplifter of the downtrodden. Reginald Heber's song recorded in Methodist hymn books bears testimony to the British mentality:

---

[32] Hiebert, pp. 166-167.

[33] Ibid., p. 167.

88

From Greenland's icy mountains
From India's coral Island . . .
From many an ancient river . . .
They call us to deliver
Their land from errors chain

Can we whose souls are lighted
With wisdom from on high
Can we to men benighted
The lamp of life deny?

We conclude that the British Protestant missionary enterprise was also unconsciously subject to ideological tendencies, that
is, strategies unconsciously generated by the society to protect
itself against others, reinforce its views and values, legitimate
its power and defend its privilges. We shall further examine the
aims and motives of both the British colonial policy and the
British humanitarian movements in order to identify some of their
"ideological" tendencies.

It needs to be understood that the avowed purpose of
the colonial enterprise was to enlighten, civilize and uplift the
backward peoples of India, Asia, Africa, and China. The fact of
the matter, however, is that "colonization is an objective relation
which demands, indeed imposes a particular political and particular
'ideological' system congruent with its objective character."[34]
In doing so, it develops justifications for colonialism by saying
that colonialism is beneficial to the colonies in the fundamental
sense of improving the quality of their lives. By this interpretation, colonialism is not self-seeking, not exploitation but "salvation." [35] The colonies are described as "protectorates" implying
that the colonial power was really fiduciary and that the **raison
d'etre** was protection of colonies. The British preferred to think
of colonialism as a "mandate" to help backward peoples. This
characterization of colonialism not only had the effect of making
it look like generosity instead of rapacity; it also enabled the
colonizers to develop some defense against the charge that

---

[34]Claude Ake, "The Congruence of Political Economics and Ideologies
in Africa," in **The Political Economy of Contemporary Africa**, ed. Peter
C. W. Gutkind and Immanuel Wallerstein (London: SAGE Publications, 1976),
p. 199.

[35]Ibid.

colonialism was racist or that it entailed treating coloured peoples as subhumans.

Furthermore, this characterization of colonialism presupposed the possibility of civilizing the colonized people of Africa, a process that could not happen all at once and so had to be done in a manner commensurate with colonized peoples' stage of development. And this, unfortunately, meant limiting their participation and their claims in the community of "civilized" British people. The idea professed was that colonialism ensured the removal of the obstacles blocking Africa's development. So with uncanny ingenuity, the British colonizers were able to reconcile racism with the proclamation of the equality of all people.[36]

Drawing on the insight of Reinhold Niebuhr in his argument on the morality of nations, [37] one could suggest that one

of the unconscious reasons why Western missionaries ventured out with the "universality" of the Christian gospel on their lips is not only for the benefit of the Third World people whose economic resources their countries have been exploiting, but, as Niebuhr would say, for the purpose of endowing their own nation with the aura of the sacred.[38] The fact of this could be seen in the adjectives: primitive, heathen, backward, foolish, benighted, and so forth, which are all part of the missionary's working vocabulary in his reference to non-Western countries, especially Africa.[39] Referring to Niebuhr's clues again, we can see that "the reason why privileged groups are more hypocritical than the under-privileged ones is that special privilege can be defended in terms of the national ideal of equal justice only by proving that it contributes something to the good of the whole."[40] The most common proof of hypocrisy among the privileged groups, says Niebuhr, is their assumption that their privileges are the just payments with which society rewards meriotorious functions.

From the point of view of the sociology of knowledge, one could suggest that perhaps one of the unconscious reasons

---

[36] Ibid.

[37] Reinhold Nieburh, **Moral Man in Immoral Society** (New York: Charles Scribner's Sons, 1932), pp. 83-112.

[38] Ibid., pp. 95-97.

[39] **The Christian Occupation of Africa:** Proceedings of the Africa Conference held in New York City, No. 20-22, 1917, p. 128.

[40] Niebuhr, p. 117.

why the British people sponsored Christian mission could be to atone for her actual pretensions.

Niebuhr contends that nations wrestle with how to justify their hypocrisies by introducing a slight measure of real international achievement; they learn how to do justice to wider interests than their own, while still pursuing their own interest.[41] He refers to one who shares the same views as his, Wilhelm Deberlius, a foreign critic and observer of English life, who said:

> England is the solitary power with a national program which while egoistic through and through, at the same time promises to the world as a whole something which the world passionately desires: order, progress, and eternal peace.[42]

Another method by which a privileged group such as Britain could secure her position is to appoint herself as the apostle of law and order. Since every society has an instinctive desire for harmony and avoidance of strife, the privileged group uses the instruments of enforcing social order to its own advantage. They proclaim how dangerous it is to disturb the peace and how they fear anarchy. This passion for peace leads them to condemn out-of-hand actions that they consider a threat to peace, such as riots and demonstrations [43] conducted by those they dominate.

On the whole, "so persistent is the cry of peace among the privileged classes and so strong the seeming abhorrence of every form of violence and anarchy that one might imagine them actuated by the purest pacifist principles were it not for the fact that they betray no pacifist scruples when they consider international affairs." [44]

Western mission and the anti-slavery movement were concerned with international affairs. So let us examine each of them, beginning with the abolitionist movement, to see if they exhibit tendencies which Mannheim describes as "ideological." The Anti-slavery crusade was an outgrowth of the British Protestant Revival. It promoted the cause of the abolitionists who believed

---

[41] Ibid., p. 97.

[42] Ibid., p. 109.

[43] Ibid., p. 129.

[44] Ibid., p. 139.

"that the chains had to be struck from the African's neck, he must be liberated, re-settled and traded with."[45] One of the areas they chose for the resettlement of freed slaves and the introduction of legitimate trade was West Africa.

William Wilberforce and his group believed that the growth of a legitimate European trade in West Africa would not only be of mutual benefit to Africans and Europeans but would tend to drive the Slave Trade out, because the chiefs would discover that the foreign goods they wanted could be got in exchange for other African products than human beings. This was the idea behind the formation of the Sierra Leone Company, chartered by Act of Parliament in 1791. Granville Sharp was the president; Thornton, chairman; Wilberforce was among the first directors.[46] Their ultimate aims were three in all: first to spread Christianity with the help of missionaries, hence their interest and involvement in the formation of missionary societies; second, commerce, to introduce and encourage legitimate European trade; and third, colonization; with the pioneer work having been done by missionaries and traders, it was then for the British government to take over the area as a Crown Colony.[47] Reginald Coupland, a British colonial historian, described this process as "unique experiment in philanthropic colonization." [48] The experiment marked the earliest conception of Christianity, commerce, colonization, the three distinct but interrelated threads that we have seen run through British activities in nineteenth-twentieth century Africa.

One of the reactions to "philanthropic imperialism," i.e., an imperialism directed by a sense of responsibility for the protection and advancement of weaker peoples, came from Eric Williams' book, **Capitalism and Slavery.** [49] Williams, a distinguished Negro scholar who later became Prime Minister of his native Trinidad, questioned Coupland's central thesis. He took Coupland to task on account of Coupland's imaginary interview with William

---

[45] Robinson et al., p. 27.

[46] Sir Reginald Coupland, **The British Anti-Slavery Movement** (New York: Barnes and Noble, 1964), p. 84.

[47] Ibid.

[48] Ibid.

[49] Eric Williams, **Capitalism and Slavery** (New York: Capricorn Books, 1944), pp. 178-196.

Wilberforce. Coupland asked Wilberforce: "What do you think Sir, is the primary significance of your work, the lesson of the abolition of the slave system?" The instant answer is: "It is God's work. It signifies the triumph of His will over human selfishness. It teaches that no obstacle of interest or prejudice is irremovable by faith and prayer."[50]

Williams contends that this imaginary response from Wilberforce is "a deliberate attempt by contemporaries to present a distorted view of the abolitionist movement." The real doubt as Williams saw it was whether the humanitarian motive was anything to be compared with the economic motive for imperial expansion. In a search for an answer to this question, Williams inquired into the British abolition of the slave trade and of the slavery. He described the abolitionist movement as "one of the greatest propaganda movements of all time."[51] The humanitarians were the spearheads of the onslaught which destroyed the West Indian system and freed the Negro. But their importance has been seriously misunderstood and grossly exaggerated by those who, according to Eric Williams, place faith before reason and evidence.

Williams' argument centers around the fact that the abolition of slavery would not have been accomplished--at least at the time when it was--had it not been for certain vital underlying economic factors. The sugar industry in the British West Indies had become increasingly inefficient and uneconomical so that the West Indian profit which had dominated British imperial thinking for over a century had come to depend increasingly on the preferential duties granted to its produce at the British customshouses. By the early years of the nineteenth century, these preferences were under attack, both by the increasing forces of British industry, anxious generally to secure cheap foodstuffs for its labour (and specifically, for the cheap sugar that could come from foreign growers, irrespective of whether they were free or slave labour), and by the growing interest of the British East Indian traders, whose sugar could not easily compete in the British market so long as the West Indians retained their preferences. In the circumstances the balance of economic advantage lay in sacrificing the West Indian interest. Thus there was no longer any need to maintain slavery and the slave trade that fed it.

---

[50] Ibid., p. 178.

[51] Ibid.

By way of a summary, we observe that Britain, in her quest to Christianize, civilize and trade with the African, manifests ideological tendencies which in Mannheim's sense refer to the set of teachings or symbols unconsciously generated by a a society to protect itself against others, legitimate its power and defend its privileges. In the light of this insight, we realize that woven into the "rhetoric of exclusion," the teachings about Christianity and the civilized institutions which the missionaries propagate are tendencies aimed at protecting and promoting the power of the misionaries and the group they represent over against those they dominate.

Religion as Ideology

The real issue that concerns us here is the "ideological" use of religion and the humanitarian sentiments that flow from it, as a cover for national economic self-interest.

Having looked at some aspects of ideological tendencies in the anti-slavery movement, let us examine the missionary movement to see if it contains any unconscious tendencies that produce views and values which tend to legitimate and reinforce its existing order and protect it against competing groups. To do this we shall analyze the aims and motives of missions, its institutional structure and the bureaucratic method by which it functions. As we have already indicated, the missionary movement is a product of the Evangelical Revival[52] which represents a de-

---

[52]The word "evangelical" (pertaining to the Gospel) has been used with various meanings. At the Reformation it designated both Luther and Reformed. This has been superseded by "Protestant." In nineteenth century Germany, it was the name given to the state churches in which Lutherans and Calvinists were merged. In England, since the nineteenth century, evangelical has been used to denote the low church party in the Church of England. In America, it is part of the names of several denominations which sprang from the Evangelical Revival. In the American Church usage, the term "evangelical" categorizes those who are concerned about the preservation of the central affirmation of the Christian faith as conveyed by the Gospels and the New Testament as a whole. Evangelical Christians are marked by their devotion to the sure word of the Bible; they are committed to the inspired scriptures as the divine rule of faith and practice. They affirm the fundamental doctrines of the Gospel including the incarnation and virgin birth of Christ,

emphasis of the institutional and doctrinal aspects of Christianity in favour of the moral and spiritual transformation of the individual. It stresses a personal religious conversion marked by consciousness of sin, awakening to grace and commitment to Christian life. The converts of the revival were characterized by moral earnestness, a vigorous standard of conduct and frequent examination of conscience. They emphasize Bible reading, private family and group prayers and an active role of the laity.[53] They were notable for their organized efforts to influence and reform society.

In order to understand the religious situation in Britain at that time, it will be necessary to set it in the context of larger European religious movements. Germany was the first to develop an evangelical movement; it was known as Pietism.[54] In large measure Pietism was a revival of Luther's emphasis on salvation by faith and the priesthood of all believers. Its major thrust was to liberate believers from the narrow confines of intellectualistic and scholastic orthodoxy into an actual practice and cultivation of Christian piety in daily living.[55] This sentiment led Philip Jacob

---

His sinless life, substitutionary atonement, and bodily resurrection as the ground of God's forgiveness of sinners, justification by faith alone and the spiritual regeneration of all who trust in the redemptive work of Jesus Christ. They tend to be more concerned with the "text" as the unchanging Word of God rather than the "context," the "changing" socio-political and economic environment which impinges on the "text." See Carl F. H. Henry, "Evangelical," in **The New International Dictionary of Christian Church**, ed. J. D. Douglas et al. (Grand Rapids, Mich.: Zondervan, 1974), pp. 358-359; Franklin H. Littell, "Evangelical Churches," in **Concise Dictionary of the Christian World Mission**, ed. Stephen Neill, Gerald H. Anderson and John Goodwin (Nashville and New York: Abingdon Press, 1971), pp. 196-198; Harold Lindsell, "The Evangelical Foreign Missions Association," in **Concise Dictionary of the Christian World Mission**, ed. Neill et al., pp. 196-198.

[53] Robert Hastings Nichols, **The Growth of the Christian Church** (Philadelphia: The Westminster Press, 1941), pp. 296-298; see also Livingstone, expecially Chapter Three on "The Breakdown of the Religion of Reason," pp. 40-80.

[54] John T. McNeil, **Modern Christian Movements** (Philadelphia: The Westminster Press, 1955), pp. 57-73.

[55] R.H. Nichols, pp. 256-258; see also J. Herbert Kane, **Understanding Christian Missions** (Grand Rapids, Mich.: Baker Book House, 1974), pp. 142-145; Philip Jacob Spencer, **Pia Desideria** [Pious Longings].

Spencer, the father and initiator of German Pietism, and his friend August Herman Francke to engage in social activities and in the founding of orphanages and the building of schools.[56]

Pietism was reinforced by a group whose tradition antedated the Reformation itself, the Moravians.[57] This group derive from the Czech, Hussites of the fifteenth century, whose radical wing was accepted as Protestant at the time of the Reformation. They were expelled from Bohemia and Moravia in the Thirty Years War. Early in the eighteenth century, a small group of Moravian refugees was given refuge at Herrnhut in Saxony by a local nobleman, Count von Zinzendorf, who had been brought up in Pietist circles. Under Zinzendorf's auspices the Moravians renewed their distinct ecclesiastical organization. In Europe they sought to work within the Protestant State Churches to bring fresh life and inspiration to them. They embarked on missionary endeavors, especially in America, where a Moravian Church was successfully planted. Missionary activity was generally characteristic of Pietism.

A decisive moment in the history of evangelicalism was the beginning of the Methodist Movement in England.[58] This rebirth of the Puritan impulse began within the established Church of England as a reaction against the cold, moralistic rationalism of the day. The leaders were John and Charles Wesley and George Whitefield.[59] Through their ministry in England, the eighteenth century Protestant Evangelical Revival had strong roots. These eighteenth century roots sprouted into several plants, among which were the abolitionist movement to which we have already referred and the missionary movement which began the modern spread of Protestantism. [60] This movement was highly stimulated through the impulse of Christian social concern generated by the revival. Until then, there were only two notable missionary agencies: The

---

[56] R. H. Nichols, p. 257.

[57] James H. Nichols, **History of Christianity (1650–1950)** (New York: Roland Press, 1956), pp. 80-84.

[58] Joseph L. Altholz, **The Churches in the 19th Century** (New York: The Bobbs Merrill Co., 1967), pp. 25-27.

[59] Ibid.

[60] Claude Welch and John Dillenberger, **Protestant Christianity: Interpreted through its Developments** (New York: Charles Scribner's Sons, 1954), pp. 167-178.

96

Society for the Propagation of the Gospel (SPG) founded in 1649 and the Society for the Promition of Christian Knowledge (SPCK) (1698). These mission societies were sponsored by the Church of England, and were designed originally to serve in the British Colonies of North America.

But as a result of the Evangelical revival, many voluntary missionary societies not connected with the established Church of England sprang up. They include The Baptist Society for Propagating the Gospel among the heathen /1792). It was William Carey, a Baptist lay preacher and a cobbler by trade, who captured the vision of the need to branch out with the Gospel to the non-Christian world. He caused the launching of the BSPG, and was its first missionary to be sent to India. Carey's example was followed by The London Missionary Society (1795) formed chiefly by Congregationalists; the Church Missionary Society (C.M.S. in 1799); and the Methodists who also took up the challenge for foreign missions.[61]

Before the nineteenth century, Protestantism had not been characterized by very great concern for missionary work in foreign lands. At any rate, much of the missionary work since the time of Constantine had been actively sponsored by the rulers of Christian countries. This pattern was true of the expansion of Christianity up to the eighteenth century when the work of Roman Catholic missionaries was strongly supported by the governments of Spain and Protugal, Russian Orthodox missionaries were supported by the Rusian government, and "Charles the Great" converted the Saxons into Christians with the sword.[62]

In Protestant nations, missions did not receive any direct financial assistance from their governments, nor were their activities directly controlled by the state per se. This was due to the fact that by the eighteenth and nineteenth centuries under the impact of Adam Smith's theory of Laissez-faire, people sought

---

[61] Ernest A. Payne, **The Growth of the World Church: The Story of the Modern Missionary Movement** (London: Edinburgh House Press, 1955), pp. 47-51. See Kane, pp. 142-145; R. H. Nichols, pp. 296-298.

[62] K. S. Latourette, **History of the Expansion of Christianity,** vol. 3 (New York: Harper and Row, 1941), pp. 25-27; cf. Richey Hogg, "The Rise of Protestant Missionary Concern, 1517-1914," in **Theology of the Christian Mission,** ed. Gerald H. Anderson (Nashville: Abingdon Press, 1961), pp. 108-111; J. Van Den Berg, **Constrained by Jesus'Love: An Inquiry into the Motives of the Missionary Awakening in Britain, 1689-1815** (Kampen: J. H. Kok, 1956), chap. 4, pp. 106-164.

to be free from state control. In general, the ideal of religious freedom was in keeping with the prevailing socio-economic philosophies of free enterprise. [63] The new movements enjoyed the participation of the rank and file in their membership. Instead of depending entirely on the resources of a few benefactors, on governments, or on the missionaries themselves, the new religious movements with their evangelical thrust for foreign missions organized their missionary societies on the widest possible base. They became essentially and increasingly a popular movement. Their moral and financial support came not only from private philanthropy, but also from a growing class of lay people of moderate income. [64]

Another new characteristic of the revival movement was their engagement in non-evangelistic humanitarian activities such as the establishment of schools, hospitals and training centers for nurses and doctors. They also engaged in anti-slavery activities. Consequent upon this, the voluntary mission organization assumed an organized and distinctive shape both for carrying out its social activities and for the propagation of the Christian faith. [65] A number of reasons have been suggested as motives for the new religious societies' engaging in foreign mission in places like Africa. At first sight, the motives seem to be purely religious. These religious motives include what we will call the eschatological motive, the motive of obedience, the motive of love and the ecclesiastical extension motive. [66] We shall look at these motives more closely.

The nineteenth century revival in Europe and North America was deeply missionary minded. With roots in the pietistic and evangelical movements of the eighteenth century, its leaders thought that souls not saved would be lost in hell's fire. These revivals were supported by people who felt they had been "saved for service" and felt their best service was to seek the salvation of others. This eschatological strain was strong especially among the Germans, yet the missionary concern it generated swept through the Protestant world of the time. It provided an ex-

---

[63] Max Warren, "Why Missionary Societies and not Missionary Churches," in **History's Lesson for Tomorrow's Mission**, ed. Audrey Abrecht (Geneva: World Student Christian Federation), pp. 149-156.

[64] Welch and Dillenberger, p. 167.

[65] Ibid., pp. 176-177.

[66] Van Den Berg, pp. 160-163.

pectancy that the millennium was soon to come, indicating that Christians ought to redouble their efforts to evangelize the world and to prepare the way of the Lord. These eschatological/millennial interests were often wedded to a theology that stressed obeying Christ's command to make disciples. The Great Commission--"Go ye into all the world and make disciples of all nations . . ." (Matthew 28:19)--stimulated much nineteenth century mission. It was imperative for Christians to obey this command.

Some missionaries not only entered their activities with a sense of duty to obey, but were activated by the Command to love. A compelling motive for Evangelical missionary work in the nineteenth century was the belief that missionaries were "constrained by the Love of Jesus"[67] to live as servants of mankind. They felt that the best response demonstrating God's love to them in Jesus Christ was for them to love their neighbor. Hence they were moved to respond in love to the needs of mankind (especially to the areas they considered to be the "heathen world," that is, non-European countries such as Asia, Africa and China). The irony here is that unfortunately this motive of love was not always free from feelings of cultural superiority.

One trace of Calvinistic influences in the nineteenth century missionary awakening was the idea of "the Glory of God" as the chief and highest end of man. This idea, though not very common in missionary theory,[68] could nonetheless be detected in some of the declarations of missionary leaders such as William Carey, who once said, "It is worthwhile to lay ourselves out with all our might to promoting the cause of the kingdom of Christ. . . . The giving of Glory to God in the highest and in the spreading of peace and goodwill among men on earth are the only motives which should influence these attempts."[69] From these Calvinistic views it was not a far step to stressing the building of God's kingdom on earth.

While the New Testament considers the proclamation of the Gospel to be the duty of the Church (1 Peter 2:9), it also attributes the work of planting the church and of extend-

---

[67] Ibid; see Charles Forman, "A History of Foreign Mission Theory," in **American Missions in Bicentennial Perspective,** ed. Pierce Beaver (California: William Carey Library, 1977), pp. 74-76.

[68] Forman, p. 75.

[69] Van Den Berg, pp. 160-165.

ing it (by the incorporation of new members into it through the act of Baptism) as part of the evangelistic task (Matthew 28:19-20). And, of course, missionaries established churches of the denominations to which they belonged. They regarded churches in the mission-field as extensions of their home church. This led to the use of such filial expressions as mother-churches and daughter-church to describe the relationship between the home church and the church in the mission-field.[70] Missionaries activated by a sense of love exported everything including their church's name, their form of organization, their liturgy, their hymns, their vestments, their church architecture and the like, to churches in the mission-field.[71] This exportation of their home denomination was also fed by an attitude which equated concern for others with reproducing one's own cultural situation abroad.[72] The goal of the enterprise from the religious perspective of the missionary societies rested on the basic Protestant tenet of the acceptance of the Bible as the standard of life. The gospel was ascribed the miraculous power to produce conversion, and the missionaries unwittingly interpreted Christianity to mean the same thing as Western civilization. The two were inextricably combined and they produced a distorted view of the original religious missionary motive. Timothy Njoya, a Kenyan graduate of the Princeton Theological Seminary, U.S.A., describes the situation thus:

> The missionary enterprise led to the conversion of Africans from village to urban life, from communalism to capitalism, from illiteracy to literacy, from superstition to medicine, from African traditions and institutions to Lutheran, Anglican, Methodist, Presbyterian and Baptist traditions and institutions.[73]

---

[70] Keith R. Bridston, **Mission Myth and Reality** (New York: Friendship Press, 1965), pp. 80-81.

[71] James A. Scherer, **Missionary Go Home!** (Englewood Cliffs, N.J.: Prentice-Hall, 1974), pp. 75-80.

[72] Forman, p. 74; Pierce Beaver, "Missionary Motivation Through Three Centuries," in **Essays in Divinity**, ed. J. C. Brauer, vol. 5: **Reinterpretation in American Church History** (Chicago: University of Chicago Press, 1968), pp. 134-137.

[73] Timothy Njoya, "Dynamics of Change in African Christianity" (Ph. D. dissertation, Princeton Theological Seminary, 1976), pp. 57-58.

This implies that the motive for mission was also based on certain cultural assumptions such as the conception that missionaries are equipped with better morals and culture than that of the people whom they went to.

However, more than this was involved in the assumptions and behavior of Western missionaries. The speed with which Western conquerors reached various parts of the world and subjugated the people there convinced the Western missionaries of their own superiority. They further concluded that the masses of people now dominated within a relatively short period must necessarily be inferior and of low morals and low cultural attainment.

As Western aggression and domination spread, Western attitudes towards the dominated unconsciously changed from curiosity, admiration, and friendliness to arrogance, pity and ridicule. This, according to Robert Rotberg, speaking of Northern Rhodesia, was because "from the start, the missionaries compromised their message. As absolute power corrupts absolutely, [so]. . . their own heightened sense of moral and racial superiority tended to corrupt the attitude of the missionaries and to perpetuate the apparent tension between sermon and action, Biblical pronouncement and observed deed." [74]

One of the outstanding achievements of the nineteenth century religious revival in both Western Europe and North America was its arousal of a sense of collective debt and the necessity to do penance for all the faults and wrongs perpetuated by the so-called "Christian nations" in their colonial and mercantile policies. It is to the great credit of the missionary movement that it recognized the debt owed to people in dominated hands, as well as the evils done to those people. It was in the matter of slavery that the "working off of white guilt" became obvious, as we read from the instructions to the first two missionaries sent in 1804 by the Church Missionary Society to West Africa:

The temporal misery of the whole Heathen World has been dreadfully aggravated by its intercourse with men who bear the name of Christians; but the Western coast of Africa between the Tropics and more especially that part of it between the Line and the Tropic of Cancer, has not only, in common with other countries received

[74] Robert Rotber, **Christian Missionaries and the Creation of Northern Rhodesia** (Princeton: Princeton University Press, 1965), p. 146.

from us our diseases and our vices, but it has ever been the chief theatre of the inhuman Slave Trade: and tens of thousands of its children have been annually torn from their dearest connexions to minister to the luxuries of men bearing the Christian name, and who had no more right to exercise this violence than the Africans had to depopulate our coasts with a similar view. . . . We desire, therefore, while we pray and labour for the removal of this evil, to make Western Africa the best remuneration in our power for our manifold wrongs.[75]

Thus many motives, cultural as well as religious, interacted to produce nineteenth century missions. This fusion and confusion of the cultural and the religious motives in mission is well illustrated in the fund-raising practices of missionary societies. This merits attention as it reveals the socio-religious mentality of the missionaries vis-à-vis the missionized.

An American example is described by William Gascoyne-Cecil who gives an account of the policy of evangelizing the world from the home base. He said:

I once saw it stated in its crudest form at a missionary meeting in the United States: a great sheet was unrolled on which there was a mass of figures; first the cost of Protestant missions was stated, then the total number of converts, from that was deduced the price it cost to convert a non-Christian. The total number of non-Christians was then given and the cost of their conversion was estimated on the preceding data; below this was the number of inhabitants in the United States; and the whole cost converting the world was then divided among the total number of her citizens. It was thus discovered that if everymember of the United States would give a certain number of dollars, the world would be evangelized within this generation.[76]

---

[75] Speech quoted in Stock, vol. 1, pp. 94-95.

[76] William Gascoyne-Cecil, "Indigenous Christianity, "**IRM** 2 (1913): 722. Gascoyne-Cecil here criticizes the assumption that money is the sole requisite to Christianize the world, while in reality conversions are a matter of men rather than money. "The money is chiefly useful in giving us the means of supporting those men."

The idea behind this method was that the "Christian West" had the financial responsibility for the evangelization of the pagan and poor non-Western parts of the world.

The other example by which missionary bodies try to raise funds for salvaging of heathens could also be seen in the role of children in the nineteenth century missionary enterprise.[77] Most of the missionary bodies (the Church Missionary Society, the London Missionary Society, the Wesleyan Methodist Missionary Society, the British and Foreign Bible Society and the Baptist Missionary Society) organized one form of the youth wing or another for fund-raising purposes. Irrespective of the society, their methods were the same: they sang identical songs lamenting the dire state of the heathen in lands far away, and after their emotions had been properly worked up, appeals were made for monetary donations to enable the Society to save the lives of the heathen. Some of the songs went like this: "I often think of heathen lands . . . far away." Thus went the opening stanza of a hymn sung by thousands of children. They sang and prayed and received the terrible facts that every day over 13,500 people in Africa passed into "Christless graves" and that in India the heathen still bowed before 330,000,000 idols.

> Can we whose souls are lighted with wisdom from on high
> Can we to men benighted the Lamp of life deny?[78]

To provide a climax to the activities of the year, all the societies held great annual children's meetings. Among the earliest were those staged in Exeter Hall by the London Missionary Society and Baptist Missionary Society. There on Easter Sunday 1842, between five and six thousand children attended the London Missionary Society's annual celebration.[79] With the juvenile associations seated in one section, Sunday School children in another and parents and teachers in the gallery, a distinguished array of officials and missionaries conducted the proceedings. Interspersed with prayers and hymns, the missionaries, brandishing fallen idols,

---

[77] Constance E. Padwick, "Children and Missionary Societies in Great Britain," **IRM** 6 (1917): 560-575.

[78] From the Methodist Hymnbook, cited by Eldon Ray, "The Christian Missionary--Vanishing Species," **The Ecumenist** (July/August 1972): 77-78.

[79] Padwick, pp. 568-569.

recounted tales of vice, atrocity and cannibalism that must have frightened the wits out of some of the children. For effect, they trotted out an Arab girl in costume, three blind Chinese girls, two of whom read from the Scripture in braille, and the Bechuana girl Sara Roby, a familiar face on the circuit, who had been r rescued by a missionary "from the grave where her mother and other relatives had consigned her." After these lurid scenes several speakers lamented the fact that the Society's income was insufficient "to meet the cries of the heathen."[80] Then the usual energetic call for action followed.

The mission societies not only engaged in rallies to raise funds to save the heathen," they also published missionary magazines and little missionary books. Despite the particular sectarian interest of children's missionary magazines, their contents were roughly the same: stories, reviews, poetry, hymns, natural science and news of associations, Sunday Schools and foreign missions. All were sentimental in tone and geared to promote sales.[81] All of them stressed over and over again the themes of thrift and self-salvation by faith, the sweetness of a Christian death, the wickedness of the heathen and the moral and cultural superiority of the British. Xenophobia was implicit, as was Anti-Catholicism, which sometimes surfaced in the form of little moral tales in which the good Protestant triumphed over the hireling of perfidious Rome. [82]

Besides the tales of horror recounted by missionaries and agents of the Societies at the missionary meetings, the invigorating hymns that embellished the magazines and meetings were also calculated to evoke positive response to the missionary appeal for funds. Up to 6,000 children sang Mrs. Gilbert's Hymn at the Exeter Hall gathering in 1842:

---

[80] Ibid., p. 569.

[81] Ibid., pp. 569-570. It was "A Decade of Publications," 1839-1849, wrote padwick, that we find a stream of magazines for children. They include: The Missionary Repository for Youth; Juvenile Missionary Instructor; Wesleyan Juvenile Offering, A Miscellany of Missionary Information for Young Persons; Missionary Magazine for Children of the LMS; in Scotland there was the Juvenile Missionary Magazine of the United Secession Church; Juvenile Missionary Herald of the B.M.S. See O.U. Kalu, The Calabar Historical Journal (1978). [82] Ibid., pp. 569-571.

Lord! while the little heathens bend,
And call some wooden god their friend
or stand and see, with bitter cries,
Theirmothers burnt before their eyes;

While many a dear and tender child
Is thrown to bears and tigers wild
Or left upon the rivers brink
To suffer more than heart can think;

Behold what mercies we possess
How far beyond our thankfulness
By happy thousands here we stand
To serve Thee in a Christian Land.[83]

It is important to see the power the missionary societies had in forming racial and cultural attitudes in the young. Before the advent of the State education in England, Sunday Schools and missionary associations were two of the most important agencies of indoctrination outside the home. If one were to ask children active in the missionary movement at the end of the nineteenth century what words were associated with, for example, "African," they would probably include heathen, sin, black, slavery, fear, dark, ignorance, evil and death. If the child is the father to the man, as psychologists warn, it is important to look carefully at the role played by children's literature and organizations in the formation of prejudice. [84] By the same token, it could be said that racism (the haughty attitude towards African cultures and religions) was bred by the ideology which pervaded the funding of the missionary enterprise. As the children in England sang:

The heathen are foolish and brutish and blind
They are mortals in body; but demons in mind.
Yet their souls we must seek though their sin be
abhorred,
For our labour shall not be in vain in the Lord.[85]

---

[83] Cited by O. U. Kalu, "Children in the Missionary Enterprise of the 19th Century," **The Calabar Historical Journal** (April/May 1978): 25.

[84] Padwick, pp. 568-570. Here Padwick comments on "Effects of Appeal in Children's Lives." See also Christine Bolt, "Victorian Attitudes to Race" (London: 1971); Peter Covency, **The Image of Childhood** (London: 1967).

[85] Padwick, p. 570.

And surely the British labour in Africa has not been in vain, as we would see from the economic and political benefits they reaped from their encounter with Africa.

Mission as an Institution

Let us briefly look at the missionary movement again, not for its motives or **raison d'être,** and not for analyzing the system of norms governing its behavior; rather, let us consider its attempt to develop an enduring organization devoted to the attainment of its missionary goals. In other words, let us look at the mission agency as a social institution and examine its merits and demerits as a missionary body. As Lewis M. Killian has pointed out in his essay on social movements, one of the most significant results of social (religious) movements is the emergence and stabilization of new institutions and new forms of social organization. "It is this appearance of a structured coordinated collectivity, not the values it promotes which is novel and which constitutes the hallmark of the social movement."[87] With the emergence of a structure as the movement endures and becomes more cohesive, a culture develops, i.e., a set of norms which exerts constant pressure to give the movement some continuity and a direction consistent with its values. In short, the movement becomes institutionalized, and therefore leans toward self-preservation. By being institutionalized, the process of bureaucratization sets in. Bureaucracy, according to Max Weber, is a "formal, rationally organized social structure with clearly defined patterns of activity in which ideally every series of action is functionally related to the purposes of the organization."[88] As it develops, it places great value on the effectiveness and efficiency of administration. It compares with other forms of organization as the machine compares with non-mechanical modes of production.

In any bureaucratically structured organization, such as a mission agency, each individual occupies an office. The duties

---

[87] Lewis M. Killian, "Social Movements," in **Handbook of Modern Sociology,** ed. Faris.

[88] Max Weber, "Bureaucracy," in **Introduction to Sociology,** ed. Daniel Hebding and Leonard Glick (London: Addison-Wesley Publishing Company, 1976), p. 198.

and tasks of the official are explicitly defined. Activities of individuals within a bureaucracy are limited by the office occupied; the office does not belong to any individual. Office claimants are those individuals who possess explicit qualifications based on the ability to perform duties. No individual can claim an office by virtue of special rank, privilege, or inherited position. No individual is indispensable within a bureaucracy. The office exists as an explicit definition of functions and duties, separate from the individual holding the office. This interchangeability of people means that the organization can continue to function even when its office-holders resign, retire, or die. It continues to function effectively by recruiting and filling the vacant positions with an appropriately qualified individual.[89]

In the bureaucracy, the behavior of an office holder is dictated by the organization's formal regulation and rules. So, to the extent that the missionary enterprise has become bureaucratized, it is not only shaped by the dynamic call of the Gospel, but also by the bureaucratic imperative that Frederick Herzog, in considering the contemporary capitalistic system under which theologians operate, observes that ". . . capitalism determines much more who we are as human beings . . . than does Jesus of Nazareth."[90]

Relationships in a bureaucracy are not between persons but between offices; they are prescribed and impersonal. A bureaucracy is also characterized by a hierarchy of offices, with a chain of command in which there is a supervision of the lower offices by the higher ones. It is further marked by a centralization of authority and decision-making within the organization. In the context of the missionary enterprise, the central authority resides with the Board of each mission agency. In a bureaucracy, only personnel who are professionally and technically qualified for the bureaucratic offices are selected to fill available positions. Finally, employment within the bureaucracy provides a career for officials based on a system of rewards consisting of tenure and seniority.

---

[89] Ibid., p. 200. See Weber's Chief Characteristics of Bureaucracy in **Encyclopedia of Sociology** (Guilford, Conn.: Dushkin Publishing Group, 1974).

[90] Frederick Herzog, "Liberation Theology at Home," **Christianity and Crisis** (May 1974): 97.

Referring then to a missionary agency as an institution, we see that it is not just a set of doctrines, a mythical or spiritual body or an edifice. It is essentially a group of individuals who function collectively towards a common goal under certain specific relationships. In effect, it comprises a number of persons whose purpose is to perform a certain social function and who enter into certain relationships with such an end in view.

Peter Berger in his book, **Sociology,**[91] elaborates on the basic elements related to institutions, noting especially the element of externality. He contends than an institution is experienced as having an external reality with an existence of its own; it is experienced as possessing objectivity.[92] In this mode, institutions tend to exercise coercive power over the individual who is part of its make-up.

Ordinarily, theological and missiological treatises on church and mission agencies dwell at great length upon "the Word," elaborating its holiness, its Catholicity, its Universality, its Biblical mandate, and so forth. In so doing, they regrettably ignore the empirical and organizational aspects that bear "the Word." The Western churches need to take into account the hard sociological and institutional facts of a church or mission agency and the degree to which its self-interests affect its theological perspectives and statements. By drawing attention to the institutional framework and bureaucratic procedure by which church or mission agency functions, our aim is to clearly distinguish the institution from **the Word,** the Gospel, which it bears. The analogy of the seed and the flower-pot helps to clarify this distinction. The "seed" is the Gospel, the Word, and the "flower pot" is the institutional structure which bears the seed. Our contention is this--that by being institutionalized and bureaucratized, the character an purpose of the missionary movement, especially the essential genius of Christianity within it, that is the "seed" it bears, is influenced or conditioned by establishment strategies of rationalization and planning of the institution. In order to press the argument further, we shall consider whether the mission agency's response to threats on its existence is a response prompted entirely by the Gospel element it bears or is due to some extent by the dynamic interplay of institutional and bureau-

---

[91] Peter Berger and Brigitte Berger, **Sociology: A Biographical Approac** (New York: Basic Books, Inc., 1972).

[92] Ibid., pp. 186-209.

cratic demands on the agency. This leads us to examine to what extent the institutional structure that embodies the Gospel enhances or hinders the operation of the Gospel.

To establish a framework for this inquiry, we shall draw from the insight of Richard Niebuhr's classic works, **The Social Sources of Denominationalism** and **The Kingdom of God in America.**[93] In these works, Niebuhr seeks to demonstrate the impact and consequences of social, national, and institutional factors on the Gospel. He recognizes the distinction between "the Gospel" (the seed) and (the flower pot, the social structure) its carrier. He also gives credit to the importance of the structure as serving a definite purpose in providing a framework for transmitting the "Gospel" from generation to generation.[94]

In spite of these merits, Niebuhr points to the dangers of confining the Gospel within the limits of an institution. He argues that the institution is static whereas "the seed it bears," the Gospel, is dynamic. He sees institutionalization as "reflecting the peculiar interests, prejudices and convictions of leaders of the organization." He analyzes the tendency for the institution to identify Gospel with the practices and doctrines of the organization and the threat of its becoming acculturated to its national setting. Niebuhr calls attention to the temptation of every religious group or institution to become intent on defending and promoting its own type of work.[95] In sum, Niebuhr says that when the church or a mission society becomes institutionalized, it has the tendency to make itself its own end, to be promoted, defended, conceptualized as though its preservation was its ultimate goal. The shift from being a dynamic, evangelical, missionary movement to becoming a divisive, defensive and bureaucratized institution struggling for survival and for relevance constitutes a compromise and a contradiction of its existence.[96] What

---

[93] Richard Niebuhr, **The Social Sources of Denominationalism** (Hamden, Conn.: The Shoe String Press, 1954); Richard Niebuhr, **The Kingdom of God in America** (New York: Harper & Row, 1937); see also Russell E. Richey, ed., **Denominationalism** (Nashville: Abingdon Press, 1977), pp. 160-180.

[94] Richard Niebuhr, **The Kingdom of God in America**, pp. 161, 167-

[95] Ibid., pp. 165-168.

[96] Ibid., pp. 174-175. See also Patrick Granfield, "The Church as Institution: A Reformulated Model," **Journal of Ecumenical Studies** 16 (Summer 1979): 425-447; Eric W. Gritsch, "The Church as Institution: From Doctrinal Pluriformity to Magisterial Mutuality," **Journal of Ecumenical Studies** 16 (Summer 1979): 449-456.

Niebuhr says of the crystalization or institutionalization of the Kingdom of God and Kingdom of Christ in America could also be applied to Britain which we have been discussing. Hence by operating as a bureaucratized institution, the missionary societies unconsciously incorporated into their structures ideological tendencies whereby they unconsciously seek to legitimise and reinforce their own views and values and tend to protect themselves against competing groups.

From the preceding discourse, we suggest that it may be the case that institutional structures which now bear the "Evangel" provide the imperative for its continuity, with the "Evangel" being used as cosmetic to hide the nationalistic, denominational and economic interests implicit in the institutional missionary agency. In view of this, we argue that the contemporary missionary enterprise is, at least in part, a response to its institutional demands. That is, those within it tend to act out of an institutional and ethnocentric urge for continuity and those who are missionized tend to react against institutional coercion and domination. In other words, the missionary organization by its institutional and bureaucratic nature has an inherent dynamic that exhibits ideological tendencies.

From the preceding description and analysis of the socio-intellectual and religious environment of Victorian Britain (in which the British saw themselves as economically viable, due to the harvest of the Industrial Revolution, intellectually advanced due to the Enlightenment movement, culturally superior and expansionist in orientation due to their military and technological capabilities and the speed with which they conquered and colonised non-Western peoples, due to their embrace of Protestant Christianity), we observe that the Victorian Briton felt self-assured and enterprising as a citizen of a powerful nation that espoused and encouraged an economic system based on privately owned property, the desire for profits, hired labour and consumer demand; he saw himself as Christian (a Protestant) and moral. This, in a sense, implies, as Daniel Defoe puts it, "clothing with Decency, not shameless and naked; feeding with Humanity and not in a manner brutal; dwelling in Towns and cities, with Economy and Civil Government, and not like Savages."[97]

---

[97] Quoted by Guy Hunter, **The New Societies of Tropical Africa** (New York: Frederick A. Praeger, 1962), p. 5.

The Victorian Briton also saw himself as educated and civilized, especially in comparison with non-Western peoples such as Africa. hence his moral urge was to spread "good government and liberty." Thomas Carlyle conveys this assumption thus: "Surely of all 'rights of man,' this right of the ignorant man to be guided by the wiser, to be gently or forcibly held in the true course by him is the indisputablest. . . . If freedom have any meaning, it means enjoyment of this right, wherein all other rights are enjoyed." [98]

It follows logically that those who believe themselves superior in morals and culture should have the tendency to branch out to educate and enlighten those whom they think to be inferior. Hence the expansionist British assumed that they had the moral responsibility to educate, enlighten, "Christianize" and uplift non-Westerners, the "heathens." With reference to Africa, this assumption was described as the "white man's burden."

The Victorian British also saw the roots of their civilization to be in Christianity itself. They seemed to believe that only with Christianity is the "good life" possible both for the individual and for the society as a whole. Hence they assumed that the birth of Christianity made possible the development of Western industrial democratic society; therefore, Christianity is the foundation of their society. [99]

Given this sense of cultural, religious, intellectual and technological superiority of the British--theWest--which in turn generated an expansionist orientation, we shall in the next chapter inquire into the encounter between the developed genius of the West and the traditional and conservative genius of Africa.

---

[98] Quoted by Hunter, p. 6.

[99] Robert T. Handy, **A Christian America. Protestant Hopes and Historical Realities** (New York: Oxford University Press, 1971), pp. 95-116; Ernest Troeltsch, **Protestantism and Progress: A Historical Study of the Relation of Protestantism to the Modern World** (Boston: Beacon Press, 1965).

. . . The Western world approached the non-Western world aggressively. This was evident in territorial conquest, commercial exploitation, and the all-pervasive Western sense of cultural and intellectual superiority. Moreover, the West had all the benefits of its industrial revolution. This was precisely the period in which Western Protestant missions emerged in full vigour. Almost inevitably, missionaries consciously or unconsciously reflected this temper of the times.

Richey Hogg, "Protestant Missions 1864-1914," in **History's Lessens for Tomorrow's Mission,** ed. Audrey Abrecht (Geneva, World Student Christian Federation, n.d.), p. 159.

. . . We cannot go on taking the Gospel to the peoples of Africa and at the same time acquiesce in national conduct which directly contravenes that Gospel. An undertaking with so deep an insincerity at its heart could not hope for success.

J. H. Oldham, "Imperialism and Missions in Africa," **International Review of Mission** 9 (1920): 462.

CHAPTER V

THE ENCOUNTER. EUROPE VS. AFRICA

Levels of Encounter

The encounter of Africa with the West marked the genesis of her subjugation and consequent colonization by European powers. The agents of this transition were the trader, the diplomat, the missionary, and the settlers who followed in their train. The encounter took place at three significant levels: slave trade, the partition of Africa, and the Christianization of Africa. Each of these requires further attention.

According to Stephen Neill, "the history of Africa can be summed up in three words--gold, ivory,slaves; and as with Charity, the greatest of the three is the third."[1] Slavery is said to be one of the most ancient institutions of mankind. It was carried on in a very low key in parts of Africa long before Africa's encounter with the West. However, as soon as the West became involved in the slave trade, it assumed staggering proportions in its traffic, volume and concentrated hardship, the type of which had never been known before.

The first European visitors to Africa were the Portuguese explorers under the leadership of Prince Henry the Navigator. They arrived on the West Coast of Africa around the fifteenth century while attempting to discover the sea rout to India. Along with them were Roman Catholic missionaries who served as chaplains to their compatriots on board the ship, and subsequently as missionaries to Africans. The Portuguese brought with them ivory and locally-woven textile with which they bought a few slaves. These slaves were acquired for exhibition purposes because there was practically no need for slaves in Portugal at the time. Later European contacts on the West Coast were different in purpose and direction. The whole period between 1500 and the British abolition of the slave trade in 1807 is a story of coastal contact by traders. During this long period of the slave trade, when about six million[2] Africans were shipped across the Atlantic,

---

[1] Stephen Neill, **Colonialism and Christian Missions** (New York: McGraw Hill, 1966), p. 266.

[2] K. O. Dike, **Trade and Politics in the Niger Delta** (Oxford, 1956), p. 10; **The New Encyclopedia Britannica**, 1973 ed., s.v. "Slavery, Serfdom and Forced Labour.

the traders were kept firmly to the coast-line by the African people of the coastal belt. The traders lived in their ships, and sometimes built barracoons on land in which to hold slaves awaiting shipment. They were all aware of the danger to their lives if they sought to break through into the interior. During this period they treated African rulers with forced respect.

Slavery and its consequences shaped vast proportions of the African-Western encounter. Yet it was not the only factor. Imperialism and the consequent partition of Africa by colonial powers also vastly determined African-Western relations.

One of the consequences of the slave trade was that it exposed the defenselessness of the African continent to external aggression. The European powers saw Africa as open to them for acquisition, and hence they "scrambled" for territories therein. In order to create some order out of the chaos caused by such scrambling, Bismarck supposedly summoned a conference of the European powers in Berlin in 1885 to determine and discuss the "spheres of influence" of each European power in Africa.[3]

The conference was in session from November 15, 1884, to February 26, 1885. It was fully representative of Western Europe with the exception of Switzerland. It was attended by Norway, Sweden, Denmark, Holland and Belgium, Spain, Portugal and Italy, together with Russia, Turkey and Eastern Europe. The United States was represented. Germany was also represented and as the host, Prince Bismarck was appointed President of the Conference.[4]

Bismarck declared three objectives for the Conference's consideration: the free navigation of the Congo, with freedom of trade; the free navigation of the Niger; and the conditions to be observed for any annexation of territory in Africa to be accepted as valid.[5] The outcome of the conference was the General Act of 1885 which was signed by fourteen European Powers. In matters of international recognition of any claim to anexation of African territory or to a protectorate, the test was to be "effective occupation." This was defined as "the establishment of authority in the regions occupied by any of the European Powers on the coasts of the African continent sufficient

---

[3]C. P. C Groves, **The Planting of Christianity in Africa**, vol. 3: **1878–1914** (London: Lutterworth Press, 1964), p. 9.

[4]Ibid.

[5]Ibid.

to protect existing rights and, as the case may be, freedom of trade and of transit under the conditions agreed upon."[6] All such claims were indicated to the Signatory Powers. In actual fact, one of the major outcomes of the Conference was the partition of Africa among European Powers. This conference was also remarkable, not only because of the "Powers" which attended it and the resolutions they arrived at, but also by virtue of the fact that no African people were represented when far-reaching decisions affecting the territorial destiny of the continent were taken. This conference marked the beginning of the loss of selfhood by the African people and paved the way for the enthronement of the political hegemony of European powers in Africa. In effect, African countries were the creation of European powers, and the situation created a master-servant relationship between the imperial European powers and the subjugated African countries.

The parttion therefore led to the occupation and exploitation of Africa by European powers. And it was during this annexation period that effective European missionary enterprise in Africa began with about 93% of the continent of Africa in European conrol.[7] In the course of the gigantic scramble, various European powers, notably France, Britain, Germany, Belgium, Portugal and Spain, sought to acquire the abundant minerals and agricultural commodities and the cheap labor of the "Dark Continent."[8] Thus, by the eve of the First World War, France held about 40% of Africa (much of it within the Sahara Desert), Britain controlled 30% and the remaining 23% was devided among Germany, Belgium, Portugal and Spain.

France controlled about 4,022,150 square miles with a population of over 44,152,600. From the standpoint of territory, France was by far the largest African power.[9] Her policy in

---

[6] Ibid., p. 11. See also S.E. Crowe, **The Berlin African Conference 1884-1885** (London 1842). Bismarck's motives have been variously interpreted. Among those attributable to him, the most popular is the longstanding German desire to establish communities overseas.

[7] E. K. Hunt, **Property and Prophets, The Evolution of Economic Institutions and Ideologies** (London and New York: Harper and Row Publishers, 1972), pp. 122-123.

[8] Ibid.

[9] John Gunther, **Inside Africa** (New York: harper and Row, 1955), pp. 16-17. See also Neill, pp. 337-358. Neill draws our attention to the fact that at the heart of French Colonial policy was her resentment at British

Africa was based on the concept of assimilation, i.e., she had the intention of making Africans (in the long run) Frenchmen. The French did not train Africans for eventual self-government, but rather tried to channel off nationalist discontent by (at least in theory) opening up the doors of French culture and civilization to the Africans. This meant that under the French rule, every African in all the vastness of French West Africa, French Equatorial Africa, Madagascar and so forth was a French citizen just as any other French citizen in Paris or Bordeaux. This policy was designed to check the problem of color bar by conferring citizenship on the residents of the colonies, irrespective of race. But the testimony of the French-speaking Africans which finds expression in "Negritude"[10] belies the achievement of the policy.

Britain, by the end of Europe's scramble for Africa's land and people, controlled parts of West Africa, East Africa and South Africa which were about 2,025,715 square miles of Africa's land.[11] The population of these places was about 62,433,645 at this time. Of the total population, about 120,00 were all-white settlers or immigrants. Britain forbade white settlers in Nigeria, but opened the door for white settlers in Rhodesia and Kenya. These settlers, according to Gunther, "will fight to the last bitter inch to maintain white supremacy." Britain adopted the policy of Indirect Rule, a mechanism by which she ruled and manipulated the Africans through their local chiefs. This policy varied from colony to colony.

Belgian Africa refers to the Congo (now Zaire), which covers 924,300 square miles and had a population of 12 million

---

success in the colonial field and her desire to thwart further British advance and wherever possible to do something bigger and better than what Britain was doing. By implication this illustrates how Africa came to be used as a pawn in the chessboard of European political rivalry.

[10]"Negritude" is the French term for the Negro (African) movement against the Western (French) dominating culture. It can be seen as a counter-movement away from the state; it constitutes a symbolic progression from subordination to independence, from alienation, through revolt to self-affirmation; see Abiola Irele, "Negritude--'Literature and Ideology,'" in **Black Africa**, ed. John Middleton (London: Macmillan & Co., 1970), pp.381-400.

[11]Gunther, p. 17; Neill, p. 302. It is difficult to accept Neill's view that only the French and the Germans were "systematic colonizers in Africa," while Britain, he claims, "was reluctant to enter African territories" (p. 302).

people, of whom 60,000 were Europeans.[12] These essence of the Belgian system was to buy off discontent by giving good wages and economic security to the Africans. Nobody in the Congo was allowed to vote and there were few, if any, civil rights or liberties. Belgian colonial rulers thought that by giving good wages and good social services, they would check the tide of nationalism. The system worked well at the time. There was little evidence of political unrest; but it is on this note that the Belgian program exposed its weakness and short-sightedness. As Chester Bowles analyzed the Belgian policy:

> The weakness of the Belgian program appears to be their reluctance to allow the African to secure an advanced education--even a technical education--for fear that he will then demand a growing share of responsibility in the shaping of his own future. Any visitor who has seen the strength of the independence movement throughout the world will wonder if the Belgians like King Canute are not trying to curb a force that eventually will become irresistible. . . . But it will be a serious mistake to underestimate the intelligence of the Belgians and to assume that they will attempt to stand like a rock in the face of strong future demands from the people. The danger lies, not so much in the possibility that the Belgians will not compromise eventually with the force of Nationalism, but that when they do, they will find the Africans almost totally inexperienced in handling the responsibilities which they are certain to demand and eventually to get.[13]

Portuguese Africa consisted mostly of two enormous colonies, Angola and Mozambique, which had a population of about 9,500,000 on 773,000 square miles.[14] Legally they were Overseas Provinces of Portugal itself. The Africans had little access to the interactions of the world outside. Thus their political maturity was greatly retarded. Protugal practised a policy of forced labor which mistreated the people. The Protuguese enjoyed the back-wardness of their colonies and in spite of their proclaimed policy

---

[12]Gunther, p. 18; Neill, pp. 359-384.

[13]Gunther, p. 662.

[14]Ibid., p. 18; Neill, pp. 284-299.

of "assimilados," they made it practically impossible for the average African to chieve a high school education, make enough money to live in the European manner or have a chance to be assimilated.[15] Angola and Mozambique were about 90% Catholic.[16]

Having quickly surveyed the colonial powers, holdings and policies in Africa, attention can be given more specifically to British coonial practices, since Britain has become our case study and since British influence was the most extensive.

Initially, the European powers had no territorial or political ambitions in Africa; in fact, they regarded having colonies in tropical Africa as an expensive absurdity. They blundered into colonial Africa accidentally, unwillingly and without any idea of what they were doing. As recorded by Stephen Neill:

> That Europe had the capacity to subjugate Africa was self-evident; but had the rulers any firm wish to do so? . . . The statesmen who drew the new frontierlines did not do so because they wanted to rule and develop those countries. Bismarck and Ferry, Gladstone and Salisbury, had no solid belief in African empire; indeed they sneered at the movement as something of a farce. A gamble in jungles and bush might interest a poor king such as Leopold II of the Belgians, or a politician on the make, such as Crispi, but the chief partitioners of the 1880's glimpsed no grand imperial idea behind what they were doing. They felt no need of African colonies and in this they reflected the indifference of all but the lunatic fringe of European busness and politics. . . . The pride and pomp of Africa did not suit the popular taste until the 1890's, when the partition was all but completed. Only after Africa lay divided and alloted did European opinion embrace the mythology of empire[17]

What really revolutionized the European attitude to Africa was not the prospect of sending Christian missions to Africa but the discovery of its potential wealth. The British and European interests in Africa may be seen to be, then and now, essentially economic and secondarily religious or humanitarian. Colonialsim, for all its noble accomplishments for Africa, seems to have been

---

[15] Gunther, p. 590.

[16] Ibid., p. 659.

[17] Neill, p. 307.

designed primarily to serve the best self-interest of the colonial powers, especially their economic interest, as Karl Marx would argue.[18] Hans W. Debrunner, A Swiss pastor and a Fellow of the Historical Society of Ghana, in his book, **A Church Between Colonial Powers: A Study of the Church in Togo** (West Africa), cites a similar typical remark by Dr. Franz Mercator, a German, who, concerning the prevailing colonizing intentions of Germans in Arica, said: "We went to Africa to earn money. . . . We need the working power of the Negroes in our interest. Our economic interests alone are the guiding principle for our colonial policy in Africa and in every case, the interests of the natives must be subordinated to them."[19]

Though the concept of imperialism dates back in European history to the Greeks and Romans, its modern manifestations are directly associated with the spread of European power to other parts of the world, either by establishing colonies or subjugating a weaker nation to their political control. In so doing, Europeans imposed systems of government and law suited to their own economic and political interest. The British colonies in Africa were effectively controlled with the aid of the British military force, and Britain exploited Africa as a source of cheap labor, of rawmaterials, markets, and areas for investment.

In order to secure these advantages, England developed the policy of "mercantilism."[20] The aim of this policy was to treat distant colonies as extensions of the parent state, rather than as autonomous communities open to international trade. Foreigners were excluded from colonial ports; colonies had to send all their exports to the metropolis and buy all imports from or through the British merchants. Colonial industries were banned if they competed with those of the metropolis, while the production of colonial staples wanted by the parent state was stimulated by preferential tariffs and bounties.

Besides the economic and political "arch" motives for imperialism, there was also the humanitarian motive,[21] which, as

---

[18] Karl Marx, **Capital**, vol. 1, part 8, chap. 31.

[19] Hans W. Debrunner, **A Church Between Colonial Powers: A Study of the Church in Togo** (London: Lutterworth Press, 1965), p. 106.

[20] **Encyclopedia Americana**, 1976 ed., s.v. "Colonial Economic System," by David K. Fieldhouse.

[21] Colin Leys, "Colonial Exploitation," in **IDOC**, no. 14: **Kenya in Search of Freedom and Unity** (1975: 2-4.

we have already seen, served the economic and chauvinistic interests of the mother country and only in a secondary sense benefited the colonized people. Foremost among the humanitarian impulses were the religious, ethical and protective motives. Christian missionaries wished to save souls and to bring people who were regarded as heathen and lost to Christ. Traders sought to make profits by selling raw materials (acquired through cheap labor and free native lands) to Europe and manufactured goods from Europe to Africa. In both ways, the trader controlled and conducted a lucrative bilateral monopoly trade between Africa and Europe. The diplomat engaged in signing "paper treaties" with local chiefs for purposes of extending the imperial power of their country over the Africans. In each case both the missionaries, the diplomat and the trader cooperated with each other in their efforts to attain their objectives. In general, all of them acted with a streak of national self-interest.

Let us briefly examine three case studies of how the missionaries brought Christ to the people of Tropical Africa by reviewing accounts of the Christianization of Nigeria, Rhodesia and Kenya. We find these in the works of E. A. Ayandele, **The Missionary Impact on Modern Nigeria 1842-1914**; Robert Rotberg, **Christian Missionaries and the Creation of Northern Rhodesia 1880-1924**; and A. J. Temu, **British Protestant Missions in Kenya 1874-1929.**

Before we examine these accounts, we need to make some preliminary remarks about the nineteenth and early twentieth century missionary movement in Africa. It was spearheaded by the British misionary societies. The movement was one-way traffic from the rich industrial, modern, capitalistic and dominant countries of the West to the ancient, primitive but dominated and partitioned societies of Africa, Asia and Latin America.

We also need to underscore the fact that historians differ vastly in their assessment of the impact of Western Christian missions on non-Western countries. There are those who take a **catastrophic view** of the impact, and portray the failure and hypocrisy of missionaries. Some take the **contributionist perspective** and have the tendency to justify claims about missionary accomplishments. Yet there are those who take a **survivalist view** and talk about the enduring character of the African religion.[22]

---

[22]Orlando Patterson, "Rethinking Black History," **Africa Report** (November-December 1972)_: 29-31. I am adapting Patterson's categories to classify African historians.

For **catastrophists,** missionary activities in Africa (and that involves the whole breadth of Western impact) are simply a chronicle of horror, replete with the exploitation, humiliation and anguish which the African suffered at the hands of the white man. This view seems to be popular with most African historians of institutional Christianity, such as E. A. Ayandele, A. J. Temu, Okot p'Bitek, Timothy Njoya and the like. For example, Timothy Njoya says this of the missionary conversion practice in Africa:

> They separated converts from pagans. They wanted to save Africans from being Africans, as if to be themselves was the greatest sin. In their scheme of Salvation, no distinction was made between sin and African custom. Sin and evil constituted such things as African homes, art, ethics, history, skills, play and beliefs. African Christians had to be saved from such imagined evils as their dress, diet, ritual, tools, market and government. It was pagan to kill with a spear and Christian to kill with gun.[23]

Okot p'Bitek compares the activities of Europeans in Africa to those of the victorious Barbarians--Goths, Samaritans, Muslims, Huns, Vandals and Marchmen--who brought proud Rome to her knees. He, however, wonders why "the European barbarians who ravaged Africa . . . are called 'civilisers.'"[24]

Those whose views tend towards the **contributionist** perspective and who have the tendency to justify mission activities include missionary scholars, secretaries of Mission boards such as Robert Speer, Stephen Neill, Max Warren, Lesslie Newbigin, and the like.[25] For example, Robert Speer, in his reply to critics of mission, said:

> That men should criticize the methods of missions and the missionaries themselves is natural and intelligent;

---

[23]Timothy Njoya, "Dynamics of Change in African Christianity" (Ph. D. dissertation, Princeton Theological Seminary, 1976), p. 28.

[24]Okot p'Bitek, **African Religions in Western Scholarship** (Nairobi: East Africa Literature Bureau, 1970), p. 45.

[25]Neill, Preface; Max Warren, **Caesar, The Beloved Enemy** (London: SCM Press, 1955), chap. 3; Max Warren, **Social History and Christian Mission** (London: SCM Press, 1967), pp. 11-15.

but that they should criticize the missionary ideal betrays a total want of appreciation of the nature of Christianity and of social obligation. Christianity claims to be the supreme good in life. The obligation of brotherhood commands us to share our good with men. . . . The task of missions and gun-boats and of "the arm of flesh" has had enough justification to create its use but not enough to keep it alive for a day.[26]

Stephen Neill also says in his book, **Colonialism and Christian Mission,** that, in spite of all the shortcomings of the European missionary enterprise, "even when measured by the strictest criteria, the good done out-weighed the evil: the future of most ex-colonies remains a Christian one."[27] Max Warren has also written two books that deal with Christian mission and colonialism: **Social History and Christian Mission** and **Caesar, the Beloved Enemy.** In the latter book, especially in the chapter on "Theology of Imperialism," Warren holds the view that God has elected the colonial powers to rule over their subjects. Therefore, colonialism should be justified as part of "the purpose of God according to His election, since the over-ruling providence of God, it has been an instrument of peace and progress and God's good-will in the world."

The **survivalist** view seems to be sponsored by those chiefly engaged in responding to men like. E. B. Taylor who glibly remarks that the untutored African cannot conceive of a high God. We have already seen the defence of the idea that the African has a sense and a belief in a high God. From their perspective, the African traditional religion has shown an indestructible potential for survival in spite of over a century of concentrated attempt to destroy it. [28] The survivalists argue that missionaries quite often estimated their success in terms of the rate at which they set up and expanded new churches and mission stations. They were hardly prepared or interested to see "the inner content of the religious behaviour stimulated by the intervention of the mis-

---

[26] Robert Speer, **Missionary Principles and Practices: A Discussion of Christian Missions and Some Criticisms Upon Them** (New York: Fleming & Revell Company, 1902), pp. 50-55.

[27] Neill,

[28] S. N. Ezeanya, "Endurance of Conviction in the Converts: The Force of the Traditional Religion of Africa," **West African Religion** (8 July 1970): 20-24.

sionaries in the existing native cultures . . . or how many different strands were woven into this religious behaviour and how
easily the Victorian missionaries deceived themselves about the
degree of Christianity reached by convers." [29]

Since we are dealing with the issues heading up to the
call for a moratorium on the Western missionaries and their funds,
we are led to select such works that have at least tendencies
towards a catastrophic view of missionary impact on Africa. We
shall begin with an analysis of the work of the Church Missionary
Society in Nigeria as presented by Ayandele.[30] We shall note the
ideological tendencies of the missionaries: how they legitimized
their power and defended their privileges through collaboration
with the colonial powers, how they justified their values through
their teachings and how they protected themselves against
competing African groups by means of institutional bureaucracy.

Ayandele gives a succinct account of the role of European Christian missionaries (British specifically) in helping European traders and administrators establish their control in
Nigeria. Ayandele's thesis is that missionaries were the path-
finders of British influence in Nigeria; their propaganda not only
prepared the way for the government and traders but ensured
the smooth and "peaceful" occupation by colonialist forces.
Ayandele posits three reasons why missionaries provided such
links: the political environment of the communities, missionaries'
patriotic instincts, and the logical outcome of their activity which
made them emissaries of both their home government and the
local chiefs. Ayandele uses the examples of the Christianization
of the Efiks, Yorubaland and the Niger Delta communities to il-
lustate the politically pernicious influence of missionaries who
ostensibly bore the Gospel but covertly insured the subjugation
of black people.[31]

---

[29] John Kent, "The History of Christian Missions in the Modern Era,"
in **Historical Theology,** Pelican Guide to Modern Theology, vol. 2 (Baltimore:
Penguin Books, 1961), p. 262.

[30] E. A. Ayandele, **The Missionary Impact on Modern Nigeria (1842–
1914)––A Political and Social Analysis** (New York: Humanities Press, 1967).

[31] Ayandele. Chapter Two deals succinctly with this paradox in missionary strategy in Nigeria. He cites a quotation from C. C. Newton to drive
home his point: ". . . War is often a means of opening a door for the gospel
to enter a country. A sword of steel often goes before a sword of the spirit.
The landing of troops here andnow may be part of the divine plan for answering
our prayers and opening Ijebu and other interior countries to the gospel"
(p.67).

One of the roles of the missionaries in the subjugation of the African to the British is seen in their role in the local politics of the Efik people of South Eastern Nigeria.[32] The Efiks were favorably disposed towards the missionaries; but a section of the people and their chiefs opposed the Christianization process. They believed that the Efiks had no use for the missionary's social teachings, that conversion would result in the eventual occupation of Old Calabar by the English. Efik customs and institutions, they reasoned, were not ideal, but were the best for the Efik environment, and had virtues and practical values which ought to commend them to missionaries, "else no man can live in this country." [33] On the other hand, another section of the people, under the influence of their chief, King Eyo, favoured the coming of the missionaries. Besides his overt display of welcome, King Eyo had the covert intention to use the missionaries for the political purpose of extending his sovereignty to other sections of the town. In order to win support he scrapped Efik customs and institutions. In a matter of two years Eyo's domain, Creek Town, had become the center of missionary activity in Old Calabar, to the chagrin of his rival, Eyamba V, who had never wanted the missionaries to establish themselves. Later in 1850, Eyo declaredhis sovereignty over all Old Calabar with the moral support of the missionaries and traders, who thereafter appealed to him to use his "almost unlimited powers" in the interest of the gospel and humanity. By patronizing missionary enterprise in order to increase his political status and by carrying out the most revolutionary social legislation in Nigeria in the nineteenth century, King Eyo made the missionaries' revolutionary program possible in a short time. [34] It was not long before Eyo observed that missionary enterprise had begun to undermine his authority. By 1856, one of King Eyo's domains, Old Town, was destroyed by the Royal Navy "in the most able manner" for resisting the cultural and religious intrusion of missionaries.[35]

The significance of the destruction of Old Town lies in the fact that it was one of the first examples ofmilitary action by the British, largely at the behest of the missionaries.[36] From

---

[32] Ibid., p. 17.

[33] Ibid., p. 20.

[34] Ibid., p. 22.

[35] Ibid.

[36] Ibid., p. 24.

124

incidents such as this Efik example, one can see that as the missionaries' political status increased, the chiefs' influence decreased, both in the eyes of the missionaries and of their wards. This was not only the experience of Efik kings who patronized the missionary enterprise but was also true of chiefs in other parts of the country (namely Abeokuta, Bonny, Brass), and in other parts of Africa (such as Kenya and Zambia).[37]

From these incidents the chiefs discovered that patronage of missionary activity implied acceptance of British influence as well. Thus, wherever missionary propaganda became successful, the chiefs noticed and regretted that they had lost considerable influence and power to missionaries and Christian groups. Missionary enterprise from this point of view became a powerful force in the expansion of British influence in many parts of Africa. One Methodist missionary ironically observed:

> Africa is a British Colony. For this England is much indebted to her missionaries. When the missionary arrives in a hitherto unknown part, he calls all the natives to him. When they have gathered around him, he makes them kneel down and close their eyes. This done, he hoists the British flag and proclaims the country British Territory. [38]

Besides this observation from a missionary, other British officials like Sir H. H. Johnson have made similar remarks to the effect that the manner in which the white man has implanted himself in Africa, as governor, exploiter, and teacher, is due more to the work of missionary societies than to the use of machine guns.

Another factor in Ayandele's account is that missionary operatons were openly supported by European military power. The reason for this may be due to the fact that the traditional Western missionary outlook was often expressed in the words, "We are militant evangelists out to capture the villages for Christ."[39] This sentence and others like it reflect Western colonial military and imperialistic sentiments and intents. This is evident in the books, sermons and hymns on mission.

---

[37] Ibid. p. 30.

[38] Ibid.

[39] Kaj Baago, "The Post Colonial Crisis of Missions," **International Review of Mission** (July 1966): 322-332.

John R. Mott, a notable American evangelist and the founder of the World Student Christian Fellowship (WXCF), in his writings used to inflame students to "conquer nations for Christ," and some leading missionaries like W. H. Findly said of his salvation in India, "We are face to face with the mighty array of heathendom, we are in the forefront in the very fire-zone of the Church's battle."[40]

The point to be made here is that Western missionaries understood mission in terms of "occupation and expansion." It is not, therefore, accidental that Kenneth Latourette entitled his monumental books on missionary history **The Expansion of Christianity.** One could also consider such popular missionary hymns as "Onward Christian Soldiers, Marching as to War." The appeal to the military, therefore, for purposes of advancing the frontiers of Western Christianity was not considered unChristian. However, it did yield a type of mentality that placed emphasis on victories and progress, elaborate statistics showing the numerical progress of the church, and the necessity for appeals to "home-base" to send more supplies to the frontier. The view that Western missions can be seen as the religious counterpart to the military and economic imperialism of the West can be sustained, and the views of the catastrophists in some respects vindicated.

The appointment of the first African Bishop, Samuel Ajai Crowther, is another issue to be examined. It is an historic issue which Ayandele examines with the expertise of a trained historian. This appointment brings us directly to the question of the attitude of British missionaries towards Africans and the institutional bureaucracy that aided them in protecting their positions against African competitors. The CMS church had been planted in several places along the Niger Delta. The churches had made good progress up to the point where it was desired that one of the outstanding ordained clergymen should be consecrated as Bishop. This was in the era of Henry Venn, the chief British secretary of the Church Missionary Society (1841-1872). His view of the role of missionaries in the mission field was to be the model or the theory of the British Church Missionary Society's endeavor. As has already been mentioned, the principle of three selves involved the stages by which the churches in Africa (and Asia) would be encouraged to become self-supporting, self-governing and self-propagating. The idea was that once the European had set the churches on their feet and

---

[40]Continuation Committee Conference in Asia, 1912-1913, Edinburgh (n.d.).

established them, his work was done. He was then expected to move on to a virgin field, the "regions beyond," and repeat the process. Chuches were to rule themselves through various councils and committees composed of European and African Bishops, missionaries and lay people. The goal was to create a full African Episcopate in which all European control would come to an end, as fas as personnel was concerned.

For Venn, this scheme was designed partly to relieve the Church Missionary Society of providing funds for further evangelization and partly to make Christianity indigenous in Africa. This dream of a native pastorate was very attractive to the Africans. Venn, in pursuance of his policy, appointed Samuel Ajai Crowther (c. 1806-1891), a Yoruba (Western Nigeria) ex-slave, to the high post of a Bishop of the Niger territories. The first African to become a Bishop, Crowther was ordained in London in 1843 and sent as a missionary to Yoruba land, where he rediscovered his mother and eventually baptised her. He later founded the first Church Missionary Society (CMS) stations in the land and was instrumental in translating parts of the Bible into Yoruba and Ibo languages. By his appointment to the bishopric, he became a romantic figure, a symbol of the Negro's ability to evangelize his people and his capacity to rule.

The white missionaries in his newly created diocese, however, would not have him. They were not willing to serve under him, they ignored him and continued to be responsible to the English Bishop of Sierra Leone. Eleven years later, in May 1875, despite Crowther's patience and conscientious work across the years, white missionaries both on the spot and in England increasingly disturbed him, believing that his appointment had been essentially a regrettable mistake. They also believed that the reins of power should be kept firmly in efficient white hands for an indefinite period.[41]

Meanwhile, the problems created by the white missionaries for Bishop Crowther had become too much for the Bishop to bear. They had deprived him of the steamer given to him by Henry Venn for his missionary work. They had assumed control of all the agents, some of whom were dismissed without prior notification of the Bishop. They were insolent and decidedly disrespectful to him. Between 1877-1890, European missionaries who arrived in the Niger Mission were determined to dislodge the Bishop from his nominal episcopate. They were in the main

---

[41] Ayandele, p. 216.

young, industrious, over-zealous and visionary Englishmen, mainly from Cambridge University, who were tainted with the quixotic idealism of the Student Volunteer Movement, [42] seeking to evangelize the whole world in a generation. In anguish, the Bishop died in 1891. "So far as the Africans were concerned, it was the Church Missonary Society which was responsible for the Bishop's death." [43]

After the death of the Bishop, instead of appointing Archdeacon James Johnson (whom the Bishop had nominated) to succeed him, the Church Missionary Society appointed a European Bishop, The Reverent J. S. Hill. Bishop Hill, in appointing his assisants, flatly ignored both Archdeacon James Johnson and Archdeacon Crowther (son of the late Bishop Crowther) who were the most senior members of the clergy. Rather, Hill chose two African non-members of the clergy: Isaac Ohiwole, Principal of the CMS Grammar School at Lagos and a holder of a B.A. degree from Fourah Bay College in Sierra Leone, and Charles Philips of Ondo, who had no collegiate training. According to Ayandele, both men were chosen because of their docility and submissiveness to white missionaries. [44]

Thus, the CMS and her European missionaries had their way as was the case with their counterparts of the London Missionary Society in Rhodesia. In Nigeria, the activities of the British missionaries and especially the events that surrounded the rise and demise of Bishop Crowther greatly fanned the embers of nationalistic feelings which protested against all foreign involvement in the affairs of the West African native Church. This sentiment was expressed by the leader of the Native Baptist Church, Mojola Agbebi:

> When we look for no manifesto from Salisbury Square, when we expect no packet of resolution from Exeter Hall, when no bench of foreign Bishops, no conclave of Cardinals "loved over" Christian Africa, when the Captain

---

[42] The Student Volunteer Movement (SVM) arose in the United States in 1886 and spread to Britain in 1892. It was a movement dedicated to the evangelization of the world in this century. It was mainly composed of university students who were recruited and sent as missionaries mainly to non-Western countries such as Nigeria.

[43] Ayandele, p. 226.

[44] Ibid., p. 228.

128

of Salvation Jesus Christ Himself, leads the Ethiopian host and our Christianity ceases to be London-ward, and New York-ward but Heaven-ward, then there will be an end to Privy Councils, Governors, Colonels, Annexations, Displacements, Partitions, Cessions, Coercions. Telegraph wires will be put to better use and even Downing Street will be absent in the political vocabulary of the West African Native.[45]

Another account of the management of mission fields in Africa is given by Robert I. Rotberg in **Christian Missionaries and the Creation of Northern Rhodesia 1880-1924.** Rotberg describes how Christian missionaries, under the auspices of the London Missionary Society, administered their areas of operation. He writes:

Of all the missions to Northern Rhodesia, only the Society carried the rule of Africans to its logical conclusion. In the absence of a substitute secular authority, each of the others likewise ruled the Africans; they too recognized the truth of an early missionary aphorism. Many a little Protestant Pope in the lonely bush is forced by his self-imposed isolation to be prophet, priest and king rolled into one--really a big duck, each, in his own private pond . . .[46]

The London Missionaries shared the presuppositions of the European colonists of his day. Frederick Stanley Arnot, the first European missionary to Rhodesia, talked mightily about the "awful heathenism" by which he was surrounded. In his eyes, his mission field was "a vast den of sin . . .," the Lozi people were without exception "utterly heathen." They wallowed in an unfathomable abyss of corruption and degradation of which he found a parallel nowhere in "heathen Africa."[47]

Members of the London Missionary Society, despite the fact that they met a people who "smelted iron into hoes and were

---

[45] Ibid., p. 174.

[46] Robert I. Rotberg, **Christian Missionaries and the Creation of Northern Rhodesia 1880-1924** (Princeton: Princeton University Press, 1965), p. 56. Northern Rhodesia is now the Independent Republic of Zambia.

[47] Ibid., p. 38.

rather superior," [48] vied among themselves in their condemnation of the "cowardly, lazy, thieving and depraved" [49] Mambwe people among whom the missionaries, like the medieval lords of the manor, exacted a price for their protection. They demanded that Africans should discard their tribal ways and conform to "Christian" practices. They compelled them to attend church at specific times and to send their children to school. As Rotberg has thoughtfully observed, "they came to govern absolutely."

The London missionaries, like white men elsewhere in Africa, frequently used force to maintain their "theocratic law." The insrument with which they maintained law and order was the **"cikoti"**--a long whip made of hippopotamus hide. The Africans were severely flogged with it on almost any pretext. As could be expected, missionaries were not restrained in their condemnation of the traditional habits, social customs and beliefs of the indigenous peoples. In their own eyes and in the eyes of their sponsors in London they had gone to Central Africa to offer a backward people the benefits of a European Christian civilization. But the irony was that the Africans resented the contempt with which the missionaries treated them. A typical example of this resentment is reflected in one of the protests to Salisbury Square by James Johnson, Archideacon in the Niger Diocese, who said:

> You in England cannot fancy how some of those who come here inflated with the idea that they are the "dominant race" do treat with something like contempt the natives of this country. The truth is that they regard us this day in pretty much the same light as our forefathers who were rescued from the iron-pangs of slavery by the philanthropists of former generation. We are not over-sensitive, but at the same time, we are not unduly pachydermatous. . . . But does anyone think we have no feelings at all, or no rights which are to be respected? . . . Having educated us, you will not allow us to think and speak and act like men.[50]

---

[48] Ibid.

[49] Ibid.

[50] Ayandele, p. 184.

In spite of protests like this, the missionaries did not relent at their efforts in swiftly destroying practices which they considered inimical to Christianity such as tribal dancing and singing which generally offended missionaries and their wives. Since drumming and other traditions seemed sinful to the missionaries, they were banned from the precincts of mission stations. The frist converts, those whom the missionaries employed and protected, were required to deport themselves in a manner befitting newly made Christians. The converts were in effect a "captive African audience."[51]

According to Rotberg, the missionaries were no different from other Europeans in the manner in which they treated and regarded the Africans. They used them as their domestic servants, as workers to maintain their station, porters to carry their wives and their luggage while touring areas distant from their station.

With this background of the dominant/dependent, master/servant pattern of relationship, the activities in the domain of the London Missonaries can well be imagined. For the Mambwe and Lungu people who built their homes near the mission station and looked to the missionaries for protection, the missionaries like medieval lords of the manor exacted a price for such a service, even though the directors of the London Missionary Society roundly condemned such a system of Christian authoritarianism. Their agents in the field refused to obey because, as Percy Jones put it, "it behoves the missionaries, as the only friends of the helpless natives . . . to stand up against adultery, cruelty, injustice, and murder."[52] Thus Western customs, law and authority were established and maintained by missionaries in Northern Rhodesia.

In order to establish their "Christian" authority, the missionaries in many parts of Northern Rhodesia, as in Nigeria and Kenya, usurped the prerogatives of the indigenous chiefs and thereby progressively destroyed tribal authority and tribal social organizations. They did not tolerate any opposition from the chiefs. When the indigenous chiefs tried to prevent the collapse of their sources of power, the missionaries countered such challenges with force. [53]

---

[51] Rotberg, p. 61.

[52] Ibid., p. 65.

[53] Ibid., p. 61.

Rotberg's account seems in every respect to represent a catastrophic view of the missionary encounter with Africans. He points out how the missionaries destroyed the basis of traditional authority, disorganized the traditional social system and dislocated the traditional religious beliefs, and in consequence legitimised their own power, defended their privileges and protected themselves against any competition from the African people.

In response to missionary action, the indigenous people of Northern Rhodesia "resented what appeared to be pretense and hypocrisy; they noted the apparent lack of congruence between utterance and action, envied the comparative wealth of the missionaries and disliked the ways in which the missionaries abused them physically and mentally." [54]

A third study of how the British Protestant missionary agencies carried out their activities in Africa is borne out of the research by A. J. Temu, **British Protestant Missions in Kenya (1874-1929).** Temu's study discusses the role of mission in the context of Kenyan society. Especially interesting is his discussion of the impact of the mission agencies on the aspirations and expectations of the Kenyan people during the period. Temu's work is very much akin to Ayandele's study of the Nigerian scene. It also assists in a further demonstration of the fact that the mission societies tended to exercise absolute control over their spheres of influence. It is ironic that their activities were not altogether religious. They were fused and suffused with economic, commercial, nationalistic and racial interests, which betrays their ideological bent.

Missionary work in Kenya was started by the Church Missionary Society between 1844 and 1874. They were joined by the United Free Methodists in the 1860's. During this period "the Africans had no wish to become Christians, but they allowed the missionaries to live among them both for economic reasons and for the prestige and military strength that an alliance with the newcomers would bring them." [55] The missionary work at this period was mainly along the coast, especially around the town of Mombasa. Its major concern was the abolition of slavery in Kenya. The missionaries were able to achieve this in 1873. Consequently, the C.M.S. established Freretown colony to resettle the liberated slaves. The first batch of settlers at Freretown were

---

[54] Ibid., p. 145.

[55] A. J. Temu, **British Protestant Missions in Kenya (1874-1929)** (London: Longman, 1972), p. 8.

repatriates from India. The majority of them came from Bombay, and hence they were called Bombay Africans. The development of this settlement was later marked by an internal conflict between Bombay Africans and the white missionaries. This was caused by the refusal of the white missionaries to grant or extend some privileges to their African members.[56] In spite of the fact that the white missionaries supposedly espoused the Venn policy of creating a self-supporting, self-propagating and self-governing church, and in spite of the fact that there were able members among the African Christians such as Rabai George-David, William Jones and Ishmael Seimler who could be assigned to positions of responsibility in the church, none of them was considered for any significant posts. This tendency of the British missionaries to destroy the African sense of self-esteem became especially clear during the tenure of J. R. Streeter, A. Menzies and J. U. Handford. By 1881, there was an open conflict between the Bombay Africans and the British missionaries over the snobbish attitude of the missionaries towards the Africans, and over the poor working conditions and extremely low wages which the missionaries paid to their African workers. The issue which brought the conflict into the open was Menzies' reference to Africans as "idle and slovenly in their habits and their women spending most of the time in gossiping . . . and sleeping!! . . ." On account of this, the Africans appealed to the C.M.S. headquarters in Salisbury Square, London, for redress. In response, Salisbury set up a commssion of inquiry headed by William Price. At the close of his investigation, Price recommended that all the three missionaries, Menzies, Streeter and Handford, should be withdrawn in the interest of mission. With regard to the Bombay Africans, Price said: "It may well be asked where should we be now but for the valuable help which these men and women have given and are giving."[57] Despite Price's recommendations and the availability of qualified Africans to man the post of the Bishopric in Kenya (as was the case in West Africa with the appointment of Samuel Ajai Crowther to the post of bishop), in 1884 when the post of the bishopric of East Equatorial Africa was created with its headquarters at Freretown, James Hannington, an Englishman, was sent from Britain to assume the post.[58]

---

[56] Ibid., p. 76.

[57] Ibid., p. 82.

[58] Ibidl, p. 84.

By this time, imperialism and the ideas of Social Darwinism were at their peak and the European scramble for East Africa had begun, so the appointment of the British Bishop reflected what was going on in the intellectual, social and political climate of the era. For the Africans, the appointment ended their hope that any African could ever be appointed to the post of a bishop. From then on, it became clear to the Bombay Africans who had remained on the stations and to the freed slaves who were training as teachers and evangelists that they were condemned to occupy inferior positions in the church hierarchy. Because of this, many of the Africans left the station at Freretown and the number of Bombay African Christians was reduced to the barest minimum.

As the treatment of mission employees worsened, the Bombay Africans and the freed slaves in general coalesced into a single group and formed a Welfare Association known as "the African Workers' Council." The council was under the leadership of F. James Deimler.[59] The Workers' Council was essentially a welfare association organized to protect an enhance the interest of the Africans working for the C.M.S. Mombasa Mission. By 1889, when all peaceful procedures to secure higher wages and better conditions of service had failed, most of the mission agents resigned. As the situation worsened, the Executive Council of C.M.S. responded by increasing their wages to stem the mass exodus of the African workers form the station.

It was the solidarity of the African workers which helped them to secure recognition and improved wages. Their solidarity and loyalty compelled the Executive Committee of the C.M.S. to recognize the importance and power of the Workers' Council. Rather than congratulate the African Workers' Council for their achievement, the C.M.S. authorities sought to undermine its activities and to manipulate it to serve their own interest. To this end, the missionaries began to patronize and fraternize with African movements. As Temu puts it: "The missionaries . . . wanted to redirect African political movements into purely welfare associations that would not challenge their own author-ity."[60]

---

[59] Ibid., p. 86.

[60] Ibid., p. 88.

What we observe from the foregoing about the missionary administration of Bombay African Christians is that the missionaries were high-handed in dealing with the Africans. There was racial discrimination in the appointment of Bishops and the ordination of ministers all in favour of the British. The conditions of service created by the missionaries for the Africans were poor and offensive to the African. In order to check the excesses of the missionaries, the Africans formed a workers union to preserve and promote their interest.

Having established mission stations on the coast in the 1890's, the missionaries moved from there to the highlands of Kenya following the railway line which was completed in 1901. By the year 1910, a number of mission stations had been established across the highlands. By the end of the decade all the three major British Protestant missions, the Church Missionary Society, the United Methodist and the Church of Scotland Mission, had begun to make their presence and influence felt. The missions and the colonial government at this time shared a common interest. Temu supports this view by reference to Charles Eliot, who acknowledged this comity of interest when he said:

> The opening of a new mission station has seemed to me to be generally as efficacious for the extension of European influence as the opening of a Government station and there are districts in East Africa, such as Teita and the lower Tana, in which European influence has hitherto been represented almost entirely by missionaries. . . .[61]

The control of the mission societies was not limited to the churches they founded, but also included the people's land which they acquired free of charge from the colonial government for commercial agriculture and other commercial undertakings. For example, the United Methodists acquired 6,000 acres of land in the Riber Tana region, 750 acres at Ribe and another 500 acres at Mazera.[62]

After the Methodists came the Church of Scotland Mission which was sponsored by the British East African Company with the alleged aim of making mission both religious, educational, medical and industrial. For this purpose, the company acquired

---

[61] Ibid., p. 93.

[62] Ibid., p. 94.

100 square miles of land on which to develop agriculture and industries.[63] The mission societies trained Africans in the brick making, carpentry, and masonry tasks that the company needed done. Very little evangelistic work was done. The mission station functioned primarily as a supply depot for caravans en route to Uganda.

The ChurchMissionary Society, at the initiative of Bishop Peel, also embarked on an industrial venture, in the name of bringing Christ to the African. His appeal led to the formation of East African Industries Limited in 1906. Peel hailed the establishment of the industrial commercial company as "a great encouragement to all who have industrial missions at heart."[64]

The missionaries eventually laid permanent claim to the lands they had been given freely by the Africans following the enactment of the Crown Lands Ordinance[65] by the British Colonial government. The Act also authorized the government to lease the land on which the native villages were located to white setlers and missionaries without excluding the portions on which the people lived. The missionaries easily obtained certificates of occupation from the colonial government without questioning the integrity of such an ordinance. This government ordinance eventually led to the Africans' loss of control over their land and to their becoming tenants on their own land and in their own country. Consequently, they became employed by the missionaries, as laborers, to develop the estates and plantations of the commercial missionaries. One of the agreements reached between the missionaries and the forcibly disposed Kenyans was for them to "work for the mission for two months every year in return for subsistence on the Estate." Further, some of the Africans were compelled to become Christians as a condition for settling on what had become mission land.

---

[63] Ibid.

[64] Ibid., p. 96.

[65] Crown Land Ordinance: This was the law passed by the British colonial government in Kenya, by which it commandeered and controlled by force the best portions of Kenya's land.

It was not long before the colonial government began to establish native reserves. One such reserve was in the Massai region. The missions acclaimed the creation of native reserves by the colonial government as "a measure that would facilitate their work among the tribes as it would give them large concentrations of people whom they could easily reach." Hitherto, they argued, "missions had been unsuccessful among the Massai because they were widely scattered over a very extensive area."[66] Thus the Protestant missions fully supported the concentration of the Massai people into one reserve. In so doing they supported the demands of their fellow British settlers and the policies of the extension of their home government in Kenya. Therefore, with the legal and military support of the settlers, the missionaries found themselves in a very strong and advantageous position to control their African converts. They have acquired the people's land with little or no pay, coerced them not only into becoming Christians but also into becoming paid labourers and approved the placing of the people in reservations in order to release land for their plantations and for settlers. All these collaborations with the colonial administration and the commercial companies glaringly indicate that the missionaries were hand in glove with their counterparts--the administrator, the trader and the settler. One of the missionaries expressed the relationship this way:

> Kenya is to be one of the most important assets of the British Empire. The missionaries are an integral part of the Colony, and must work with the Government and settlers for the good of the whole. . . . Therefore, it is . . . impossible for us--nor would we wish to do so-- to dissociate ourselves from the members of the British Empire and of the Kingdom of God from the political life of the country. . . . The other great force--settlers. Here there is no desire on our part to dissociate ourselves from their lives. . . . We can help the settler in many ways: supplying him with trained boys, clerks, artisans and hospital dressers etc. . . .[67]

Perhaps the "unkindest cut of all" which the missionaries inflicted on the Africans was their tacit approval of the Forced Labour Act. By this Act, the Kenyans were compelled both by

---

[66] Temu, p. 98.

[67] Ibid., pp. 118-119.

law and by high taxation to work for little or no pay for the benefit of the white settlers, the missionaries and the colonial government. The argument for the missions support, according to their spokesman and the head of the CSM group of missionaries, J. W. Arthur, was based on the belief that "every native ought to work and that work was a necessary part of Christianity. To Christiasnize natives, to educate them and to make them work were complementary principles."[68] This attitude of British missionaries to political questions in Kenya soon earned them the indictment of the International Missionary Council which met in Geneva in June 1920. From there the secretary to the council, J. H. Oldham, warned:

> For the welfare of the peoples of the African continent A right solution to the questions of land and labour is vital. . . . Policies of European governments which are dictated by the economic advantage of citizens of the ruling power with small regard to the interests of the governed are essentially un-Christian; and there would appear to be a fatal insincerity at the heart of the missionary undertaking if missions acquiesce without protest in policies which deprive the natives of their rights to land and degrade them to be mere instruments of the White Man's gain. . . .[69]

Encounter: A Theoretical Analysis With Introductory Overview

What we have seen in the preceding discussion is the coming together of two widely different populations and civilizations, which having met are obliged to live side by side. But their chances are not equal. We saw that African life, in its various expressions, is infinitely weaker than that of the European invaders; hence the Africans tend to lose ground. What we are about to discuss now is the struggle between a civilization that has conquered the world, and is equipped with an almost infinite political and military power and can boast of unheard-off technical and scientific achievements, and that of small congeries

---

[68] Ibid., p. 124-125.

[69] J. H. Oldham, "Christian Mission and African Laboru," **International Review of Mission** (1921): 183.

of tribes in a more or less "primitive" state. It is inevitable that the stronger should dominate the weaker and impose upon him his own ideals--be it by force or by fair means (in Africa the former was applied much more than the latter). Hence Africa lost his self-control and self-respect. And being overwhelmed by the West, he sought for salvation and survival by adopting the civilization of his conqueror. This is what happened and why Arican and why African countries became incorporated, often involuntarily, into states and empires whithin which they occupied a subordinate position. Africa's resources in land and labor came to be affected by and linked in a number of ways to the money economy of the modern Western state and to the world market. It is, in short, impinged upon by external forces which in most cases constitute significant forces in shaping its response to the situation of dependency and domintion.

In other words, Africa became colonized as a result of her encounter with the West. The colonial situation manifested itself in different dimensions. Colonialism "is a system of rule which assumes the right of one people to impose their will upon another. This situation invariably leads to a situation of dominance and dependency which . . . systematically subordinates those governed by it to the imported culture in social [religious] economic and political life."[70] This is the context in which we have to analyze Africa's response to European domination. It is a context created by the violent penetration and rupture of tradi-tional precapitalist societies and the subjugation of their economic, political and religious life to the profit impulse (spiritual and material) of the Western burgeoisie. As a result of this situation, the people of Africa found their resources and their land developed and explited (by their own labor power) not for their own benefit, but for the benefit of the capitalist classes of Europe. For the first time Africans began to produce not to meet their needs but for export to meet the needs of the white man in Europe. And for all this labour, their reward is well sum-med up by K. O. Dike, an African historian, who, speaking of the West African typical example, says:

---

[70] Claude Ake, "The Congruence of Political Economics and Ideologies in Africa, "in **The Political Economy of Contemporary Africa,** ed. Peter C. W. Gutkind and Immanuel Wallerstein (London: SAGE Publications, 1976), p. 99.

It is a matter for reflection that little of permanent value came to West Africa from the 400 years of trade with Europe. In return for the superior labour force, the palm oil, ivory, timber, gold and other commodities which fed and buttressed the rising industrialism, they received the worst type of trade, gin and meretricious articles.[71]

In response to a situation like this, Lord Lugard, one of the most impressive of the British colonizing agents in Africa, the conqueror who brought both Uganda and Nigeria under the heels of Britain and the architect of Britain's staple colonial policy of "indirect rule," replies in a tone like this:

It is a cheap form of rhetoric which stigmatizes as "common greed" the honourable work by which men and nations earn their bread and improve their standard of life.[72]

The conquest and colonization of Africa by the European powers, i.e., the partition of Africa, "was due primarily to the economic necessity of increasing the supplies of raw materials and food to meet the needs of the industrialized nations of Europe."[73]

The encounter (slave trade, partition, Christianization) between Africans and Europeans was not a friendly one from the beginning. Though the host group was more numerous than the European invaders, the latter, with its superior weaponry, conquered and subjugated the Africans, and coerced them to conform to European culture which they thought to be the best in the world. This "forced acculturation" is what E. A. Hobel describes as "the process of interaction between two societies by which the culture of the society in the subordinate position is drastically modified to conform to the culture of the dominant society."[74]

---

[71] Dike, p. 114.

[72] Cited in Chinweizu, **The West and the Rest of Us** (New York: Random House, 1975), p. 25.

[73] Sir Frederick D. Lugard, **The Dual Mandate in British Tropical Africa** (London: William Blackwood and Sons, 1923), p. 613.

[74] E. A. Hobel, **Man in the Primitive World**, 2nd ed. (New York, 1958), p. 643.

The means by which the Europeans achieved forced acculturation was through a combination of military and missionary power. The Europeans strove to make their culture the point of reference, thereby reserving to themselves the right to accept, reformulate or reject elements of the subordinate African culture. They acted ideologically to perpetuate their own ideas of what was "right," "desirable," and "good." The dominant European group believed that the survival of the African society depended on the African espousing the values of the dominant group and behaving accordingly.

In order to analyse the dynamics at work in such a dominant/dependent situation, we shall employ the model of interpretation of dominant/minority relationships developed by Charles Marden and Gladys Meyer in their work, **Minorities in American Society**.[75] Although the African situation is not identical with the American scene (the Africans being numerically more than Europeans in Africa while the minorities in America are minorities both in number and in influence), yet both groups occupy a subordinated status in the society. Hence Marden and Meyer's categories such as the mechanics by which the dominant group establishes and maintains its power in society and the generic problems arising from such a relationship are helpful for our analysis. Hobel has remarked that one of the methods by which a minority group is incorporated into the dominant culture is by acculturation. Another response is "assimilation." This is the process by which individuals at all class levels are allowed to become part of the dominant society.[76] These processes were operative in the case of Afro-Euro relationships but were applied through the use of force (military, technological and religious propaganda),[77] law and custom.[78] As we have already noted, force or the threat of force remains the ultimate sanction for maintaining dominance.[79] In Euro-African context, this had become inevitably so. With the loss of political autonomy, the very nature

---

[75] Charles R. Marden and Gladys Meyer, **Minorities in American Society**, 4th ed. (New York: D. Van Nostrand Company, 1973), p. 37.

[76] Ibid., p. 58.

[77] Guy Hunter, **The New Societies of Tropical Africa** (New York: Frederick A. Praeger, 1962), pp. 8-9.

[78] Marden and Meyer, pp. 47-48.

[79] Ibid.

of contact came to be determined by the character of the dominant European culture. In other words, the Europeans called the tune to which the African danced. This tune was composed of certain European social, economic, political and religious concepts enforced by the power of the British gun-boats.[80]

The gun-boats were also employed to ensure the preservation and maintenance of established relationships in periods of tension. Sometimes they were used in defiance of the law. Whichever way you look at it, their use was geared to upholding dominant values. Besides the use of force to support dominant values, certain public rituals and symbols were also employed to stimulate and reinvoke sentiments of loyalty, affection and commitment to dominant values. For example, when Nigeria was a colony of Britain, Nigerians celebrated what was known as "Empire Day." This celebration was marked by letting all school pupils from primary to secondary schools troop out into a big open field. They marched past the British administrator, chanting such songs as "God save our gracious Queen" and "British Empire shall never perish . . . Amen, Amen, Amen!" Rituals like these serve to uphold dominant British values. For the mission Churches, there was the custom of using prayer books, hymn books, orders of worship, forms of church organization drawn up in Britain and clerical vestments designed and sewn in Britain; all these visible signs and symbols tended to reinvoke sentiments of loyalty, affection, and commitment to dominant missionary values. Custom seemed to govern the whole web and patterns of established relationship between the groups. These customs tended to be elaborated into a rigid etiquette which amplified the fact of dominance in almost all spheres of life. Hence in order to maintain a stable pattern of dominance, specific patterns of action and attitude were incorporated into the social system. Such attitudes and actions are sustaining processes; they also ensure the restriction of the minority group from full participation in the overall social, economic, and political opportunities available.

Consequently, discrimination--the differential and unequal treatment by the dominant of the dependent--becomes an essential feature of the dominant-dependent relationship. Discrimination becomes categorical, according to Marden and Meyer, when it is applied to all members of the minority group.[81] So what we find in Euro-Afro relationship especially amid the colonial days

---

[80] Hunter, pp. 8-9.

[81] Marden and Meyer, pp. 55-56.

and also within the missionary churches, is a whole series of political, economic and social discriminations which are practised to ensure a stable pattern of dominance.

We find examples of political discrimination in Kenya, where Europeans are appointed to Kenya's parliament in preference to Kenyans. Also in Kenya, we find glaring examples of economic discrimination in practices such as forced labor laws, lack of employment opportunities, poor salaries and poor conditions of service for the Kenyans. There was also in Kenya social discrimination whereby Kenyans did not share the same public facilities such as hotels, libraries, swimming pools, and the like with the Europeans living on Kenyan soil. Within the missionary church, we saw how Africans were deprived of such high posts as Bishops. That is also a case of categorical religious discrimination. As Marden and Meyer have defined it, "all practices, formal and informal, which limit admissions to groups or situations that are primarily sociable or prestige-defining are what . . . we refer to as social discrimination without particular reference to their institutional base."[82]

Another factor in the dominant/dependent relationship which the dominant group uses to maintain itself in power is "segregation," that is, an enforced pattern of settlement. This form of restriction has the effect of categorically defining inferior status. The dislike of many dominant white groups entering into close contact with the minority African group has in some cases such as in Kenya (South Africa and Rhodesia are the extreme examples) brought about the creation of reservations where segregation becomes formally established. In Kenya, the Masai people were victims of this enforced segregation. Like other Kenyans, they were restrained and restricted from full participation in the political, economic, social and religious privileges of the society. Initially, they responded to their subordinate position by way of acommodation, that is, when both accepted the situation as it was and functioned within it, with the dependent group incorporated into the dominant and more powerful culture. Since the dominant European group assumes that their values and social system are the best, they expected the dependent group to acculturate, i.e., to learn and practice traits from the dominant group such as the English language which was essential for reciprocal comunication.

---

[82]Ibid., pp. 46-47.

Once the dynamics of dominant-dependent relationships are established, they set in motion a continuous series of reciprocal stimuli and responses. Discriminatory practices tend to become legitimized to keep the Africans at a disadvantage in matters relating to education, job opportunities, health care and housing facilities. This fact is glaring in Kenya where, for example, the Kenya people are kept at the bottom of the colony's socio-economic hierarchy. The vast majority of the people are forced to live in the overcrowded and steadily deteriorating native land units "reserved" for them. The majority of them engaged in subsistence patterns of agriculture. Another group, comprising of unskilled and semi-skilled labourers, are employed primarily on the European farms and plantations. Cost in terms of earning capacity is indicated in the statistics that "in 1948, 385,000 African workers in Kenya earned 28 million dollars--an average of $73 per worker per year. And the European wage earners numbering 11,500 garnered a total of 20 million dollars--an average vo $1,739 per year."[83]

Encounter-Socio-Cultural Consequences

In the light of the preceding chapter, we shall consider some specific consequences of the enforced change that took place within the African culture as a result of the encounter.

One of the areas of directed change is in the domain of traditional African religious beliefs. Implicit in the theory that undergirded the action of the missionaries and social anthropologists, as we have observed, was the unilinear evolutionary conception. In this conception, the small scale or primitive societies were seen as evolving towards the higher position occupied by nineteenth century Europe. To aid in such evolutionary change the anthropologists and missionaries reasoned that there was to be a displacement of the traditional religions and social practices by Christianity and Western civilization. In view of these assumptions, they reasoned that the lost heathen had nothing of value in his primitive system and that his religious mind was totally void of insight. They saw the African as a heathen, but at the same

---

[83] Donald L. Barnett and Karari Njama, "The African Masses on the Eve of the Struggle," in **ICOC** No. 14: **The Future of the Missionary Enterprise, Kenya in Search of Freedom and Unity** (1975): 2-4.

time as **tabula rasa,** an inert and passive field, a clean slate on which Western religion was to be engraved. This ambivalence in viewing the African on the one hand with contempt as a heathen, a savage, belonging to the lowest condition of normal human development, and on the other hand with admiration as somehow belonging to the classical heroes of the Golden Age, admired for their bravery, their hospitality, their simple mode of life, their goodness and happiness, plagued the European mental picture of the African. In spite of the long list of virtues attributed to the savage people, they were occasionally described as brutal. Whatever the Europeans lacked was to be found among the savage people.

Hence African beliefs still fell in the missionary categories of superstition, fetishism, magic, and sorcery, with underlying religious beliefs often discounted. The European missionary had to approach his work in Africa with this attitude because his own history had proved to him that, given enough scientific knowledge and rational thought, all non-rational phenomena could be disposed of as superstitious. But it did not take much time before the African Christians became aware that the missionaries discounted their own world of mysterious phenomena as being devilish or at least not valid. As a result of this, the Africans practised their religion in secret.

This was because the official position of the Church denied the spiritual reality of the African world and disciplined members who openly practised their traditional religion. In view of this, the African chose to hold onto his traditional religious beliefs in private and at the same time practise the new religion because he sought to acquire the "force vitale" of the white man. This was beause Christianity itself came as part of a larger order comprising Western education, colonial administration, commerce and industry. These accompaniments attracted the Africans to Christianity but did not cause them to abandon their original religious beliefs. This ambivalence in the African religious mentality is captured by Chinua Achebe in his novel, **Arrow of God.** Here, Achebe portrays a typical African situation in which a traditional chief priest tells one of his sons why he had to send him to church:

> I want one of my sons to join these people and be my eyes there. If there is nothing in it you will come back. But if there is something there you will bring home my share. The world is like a mask, dancing. If you want to see it well you do not stand in one place. My spirit

tells me those who do not befriend the white man today will be saying "had we known" tomorrow.[84]

So, the introduction of Christianity by European missionaries accounts, to a great extent, for the ambivalence, the schizoid religious mentality of the African.[85] On the one hand he clings on to his traditional religion that he is used to, and on the other hand, he attempts to embrace the new religion, Christianity, whose trail is blazed by the symbols of European power. The outcome of this is that African converts who profess mission Christianity tend to be capable of keeping their traditional religion along with Christianity simultaneously. As J. B. Schuyler, S.J., writing on Nigerian reactions to Christianity, has observed, many conversions to Christianity have been for material reasons. Thus Christianity is quite superficial, and so has not touched the cultural substratum of the African life. George Williamson, who was a missionary in Ghana, West Africa, for 26 years, arrived at a similar conclusion in his book, **Akan Religion and the Christian Faith.** He observes in this study that "the Akan became a Christian by cleaving to the new order introduced by the missionary rather than by working out his salvation within the traditional religious milieu. . . . The result has been that Christianity 'has proved unable to sympathize with or relate its message spiritually to Akan spiritual outlook: Its impact is thereby dulled.'"[86]

---

[84]Chinua Achebe, **Arrow of God** (London: Heinemann, 1964), p. 35. See also: T. O. Ranger and Matthew Schoffeleers, "Interaction Between African Religions and Christianity in the Twentieth Century," in **The Historical Study of African Religion,** ed. T. O. Ranger and I. N. Kimambo (Los Angeles: University of California Press, 1972), pp. 219-252; Hunter, pp. 71-92; F. B. Welboum, **Religion and Politics in Uganda, 1952-1962** (Nairobi, 1965); Marshall W. Murphree, **Christianity and the Shona** (London, 1969); Robin Horton, "African Conversion," **Africa** 41 (April 1971): 86-107.

[85]O. U. Kalu, "Gods in Retreat: Models of Religious Change in Africa," in **Nigerian Journal of Humanities** (Benin, 1978). See also J. B. Schuyler, S.J., "Conceptions of Christianity in the Context of Tropical Africa: Nigerian Reaction to its Advent," in **Christianity in Tropical Africa,** ed. C. C. Baeta (Oxford: Oxford University Press, 1968), pp. 220-225.

[86]S. G. Williamson, **Akan Religion and the Christian Faith** (Accra: Ghana University Press, 1965), pp. 170-176.

146

A second vital index of change produced by the encounter lies in the introduction of many new roles--managers, district officers and councilors, civil servants, engineers, accountants and the like. In the traditional setting, these new roles upset many things; for instance, a man may have different roles in society as head of the family, as chief or priest in a ritual capacity. The number of roles was small and each role had a moral code attached to it, but the new roles operated on a different scale of reference, on a new key. We must stress also the enduring strength of the family relationship in African society. Africans invest in personal relationships because they supply their ultimate security. Until an alternative system of social security appears, family obligations are likely to remain paramount, even where they conflict with the obligations of the new type of society.

The place of authority is another point of difference. Most Tropical African societies recognize authority in age, in traditional office, in high lineage or in another tribal group felt to be superior. But the industrial hierarchy is built on technical skill and experience in employment, criteria which have little to do with age and nothing with lineage or tribal history. They undermined the African traditional system. An African who finds himself within such a hierarchy is in a very strange world; a world created by contact and conquest with the West.

Closely related to but not identical with concepts of authority are those of status. The new Westernized society introduces new status ranks--for example, to have a university degree is a high status symbol. These new symbols replace the old ones, or at least co-existed with them. To be a medical doctor or an engineer irrespective of your age or lineage or to be a high executive officer--your tribal history notwithstanding--placed the holder in a comfortable social and income bracket. The new symbols are what confer and carry real influence and wealth, rather than age, traditional ranks and titles.

Another consequence of the African's encounter with the West is in attitudes and interpretation of work. There seems to be a compulsive attitude to the virtues of hard work which is present in European societies. Whether or not this springs from the Protestant ethic, as Max Weber has persuasively argued, is not a matter for discussion here. The fact is that the missionaries, as the products of Western world view, considered work or production, not only as a condition of progress but as a posi-

147

tive moral good.[87] Hence the Africans who had not developed any large scale industrial skills as the West were described by the missionaries as lazy, corrupt, undisciplined and ignorant. This tendency, as we have already mentioned (Chapter III), is in keeping with the Aristotelian and The Enlightenment thinking that knowledge is virtue. Therefore, the missionaries thought that the way to raise the production level of the Africans was by converting them to Christianity and Western institutions which they considered as the two sides of the same coin. Thus the direction of change was towards Western education and the infusion of the attitude of "Time is money."

The African's attitude to land, too, was changed by his contact with the West.[88] Land to the African is the symbol of a world where everyone has access to food and basic security. The transition from a society where security is based on land to one where it rests on social organization--and full employment -- is a profound change and one which stirs deep emotion and fears.

Another area of forced change is in the African's attitude towards economic exchange and the use of money. Karl Polyani, in a symposium on the nature of the market in early civilizations, has pointed out that modern conceptions of the economy are entirely alien to societies which redistribute goods through multiple reciprocal obligations based on kinship and other ties. He said:

> The disembeded economy of the 19th century stood apart from the rest of society, more specifically from the political and governmental systems. In a market economy the production and distribution of material goods in principle is carried on through a self-regulating system of price-making markets. It is governed by laws of its own, the so-called laws of supply and demand and motivated by fear of hunger and hope of gain.[89]

In contrast, in societies relying on reciprocity regulated by status rather than contract, Polyani said:

---

[87] Hunter, pp. 78-79; R. H. Tawney, **Religion and the Rise of Capitalism** (London: Penguin Books, 1942), pp. 200-204.

[88] Ibid.

[89] Karl Polyani, **Trade and Market in the Early Empires** (Glencoe, Illinois: The Free Press, 1957), pp. 5-10.

148

The element of the economy is here embeded in non-economic institutions, the economic process itself being instituted through kinship, marriage, age-groups, secret societies, totemic associations and public solemnities. The term "economic" life would have no obvious meaning.[90]

Thus, land, cattle, or goods would pass at betrothal or marriage, making a change of status; and gifts of food would move from person to person according to rules of social situation. Nor is there an exact quantitative measurement--reciprocity demanded adequacy of response, not mathematical equality.

L. P. Mair also illustrates this difference in approach when she said: "The possession of most goods is prized for its own sake rather than for the sake of other goods which might be acquired by disposing of them."[91]

Finally, at the personal level, we observe the direction of change away from a life in community to an "individualistic" type of life. The life in community implied an existence in which the community comprehended the individuals within it, supported and sanctioned them, surrounded them with a cocoon of fine spun relationships, related them to the ancestors of the tribe and to its posterity and in return exacted certain disciplines and obligations. Community life involved the choice of marriage partners which would best serve the harmony and prosperity of the family life, the duty to takecare of one's old parents and the obligation to contribute in work and wealth to the common good.

Against this world must be set the Western emphasis on the free individual, free to develop capacities and powers, to choose friends and husband or wife, from wherever one likes, to move beyond home community into a wider society, to insulate oneself against demands from less successful relations and neighbors--but free also to fail and to find little but the impersonal support of state charity if one does. The new opportunities carry with them the new burden of individual freedom to the deepest level of personality. They involve personal moral responsibility. They involve the strength to live without dependence.[92]

---

[90] Ibid.

[91] L.P. Mair, **An African People in the Twentieth Century** (London: Routledge, 1934), p. 60.

[92] Gunther, pp. 82-83.

The Encounter Paradox

So the encounter between these two opposed worlds of values involves religion, family, status, authority, land, work, economics, choice of marriage and personality itself. The encounter coupled with the enforced subordination of one over the other produced, among other things, tensions, protests and revolts on the part of the African against the European overlords. Let us consider the causes and consequences of these strains and tensions on the African traditional culture.

The paradox of the encounter is that the European invader had as his avowed objective the development of native life, but the results of his endeavours were the destruction or the radical modifications of native institutions. The new free enterprise economy introduced destroyed all traditional values, leaving only the cash value. As Mair has put it: "The African has been entrapped in a utilitarian world deprived of higher values and ideals."[93] Within the context of this enforced utilitarian philosophy arising from the impact of Western civilization and the advent of missionary work, the spirit of the African was suppressed. Missionaries did not give Africans Christ and leave them to repent and relate directly to Him. They went on to say: "If you want to belong to Christ, you must speak and act like the white man."[94] Given this dominant/dependent situation arising from the encounter, Karl Mannheim shows that the dominant group ideologically seeks always to preserve and reinforce its position of dominance while the dominated group (like the Anabaptist-Chiliastic group) in a utopian fashion demands a total change of condition that would release them from their subordinated status. Therefore, the roots of the tension we find in Euro-African relations, be it on the political, social or religious levels, lie in the disorganization and subordination of the African culture and people to alien culture. Since African culture is permeated with religion and whereas secular political protests and even organizations were prohibited during the colonial period, social tensions at that time found release in religious protests. In some ways, the Christianity introduced by the missionaries offered the African the fantasy equivalent of a social and political revolution aimed at reconstructing and reestablishing their culture.

---

[93] Mair,

[94] Njoya, pp. 16-22, 72-78.

150

The African independent churches were a movement away from the churches funded and controlled by missionaries. They represent, among other things, a protest against the monopoly of Church authority by the missionaries. Their resentment was exacerbated by strongly authoritative patterns of church organization. The result was the emergence of "African churches." These were breakaway bodies; for example, the Aladura churches in Western Nigeria broke away from the Anglican Church in 1922,[95] and the Kimbangu church in the Congo, now Zaire, broke away in 1921 from the Baptist Missionary Society where the leader and founder, Simon Kimbangu,[96] served as a catechist. These breakaway ecclesiastical bodies are now generally referred to as independent churches since most of them lay emphasis on independence from missionary control. Independence, as Mbiti points out, is chiefly in terms of "organization, leadership, decisions, finance and direction."[97] A. F. Walls has clarified the term "independent" church to include African churches where the leadership is African, their ministry overwhelmingly African, and their missionary direction minimal. According to him, some of the "independent" churches are nowadays virtually indistinguishable from the mainline churches from which they sprang; they are "new religious movements" only in a historical and no longer in a qualitative sense.[98] This means that the movement from "sect to denomination" has set in on the independent churches in Africa.

In order to examine this phenomenon of independent churches further, let us inquire into some of the causes for their emergence, bearing in mind that they did not protest against the Christian faith which had become common to both the African Christian and the missionary. At best it could be said that they

---

[95] Horton, pp. 86-87; for a full account see J. D. Y. Peel, **Aladura: A Religious Movement Among the Yoruba** (London, Oxford University Press, 1968).

[96] Marvin D. Markowitz, **Cross and Sword: The Political Role of Christian Missions in the Belgian Congo, 1908-1960** Standford, Cal.: Hoover Institute Press, 1973), pp. 135-143. For a full account of Kombangu Movement see Marie Louise Martin, **Kimbangu--An African Prophet** (Grand Rapids, Mich.: W. M. B. Eerdmans, 1978).

[97] John Mbiti, **African Religions and Philosophy** (London: Heinemann, 1967), p. 235.

[98] A. F. Walls, "The Anabaptists of Africa: The Challenge of the African Independent Churches," **Occasional Bulletin of Missionary Research** 3 (April 1978): 48-51.

broke out of the Western churches' mold in an attempt to develop an authentic African Church. The independent church movements we find in Africa especially in the last twenty years are to a large extent the symbol of the struggle of the African spirit to be free, first of all, from all external controls and subsequently from internal constraints.

In view of the number and variety of these churches, they have been classified as **Ethiopian, Zionist** or **Aladura** and **Messiaic** churches. The **Ethiopian** churches are those in which the emphasis is on independence, with the retention of pre-existing church patterns. **Zionist** or **Aladura** (in Yoruba **Aladura** means one who prays) churches are those in which the emphasis is on the work of the Holy Spirit, with particular reference to various forms of revelation and healing, reinterpreted in forms of the felt needs of the local culture. The term **Messianic** is used to describe groups like the Kimbangu movement (of Simon Kimbangu of Bakongo-Zaire) which is centered on a dominant personality, who claims a special power involving a form of identification with Christ.[99]

Some church historians have studied the history of some of these movements. We shall refer to some of the reasons adduced for their development using David Barrett's theory for the rise of schism and renewal in Africa.[100] The insight gained from this inquiry into the emergence and development of independent church movements will constitute the background information that will enable us to comprehend the remote sentiments, feelings, and values that inform the African call for moratorium on Western missionaries.

Among the studies that have been carried out in this field, David Barrett's theory of the rise of schism and reneural in Africa constitutes an important contribution. Barrett is an Anglican priest and his book, a Ph.D. dissertation for Union Theological Seminary, is a study of extraordinary breadth: it is no less than an attempt to describe all the independent Christian religious movements in Africa and to develop a theory which explains their emergence. We shall summarize his main thesis for the rise of "secessionist groups" from the mission churches.

---

[99]Victor E. W. Hayward, "African Independent Church Movements," **International Review of Mission** (1963): 166-167.

[100]David Barrett, **Schism and Renewal in Africa, An Analysis of Six Thousand Contemporary Movements** (London: Oxford University Press, 1968).

Barrett starts his analysis of the phenomenon of independency by examining the foundations of African society as we have shown in a preceding chapter. He recognizes that for centuries the basis of African society was founded on a number of institutions--family and kinship, the economic, political, and religious institutions. Within this traditional social grouping, every person knew his/her rights and responsibilities. Facts about religion, family, status, authority, land, work, economic choice, marriage and personality were well known. All these features of a tribal social structure, the outcome of a long and complex history, were so closely knit together that no enforced change could take place in one without affecting all the others.

Missions at the outset were preoccupied with the task of church building. They had little time for any real encounter in depth with indigenous beliefs and systems of thought which in any case they expected would disappear in favour of "the higher" European culture and religion. Consequently, little attempt was made to discern points of preparedness for the Gospel in traditional religion.

The early missionary attitude of courtesy towards African society and religion gave way to a disparaging of traditional institutions unacceptable to European morality and mentality. The reasons for this shift in attitude came especially during the period after the partition of Africa--1885 and on until the First World War of 1914. By this time a change had taken place in mission thinking concerning European colonial rule which they thought was the only way of ending the slave trade and all the abuses associated with it. By comparing their European culture with the African culture, the latter seemed inferior and doomed to peter out with time. With the advances made in medical science at the turn of the century, Europeans thought they could now live indefinitely in the tropics. So increasing numbers poured out both as settlers and as missionaries. Day-to-day mission affairs came increasingly under direct control from Europe with the introduction of the electric cable. The absence at this period of serious ethnographic literature left the new recruits woefully ignorant of African world views and of the social functions of traditional religion. All they knew about was a catalogue of African practices and customs to be wiped out, because they believed all of Africa was heathen and like a wild forest needed to be cleared so as to plant Christianity.

While Africans appeared to accept the new religion, a subconscious alarm at the assault on their society took root across the continent. As a result, most of the Africans began to realize with some bitterness that the hopes aroused by the early day of Christian searching would not materialize. They had least antici-pated the consequences of the severe strain being put on their traditional institutions. They had failed to obtain the "force vitale," the mysterious power of the whites[101] --either material, financial, cultural, religious, spiritual or ecclesiastical. Their lives were not being fulfilled. The new religion they embraced did not satisfy their needs for security and material well-being. Hence they became disillusioned. In the place of secure religion of old, there was now a "religious void"--a widespread sense of uncertainty and insecurity arose. "Hope was replaced by frustration and resent-ment as they saw their traditional culture further disrupted by the expansion of white settler areas and growth of towns."[102] This atmosphere of resentment at first simmered at the unconscious level of unrest and later erupted into a conscious awareness of disaffection.

Barrett also noted that with the translation of the Chris-tian scriptures into the language of the people and their access to reading it raised the people's hope. They saw that the Biblical vision of societal renewal, power, prosperity, peace, love, racial equality and so forth was consistent with their traditional religious aspirations. So they began to discern a serious discrepancy be-tween mission institutional religion and Biblical religion in connec-tion with the attack on traditional institutions by the missionaries. Gradually the vernacular scriptures became for African society an independent standard of reference to legitimate their griev-ances. Consequently, says Barrett, the major Christian attributes of God such as love (**agape, philia, philadelphia**), which means servi-ce, sacrifice, forgiveness, caring, compassion, charity, peace, and also love as listening, sharing, sympathizing, and sensitive understand-ing in depth between equals were understood by Africans to have been distorted by the missionaries.[103] "Instead of Biblical love, there was paternalism; instead of philadelphia, there was com-petitiveness between missionary agencies."[104] So the root cause common to the entire movement of independency could be seen in

---

[101] Ibid., pp. 154-170.

[102] Ibid.

[103] Ibid., p. 184.

[104] David Barrett, "The African Independent Churches," in **World Christian Handbook**, ed. H. Wakelin Coxill and K. A. Knapp (London: Lutter-worth Press, 1968), p. 24.

154

the failure in sensitivity, the failure of mission to demonstrate love, together with the African perception from the vernacular scriptures of the catastrophic nature of this failure and of the urgent need to remedy it if Christianity were to survive on African soil.

In their attempt to re-establish love among the brethren, says Barrett, the Africans embarked on various types of protests. These protests, hitherto lying dormant, erupted as popular resistance movements

> built on political, economic, social or religious factors. These reactions were not only directed against missions but also against the evils resulting from their encounter with the whites. On such occasions, the white government in control employs various repressive measures to deal with the protest movements. But instead of destroying them, they drove them underground and in so doing provided the movements religious legitimation for their protest.[105]

All in all, the burden of Barrett's theory is that the African Independent Church Movements represent a resentment of, and a reaction against missionary interference with the African culture and world view. Since the missionaries are representatives and bearers of Western religion, culture and power, the Independent Church Movements, therefore, represent on a broader scale a total reaction, not only against the ill-conceived approach of the missionaries, but also a reaction against the colonial political situation and the social inequality existing between the two races.

A closer analysis of these movements has revealed that certain facts have to be taken into account in any assessment of the movements. These, according to Barrett, inculde: "A central confession of Christ as **Kyrios**; a marked resurgence of traditional African custom and world-view; and a strong affirmation of their right to be both fully Christian and fully African, independent of foreign pressures."[106] So the independent churches are marked by a "complex of the religious forms which . . . combine cultural integrity and spiritual autonomy."[107] Independ-

---

[105] Ibid., p. 26.

[106] Ibid.

[107] Walls, p. 48.

ency, says Barrett, therefore produced an unorthodox but properly indigenous churchmanship, and represents a creative response to the breakdown of old forms, and an attempt at introducing traditional religious forms into Christianity.[108]

The independent churches, it should be noted, have not generally been founded by theologians or even clerics. They are not even the creation of the highly educated or the rich, but of concerned laymen or alienated church workers. These new religious movements adopted a traditional African world-view in which human events are seen to be primarily controlled by spiritual forces.

Harold Turner has shown that the new religious movements in Africa of which the independent churches are a part have their analogues elsewhere--in North and South America, in Oceania, some in Asia, even a few in Europe. He defines these movements as: "a historically new development arising in the interaction between a tribal society and its religion and one of the higher cultures and its major religion, and involving some substantial departures from the classical religious traditions of both the cultures concerned, in order to find renewal by reworking the rejected traditions into a different religious system."[109]

Bengt Sundkler, an expert on African independent churches, described the indigenous religious movements as groupings in Africa which have taken seriously their existentialist conditions and their local culture and have sought to interpret the Western faiths as they could be relevant to those situations. In a later study on the African Independent Churches, he claims that the independent churches arose as a result of the older churches' failure in "personal relationships, especially pastoral care."[110] Sundkler and Welbourn also suggest that the real reason for the emergence of the new African religious movements goes deeper to "an urge on the part of the African to have some place, amidst

---

[108] Barrett, "African Independent Churches," p. 25.

[109] **Encyclopedia Britannica.** 1974 ed., s.v. "Tribal Religious Movements," by Harold Turner. See Turner's major work: **African Independent Church: The Life and Faith of the Church of the Lord (Aladura)** (Oxford: Clarendon Press, 1967); see also Harold Turner, **History of an African Independent Church: The Church of the Lord** (Oxford: Clarendon Press, 1967).

[110] B. G. M. Sundkler, "What Is at Stake?," in **African Independent Church Movements,** ed. V. E. W. Hayward (London: Edinburgh House, 1963), pp. 84-94.

156

the accumulating debris of African life, where he can feel at home, where he can recognize his fellowmen face to face, salute them as his brethren and have an identity himself. He wants to belong to a fellowship where his whole personality is at home, and where the Western Christian's distinction between 'religion' and 'ordinary life' is, at least momentarily, abolished."[111]

For Odhiambo Okite, an African church journalist, the growth of African independent churches is as a result of the failure of the majority of missionary-led churches in Africa to envision a politically free Africa in which everyone enjoyed equal political and economic opportunity. They defended the "lawfully constituted authorities" and were passionate in favour of peace and order. They condemned African Christians who got involved in political activities as subversive elements.[112]

Vittorio Lantenari saw the new African religious movements as vehicles for social and political protest in the colonial situation. He associated the religious reaction of the indigenous people to various manifestations of white man's policy. Therefore, he contended that "the birth of these movements can only be understood in the light of historical conditions relating to the colonial experience and to the striving of subject peoples to become emancipated."[113]

Many reasons, as we have referred to, account for the origins and growth of the independent church groups. A considerable amount of literature totalling over 1,400 books and articles has appeared.[114] They suggest that Western Christianity has yet to discover the clue to the religious heart of the African because all these independent groups are spontaneously and essentially African, founded, as we have already mentioned, either by direct separation from parent churches or under the initiative of African leadership outside the missions. Their number exceeds seven million[115] drawn predominantly from 270 different tribes

---

[111] F. B. Welbourn and B. A. Ogot, **A Place to Feel at Home: A Study of Two Independent Churches in Western Kenya** (London: Oxford University Press, 1966), pp. 8-20.

[112] Odhiambo W. Okite, "The Politics of African Church Independency," **Risk** 7 (1971): 42-45.

[113] Vittorio Lantenari, **Religions of the Oppressed: A Study of Modern Messianic Cults** (New York: Alfred A. Knopf, 1963), p. xii.

[114] Barrett, "African Independent Churches," p. 25.

[115] Ibid., p. 24.

in all parts of the continent south of the Sahara. Almost all of them have risen out of a remarkably similar pattern of background circumstances in each of the ethnic groups concerned.[116]

The phenomenon of the independent church movements is not new in the history of Christendom, as scholars in the field of church history would affirm. Harold Turner has already said that African independent churches have their analogues in North and South America, in Oceania, Asia and so forth. Andrew Walls sees their place in church history as the Anabaptists of Africa. Christopher Dawson confirms these views about independent churches in "underdeveloped" countries when he said:

> The same spiritual forces which produced monasticism remained active in the Protestant world. This activity is to be seen in the formation of the sects, considered not as theological doctrines but as new ways of religious life. And accordingly, if we wish to find the sociological analogies of the religious orders in the Protestant world, we must look to such organizations as the Anabaptists, the Puritan sects, the Pietists, the Quakers, the Methodists and the Plymouth Brothers. . . . This sectarian development has had considerable influence on the culture of Protestant Europe and America. . . . As we cannot understand Western culture as a whole without a study of the great Christian culture which lies behind it, so also we cannot understand the culture of modern England and Wales and America unless we have studied the underworld of sectarian Christianity, a world which has been so neglected by the political and economic historian, but which nonetheless contributed so many vital elements to the complex pattern of nineteenth century society.[117]

The reality of the independent church movements in Africa therefore calls into question the spiritual leadership of Europeans. It seriously challenges old assumptions of European superiority in the church and opens the way for a recovery of African responsibility for leadership in the church.[118]

---

[116] Ibid., pp. 24-25.

[117] Christopher Dawson, **The Historical Reality of Christian Culture** (London: Routeledge and Kegan-Paul, 1960), pp. 75-76.

[118] J. V. Taylor, **The Growth of the Church in Buganda** (London: SCM Press, 1958), pp. 102-105.

Since our overall objective is to establish the Utopian tendencies in dominated groups, we shall consider how this mentality is characteristic of the African independent churches.

What has happened to the African entrapped in colonial bondage (either in the church or state) is that he feels like a lion in a zoo, smitten by a keen sense of alienation. He feels separated from his own world and thrown into a social system with cultural values he can strike no personal relations with. He sees himself as an alien in relation to the West which controls the total universe in which "he lives and moves and has his being." This sentiment of belonging no longer to oneself but to another goes together with an awareness of inferiority which has the effect of vitiating one's sense of self-esteem. There are profound psychological consequences involving shame and self-hatred. These negative emotions lead inevitably to a call to arms, to revolts, criticisms, accusations, to secessions aimed at reversing and restoring the proper image of the self and of the culture in general.

They are, therefore, manifestations not only of self-affirmation but also of self-differentiation and self-awareness. This condition of alienation, and the impulse to remedy it, accounts for one of the major factors that lie at the heart of the rise of the African independent churches. It strikes an identical note with Mannheim's portrayal of the Anabaptist-Chiliastic group, that oppressed radical religious Movement of the late Middle Ages which rebelled against the domination of the institutional religious establishment of their day in their quest for a new age when the injustices and contradictions of the old will be overcome.[119] Mannheim describes their mentality as utopian.

This utopian mentality of the Anabaptist-Chiliastic group informs the African independent churches whose mentality is utopian in the sense that it constitutes a rejection of the oppression and the domination of external institutions. Their mentality is also a quest for a new order of freedom and independence.

The moratorium call is prefigured by the African independent church movement. The difference between the two is that the leadership in the independent churches is drawn from dissident church workers and ordinary men and women who have little education, while the advocates of moratorium are highly

---

[119] Karl Mannheim, **Ideology and Utopia: An Introduction to the Sociology of Knowledge,** trans. Louis Writh and Edward Shils (New York: Harcourt, Brace, 1954), pp. 211-218.

educated church leaders. The independent church movement is essentially a grassroots movement, while the moratorium is essentially bureaucratic, institutional and elitist. Just as the independent churches are a product of socio-political, economic and religious factors, so, too, is the moratorium call a product of similar factors. Therefore, in order to account for the moratorium call we shall examine socio-economic, political and religious context out of which the call was made.

Dominant classes are always slowest to yield power because it is the source of privilege. As long as they hold it, they may dispense and share privilege, enjoying the moral pleasure of giving what does not belong to them and the practical advantage of withholding enough to preserve their eminence and superiority in society.

Reinhold Niebuhr, **Moral Man and Immoral Society** (New York: Charles Scribner's Sons, c. 1932), p. 121.

. . . The injustices in society which arise from class privileges, will not be abolished purely by moral suasion. That is the conviction which the proletarian class, which suffer most from social injustices, has finally arrived after centuries of disappointed hopes.

Reinhold Niebuhr, p. 141.

CHAPTER VI

THE GEO-ECONOMIC AND POLITICAL
CONTEXT FOR MORATORIUM

In the preceding chapter we discussed some aspects of the consequences of Euro-Afro encounter which, among other things, led to the establishment of a dominant-subordinate relationship between the two groups. This pattern of relationship was, on the one hand, achieved through power politics (politics used in Mannheim's sense). This entailed conquest and colonization of Africa by Europe. On the other hand, the relationship has continued to last through the economic power of Europe over Africa. Having considered the political aspect of the encounter in the last chapter, we shall in this chapter inquire into the economic aspect by examining the evolution of capitalism in the West and the historical incorporation of Africa into the Western capitalist system. For that purpose, we will examine the evolution of the spirit of Western capitalism as analyzed by Max Weber in **The Protestant Ethic and the Spirit of Capitalism.**[1] We will pay attention to Weber's explanation of the paradoxical relationship between intense economic activity and intense religious activity which he observed in Western Europe. Our aim will be to examine Weber's analysis of the countries of Western Europe where Weber found the unique evidence of the evolution of mature capitalism and the places where such developments were non-existent. Then with the application of Marxian framework of analysis we will examine the nature of the socio-economic relationship between the two areas where mature capitalism exists and where it is non-existent.

Important to our discussion, therefore, will be Weber's division of the world into two groups--one informed by the spirt, i.e., principles, of "Traditionalism"[2] and the other by the spirit of "Capitalism."[3] Weber contrasts both groups, showing that the economic calculus of the former is characteristic of pre-capitalist or traditional societies such as we described in Chapter III, while

---

[1] Max Weber, **The Protestant Ethic and the Spirit of Capitalism** (New York: Charles Scribners, 1952), pp. 175-176.

[2] Ibid., pp. 16-26. See Reinhard Bendix, **Max Weber: An Intellectual Portrait** (New York: Doubleday & Co., 1962), pp. 50-55.

[3] Weber, pp. 36-46.

162

the economic enterprise of the latter is marked by a rational calculation and this, according to Weber, originated in Western civilization. It was expansionist in orientation and promoted by trading and colonization.

In order to explain the distinction between the two spirits--of traditionalism and of capitalism--Weber examined certain doctrines of the Protestant reformers. His analysis of Calvin's doctrine of vocation and election revealed how modern mature capitalism emerged in Western Europe not simply by inner economic necessity as Karl Marx had argued, but, as it were, pushed by another rising force--the religious ethic of Calvinist Protestantism.[4] The points of convergence, therefore, were the Spirit of Protestantism and the Spirit of Capitalism.

His point of emphasis is the Calvinist doctrine which held that the gift of grace (salvation) was predestined by God. As predestination was an immutable decision of God, one can do nothing to achieve salvation. Since salvation, however, was the focus of one's religious life, one was necessarily interested in knowing whether or not one was among the chosen. Success in one's secular or worldly calling was, therefore, believed to be an almost infalible indication of being one of the chosen.[5] Whatever one's calling, one should conduct oneself in a disciplined, rational and orderly manner to exhibit the gift of grace (salvation). The individual Calvinist thus regarded the performance of acquisitive behaviour as a kind of calling, and laid stress on economic success not for the sake of the joys derived from it, but because economic success was an evidence of God's grace.

Weber, therefore, observed that the principles of religious and secular conduct were in agreement and that the rise of Protestant ethical orientation--the Calvinist inner-worldly asceticism --was a necessary, though not sufficient condition for the emergence of modern capitalism. The Calvinists did not set out deliberately to establish the capitalist mode of production. Rather in their conscious attempt to rationally transform the world, thereby gain salvation, they unwittingly sowed the seeds of modern capitalism which was predicated on entrepreneurship, rationality, calculability, science and technology, investment and profit motivation. Puritan wealth was, therefore, according to Weber, the unintended consequence of anxiety aroused by the Calvinist doctrine of predestination and, paradoxically, a rational

---

[4] Benedix, pp. 55-57.

[5] Ibid., p. 58.

163

attempt to win or at least look as if one had won salvation through secular economic success.[6]

Weber further tested the thesis regarding the role of Christian ethics in generating modern capitalism in Western Europe by undertaking a comparative study of major world religions--Confucianism, Buddhism, Taoism, Ancient Judaism and Hinduism. This was a kind of quasi-experiment in which situations which were otherwise similar differed only in the particular factor under consideration, namely religion. Weber sought to determine what took place in Asia where general conditions were as favourable to the rise of mature capitalism as they were in Europe about the time of the Reformation, except for the religious ethic.[7] To what extent was the absence of mature capitalism in these Asian societies due to the variation in the ethics of their respective religions?

Weber's comparative study of these religions led him to conclude that economic rationality--the basis of modern mature capitalism--was only possible where religious leaders were outside the secular administration and were, therefore, forced by their circumstance to attempt to master and control the world. He categorized these religions into (1) those which emphasized acceptance of the world, e.g., Confucianism, and (2) those which emphasized rejection of the world, the ascetic type of which there are two variants--those which stressed an attempt to escape from the world even after rejecting it (e.g., Hinduism and Buddhism) and those which stressed inner-worldly asceticism and attempted to control the world which has been rejected (e.g., Calvinist Protestantism). The African traditional religion fits into the last category. It differs slightly only in the sense that it seeks to cooperate with, not control the natural order.

The Calvinist inner-worldly asceticism emphasized mastery of the world, an intervention to control nature, a rational, calculated attempt to prove one's attainment of the gift of grace by excelling oneself in rational, secular pursuits. The personal traits of early Calvinist Protestants--their honesty and trustworthiness, their diligence, their sobriety, their modesty in personal tastes, and their subsequent ability to save money--all contributed toward the business success of this class of people who, though perfectly law-abiding, were impatient of authority (religious or political),

---

[6]Ibid., p. 60.

[7]Ibid., pp. 81-84.

and felt themselves only answerable to conscience as the inner voice of God. They thus established freedom of inquiry and the right of economic innovators to the rewards of their enterprise-- the essential features of industrial capitalism as developed in the nineteenth century England, Europe and America.[8]

According to Weber's thesis, this was due to the new spirituality. Weber did not deny that this new inwardness was, in part at least, an adjustment to the growing commercialism and entrepreneurship present in certain parts of Europe. For him, it was not simply a giving in to social pressure. An original, creative and religious breakthrough took place in Calvinistic Christianity. God's call was experienced as a secular calling. Christians experienced the meaning and power of the Gospel in their dedication to hard work and personal enterprise and they regarded success of their undertaking as God's approval and blessing.

This new spirituality removed the religious obstacles to capitalist expansion. It differed from the Middle Ages when the Church condemned the taking of interest on money loans and held up contemplation, otherworldliness, patience in one's providential position, and even recommended poverty as an ideal to be followed by dedicated Christians. The net effect of these developments was the emergence of a symbiotic relationship between Western Protestantism and Capitalism. Protestantism provided the religious motivation for capital acquisition through the Calvinist doctrine of salvation and vocation, while the principles of Capitalism provided the method for ascertaining God's smile on one's endeavour.

These two concepts explain at least in part the relationship between the principles governing the expansionism of Western Protestantism through mission to the non-Western world, and of Capitalism in its drive for profits through saving, conquest, colonialism and imperialism of the non-Western world. One of the factors common to both is the "region beyond" the Western boundaries, where the missionaries go in search of the 2.7 billion[9] who would otherwise die unless they hear the Gospel preached to them from the West and where the capitalists hurry to

---

[8] Ibid., pp. 68-69.

[9] Russel A. Cervin, **Mission in Ferment** (Chicago: Covenant Press, 1977), p. 74. See also Edward Dayton and Peter Wagner, eds., **The Unreached People**.

"develop"[10] or else the people will die of hunger and backwardness.

We shall now attempt an analysis of the socio-economic relationship between the West equipped with the combined spirit of Capitalism and Protestantism and the Third World (e.g., Africa) equipped with little or none of such drives. We shall adopt a Marxian framework of analysis of the relationship between a dominant structure and a subordinate structure.[11] The aim here is to try to understand the causes and consequences of the integration or historical incorporation of the Third World (Africa) into the orbit of the Western capitalist system. That is how, for example, Africa was incorporated politically, economically, or geographically, often involuntarily, into states and empires within which it normally occupies a subordinate position and in which its resources in land and labor have, to one degree or another, been affected and linked in a number of ways to the money economy of the modern state and world market. In other words, it is how Africa was impinged upon by external forces which are beyond its power to control and which in most cases constituted significant factors in shaping its present structure and future development.[12]

In examining the incorporation of Africa under imperialism into the orbit of Western capitalism one has to study the activities and structure of British, French, Belgian, Portuguese and American finance capital in Africa. This involves the study of how the Western nations, that is, the owners of the means of production, the dominant group who wield power, exploit those who are dependent and subordinated to them. When we translate this relationship between countries of the center that developed through autonomous capitalist evolution and those on the periphery that developed through historical incorporation and integration,

---

[10] Emilio Castro, "Liberation, Development and Evangelism: Must We Choose in Mission?," **Occasional Bulletin of Missionary Research Library** 2 (July 1978): 87-90.

[11] Karl Marx and Friedrich Engels, **The Communist Manifesto,** with an Introduction by A. J. P. Taylor (Middlesex, England: Penguin Books, 1967), pp. 79-94.

[12] Cf. Orlando E. Costas, "Evangelism in a Latin American Context," **Evangelical Review of Theology** 3 (April 1979): 53-67. What Costas says about the fate of Latin America at the hands of Western culture and civilization is similar to that of Africans and the West.

we come up with an international network of unequal social and economic relations between the rich and industrialized nations of North America, Western Europe (the West), and the non-industrialized nations of Asia, Africa and Latin America. This network of international relations is controlled largely by the countries in the center of the capitalist system, i.e., by the Western nations. It involves the dominance of weaker, non-industrialized nations by the stronger, industrialized nations. It connotes a relationship of dominance-subordination.

It is a system built on hierarchy and inequality, and it is for this reason that **imperialism** is used to characterize international relations within the world capitalist system. Imperialism refers to the dominant relationship of the most powerful nations within the world capitalist economy over the other weaker nations with which they enter into social, political, economic and religious relations. The domination of weaker nations by stronger ones is not unique to the capitalist system. A reading of world history sugests that empire building has been the rule rather than the exception for human societies. The point we wish to make, however, is not to argue that the imperialist drives arise only out of a capitalist society, but to pose the capitalist system as the context in which we have to understand and analyze the cross-cultural missinary endeavor between the West, North America, and Africa. Our task will be to examine the particular form and stages through which this imperialism developed under the capitalist system and the role of the Western-North American missionaries within the system.

As it stands today, the capitalist world comprises two mutually dependent groups of people. There is the group at the "center" and a group at the "periphery." The center includes those nations in which capital accumulation is centered, i.e., the major sources of economic management, financial control and technological progress. The periphery refers to those countries that are linked to the center in an economically subordinate manner. This world of the capitalist system evolved through three broad stages of imperialism: the stage of plunder, then of legitimate trade and finally of direct investment.[13] In the first stage, the capitalist center (which at the outset included England and a few coastal regions of Continental Europe) made use of the periphery (Asia,

---

[13] G. D. H. Cole, "Capitalism," in **Dictionary of the Social Sciences,** ed. Julius Gould and William L. Kolb (New York: The Free Press, 1964), pp. 70-72.

Africa, the Americas) primarily as their object of plunder, or source of exotic products and slaves. This predatory relationship between the center and the periphery was dominant for several centuries following the initial overseas exploration of the late fifteenth century. Concerning this first stage Karl Marx said: ". . . The treasures captured outside Europe, by undisguised looting, enslavement and murder, floated back to the mother country and were there turned into capital."[14] By the beginning of the nineteenth century, Western Europe began to industrialize on a significant scale and became interested in the periphery primarily as a partner in trade for supplying food and raw materials in exchange for industrial goods.

By this second stage many of the American territories previously colonized by the European powers had become politically independent nations. But in the Caribbean, in Asia, and (by the end of the nineteenth century) in Africa, the Europeans strengthened their political control, established direct rule over their overseas territories and formed a world-wide system of rival colonial empires.[15] In spite of the differences in political status of the different countries on the periphery, their economic relations to the center were quite similar. Each major European power, as we saw in Chapter V, sought to preserve for its own capitalists the economic gains accruing from trade with those parts of the periphery which it dominated. In the process of promoting a rapid growth of world trade, capitalists from the center exported increasing amounts of capital to the periphery. With the aid of their national governments they invested in mines, plantations and related infra-structural facilities designed to improve access to needed raw materials and to create expanded markets for the exports of manufactured goods from the center. In this process the peripheral economies were shaped to meet the needs of the center. As is turned out, imperialism in its second stage had the effect of inhibiting industrialization on the periphery. In fact, the competition among the capitalist powers during the second stage of imperialism greatly contributed to the tensions that led to World Wars I and II and ultimately resulted in a major transformation of the world capitalist system.

The third stage of imperialism emerged in the second half of the twentieth century following the disruptions of two world wars and the rise of socialist states in most of Eastern

---

[14] Karl Marx, **Capital**, vol. 1, pt. 8, chap. 31; also Cole, p. 71.

[15] "The Berlin Conference of 1855" see Chapter IV.

Europe and mainland China. The weakening of the European colonial powers led to the dissolution of their colonial empire; within a short time after World War II almost all of the former colonial territories had gained their political independence. Imperialist relations between the center and the periphery were no longer mediated by colonial rule; instead they operated in a "neo-colonial" manner between formally independent nation-states. Moreover, the emergence of the state socialist nations removed a substantial part of the world from the capitalist orbit.[16]

With the erosion of colonial barriers since the Second World War and the establishment of a new international economic framework under the leadership of the United States,[17] economic relations among the nations of the capitalist center and between the center and the periphery have developed on an unprecedented scale. This increasing integration has involved a great expansion of foreign trade marked by the rapid growth of direct foreign private investment. Rather than simply export their products to foreign markets, capitalist firms have found it increasingly profitable to set up or buy out production facilities in foreign countries. Thus the "multinational corporation" has become the hallmark of modern capitalism and the primary vehicle of imperialist reltions between the center and the periphery.[18] The dominance of the center over the periphery in the contemporary stage of imperialism has been maintained not by direct political control but by virtue of the economic power of the center-nations and their multi-national corporations. Virtually all of the foreign investments within the world capitalist economy are undertaken by corporations based in the center-nations.[19]

---

[16] It is difficult to draw a precise line between the center and the periphery. The latter is now confined to Latin America, Southern Europe, Africa and Asia, exclusive of countries like Japan, China, Israel and South Africa.

[17] Arthur MacEvan, "Changes in World Capitalism and the Current Crisis of the U.S. Economy," **Radical America** 9 (January-February 1975); Cole, p. 71.

[18] Stephan Langdon, "A Paradise for Multinationals," **IDOC project 14: Kenya in Search of Freedom and Unity** (1975): 27-32; S. L. Parmar, **A Third World Perspective on the International Economic Order and the Role of Transnational Corporations in It,** WCC Consultation Paper No. 3 (Geneva, n.d.).

[19] MacEvan.

As the dominant capitalist power in the post-war period, the United States accounts for the lion's share of foreign investments. Out of a total value of direct private investment assets estimated at $165 billion in 1972, slightly over 50 percent were owned by U.S.-based multinational corporations. British firms owned about 15 percent of the total. No other country accounted for more than 6 percent.[20]

In order to have a glimpse of how imperialism functions in our contemporary world, let us by way of an example examine the role of the United States as an imperial power vi-à-vis the Third World. We shall cite two concrete areas of the U.S. involvement on the periphery. The first is in the exercise of military power calculated to subjugate and disrupt the productive forces of a host counry to serve the U.S. economic and political interest. Examples published by the Committee on Foreign Affairs on the United States House of Representatives include:

1953 Iran: CIA-sponsored coup overthrew popular government, installed Shah as ruler.

1954 Guatemala: CIA-sponsored coup overthrew popular Arbenz government and installed pro-U.S. ruler.

1961 Cuba: Bay of Pigs invasion organized by CIA to overthrow revolutionary government.

1962 Cuba: Missile crisis, naval blockade.

1961-1975: War in Vietnam.

1964 Brazil: CIA-supported coup overthrew elected Goulart government, installed dictatorship.

1965 Indonesia: CIA-sponsored coup overthrew government installedmilitary regime.

1967 Greece: CIA-sponsored coup overthrew democratic government, installed "colonels" regime.

1973 Chile: CIA-supported coup overthrew elected government, installed military regime.

---

[20]See United Nations, Department of Economic and Social Affairs, **Multinational Corporations in World Development** (1973), Table 5.

1975-76 Portugal, Angola: Support of right-wing factions.[21]

The second area of involvement is in the sector of capital investments in the Third World countries.[22]

Here,the overall impact of the high profit earned by the countries on the center leads to the overall heavy debt owed by Third World countries to national governments, international agencies, and commercial banks of the center. The U.S. magazine, **Business Week,** puts the total debt at $130 billion, almost double the total of long-term debt at the start of 1974. Other sources give estimates of $150 billion or $200 billion. Somewhat more precise are the figures for the annual payments deficit of non-oil producing countries: these mounted from $9 billion in 1973 to $28 billion in 1974 and $38 billion in 1975. The executive director of Chase Manhattan's London bank appraised the total debt of Third World countries at $145 billion in December 1975, and estimates that $150 billion more will be needed to cover deficits from 1976 through 1980.[23]

One of the pressing problems facing the Third World is how to pay back this immense debt. Given the fact that the profit of the center is earned through capitalist organization of

---

[21]See Appendix for details on U.S. Congress House Committee on foreign Affairs. Use of U.S. Armed Forces in Foreign Counries, 91st Cong., 2nd sess., 1970.

[22]Thomas E. Weisskopf, **American Economic Interest in Foreign Countries: An Empirical Survey,** Discussion Paper 35 (Ann Arbor: University of Michigan, Center for Research on Economic Development, April 1974), p. 16.

[23]Cheryl Payer, "Third World Debt Problems: The New Wave of Default," **Monthly Review** (September 1976): 1-18; see also Cheryl Payer, **The Debt Trap: The International Monetary Fund (IMF) and the Third World** (London, New York: Monthly Review Press, 1974), p. 209. Here Payer calls attention to the rapid rise in "Eurodollar" lending to the Third World countries which rose from $455 million borrowed in 1970 to $10,000 million in 1973. These loans, according to Payer, carry extremely high interest rates and thus represent a new burden to balance of payments of the Third World countries in the long run while relieving it in the short run. See also Samir Amin, **Unequal Development: An Essay on the Social Formation of Peripheral Capitalism,** trans. Brian Pearce (New York: Monthly Review Press, 1976).

production for the extraction of profit rather than the benefit of the people, a time may come or has already come when the imbalance created by the rich nations disrupts the Third World countries so severely that it creates the occasion for a revolution.

These inequities between the "First World" and the "Third World" are attributable to the main institutions created during the coloial era by the industrialized countries to enhance their industrial and economic advantage and well-being. It was an era when the vics of the world's dominated and exploited people were unheard in international fora. The system supported by these institutions is antiquated, inequitable and ill-functioning. To give some eidence as an illustration of this glaring internatio- nal inequity will be helpful at this point.

For example,

--91% of all exports, 85% of armaments production and 98% of research and science are controlled by in- dustrialized countries, whose population is 30% of the world's total. These countries consume 87% of world energy production, 78% of all fertilizers, 94% of aluminum and 94% of all copper supplies. A. country such as the U.S.A. has 6% of the world's population but uses nearly 40% of global resources. 5% of the increase in GNP of the U.S.A. in 1976 was equal to the combined GNP of more than 70 countries of the Third World.[24]

--Mr. MacNamara, President of the World Bank, said that between 1960 and 1970, 80% of the world's in- creased production of wealth accrued to countries where the per capita income was over $1000 per annum at the beginning. Only 6% of the increase went to the 50% of the world's population where the per capita

---

[24] Data based on United Nations Council on International Aid and Development (UNCIAD) sources: **Handbook of International Trade and Development Statistics,** supplement (1973).

national incomes started the decade at $200 or less.[25]

--In industrialized countries each person uses on the average of 497 kg. of cereals per year (U.S.A., 910 kg.) of which 396 kg. are used for animal feed, i.e., meat production (in U.S.A., 810 kg.). The average for developing countries is 194 kg. of which only 20% is used for animal feeding. The livestock population of the U.S.A. alone (excluding house pets) is estimated to consume enough food to feed 1.3 billion people.[26]

--The gap in per capita incomes in 1976 at the extremes was estimated at 1 : 127.[27] As James Grant puts It: "For an Asian starting with a $60 per capita income, a 3% growth rate would mean an income of $120 at the end of 24 years; but for an American with a $2600 annual income, the same growth rate would mean an income of $5200 in the same 24 years. The effect clearly would not be one of increasing equitability."[28]

--Looking at **trade** relations one finds that the share in world trade of non-oil-exporting developing countries has steadily dropped from 19% in 1960 to 15% in 1970 and 14% in the mid-seventies. The deficit in their balance of payments rose from $10.7 billion in 1973 to $26.1 billion in 1974 and $42 billion in 1975. Consequently, the size of their foreign debts keeps on increasing. From $85 billion in 1974 it jumped to $172 billion in 1976 and according to a World Bank estimate may reach $200 billion by 1980. The debt of the Third World increases by approximately 17% annually. For example, in 1960, 25 tons of rubber could buy 6 tractors. In 1975 they could buy only 2 tractros. In 1963

---

[25] Quoted by President Julius Nyerere of Tanzania in "The Economic Challenge: Dialogue or Confrontation?," paper presented to the Royal Commonwealth Society, London, November 21, 1975.

[26] United Nations, Food and Agriculture Organization, **UNO: Assessment of the World Food Situation,** table 6.

[27] Nandini Joshi, **The Challenge of Poverty** (New York: Arnold Heinemann, 1978), p. 20.

[28] James P. Grant, "Development Today: In Search of Global Justice," **Report of the Aspen Consultation,** p. 11.

Tanzania would pay for a tractor by exporting 5 tons of sisal, but in 1970 it had to sell 10 tons of sisal. From the mid-fifties non-oil-exporting countries of the Third World have increased the volume of their exports by over 30% but their earnings increased by only 4%.[29] Price fluctuations, often in a downward direction, have characterized many important export commodities of developing countries, such as natural rubber, sugar, copper, jute products, sisal, tea, etc. The prices of industrial goods and foodgrains exported by the developed countries have steadily risen. Moreover, nearly one-fifth of export earnings of the Third World is paid back to Western shipowners for transport-charges. In addition, there are high costs for services like insurance, marketing, banking, etc.

--World Bank sources show that by the end of 1974 the total debt servicing of the Third World was $12,462 million. Official aid received during this period was $11,300 million. That means that the inflow of money into the rich world exceeds the outflow.[30]

--Regarding investments, for a country like the United States, corporate investments abroad between 1950 and 1965 amounted to $7.8 billion from Latin America and $9 billion from Asia and Africa.[31] One estimate charges transnationals in Brazil for generating "surpluses five times greater than the initial investment."[32] A substantial part of this goes to developed countries in the form of profits, royalties and transfer pricing (charging higher prices for goods supplied to subsidiaries in Third World countries). According to a U.K. study, some drug companies of the U.S.A. showed a 50% return on capital in 1973.[33] The

---

[29] Data based on UNCIAD and World Bank sources.

[30] Cited by S. L. Parmar, "A Third World Perspective on the International Economic Order and the Role of Transnational Corporations in it," Consultation Paper No. 3 (Geneva, World Council of Churches, n.d.), p. 16.

[31] **New Internationalist** (January 1976): 26.

[32] A. Furtado, member of Brazilian opposition, **New Internationalist** (March 1976): 28.

[33] **New Internationalist** (March 1976): 18-21.

top 298 U.S. based transnational corporations earn 40% of their entire net profits outside the U.S.A.[34]

--Transfer of **technology** is also proving burdensome to developing countries. According to a United Nations Council on Trade and Development (UNCTAD) estimate, these countries pay $1-1/2 billion a year for imported technology, which is roughly equal to half the total amount of private investment. A 1964 UN study shows that "more than 89% of all outstanding patents were owned by foreigners. Nothing has happened since to suggest that the trend is slackening."[35]

--Facilities for international **liquidity** have also been stingy towards the Third World. Out of $102 billion of international reserves created between 1970 and 1974, the developing countries received less than 4%. "The system . . . is inherently skewed in favour of the economically powerful countries[;] the U.S. has received a grossly disproportionate share of over $1 billion each year--which is more than the share of the entire developing world."[36]

Such evidence shows that the important constituents of the international economy are heavily weighted against the Third World, because of its weaker bargaining position, limited voice in the decision-making bodies of international agencies, and its overall postion of economic subservience to the industrial nations of the Northern Hemisphere. The pressure for an equitable international order is, therefore, justified, and can now be heard from the Third World. The pressure is even more justified on the grounds that Africa is a source not only of profit for the West but also a source of a host of raw materials needed in the West. For example, the U.S. depends 100% on Africa for its suply of industrial diamonds, 58% for its supply of uranium and 49% for its supply of cocoa.[37]

---

[34]Richard J. Barnet and Ronald E. Muller, **Global Reach** (New York: Simon and Schuster, 1974), p. 16; see also Weisskopf, p. 16.

[35]Barnet and Muller, p. 140.

[36]Grant, p. 12.

[37]Eleanor Goldstein and Joseph Newman, eds., **What Citizens Need to Know About World Affairs** (Washington, D.C.: U.S. News and World Report, 1978), p. 139.

The rapid growth of multi-national corporations in recent years has greatly enhanced their economic power over the countries on the periphery and thereby exacerbates the inequities. For example, they have a great deal of bargaining power in setting the terms on which their capital will be deployed in host countries. They control technology and can regulate its dissemination according to their own priorities. They have the power, through international pricing and bookkeeping adjustments, to artifically adjust the international location of their revenues and outlays and thereby affect the finances and balance of payments of host countries.[38]

The imperialist control by the capitalist center operates through political as well as economic channels. For example, the role of U.S. diplomatic missions throughout the world is defined as looking after the interest of its nationals, and this means in practice loking after the interest of U.S. business. Modern imperialist operations depend on the actual deployment of the military when problems arise which economic power and quiet political dealings cannot handle. So with the rise of the socialist countries the capitalists' system feels threatened, and hence military responses become increasingly necessary. This accounts partly for the increase in the United States defense budget from $75.5 billion in 1967 to $91 billion in 1976.[39] The challenge occasioned by the successful revolutions in Russia, China, Korea, Vietnam and Angola places the political position of international capitalism on the defensive. Hence the establishment of over 384 major and 3,000 minor American military bases around the world to protect U.S. business interest and to check the spread of socialism.[40] Added to this heavy defense spending are the stag-

---

[38]Stephen Hymer, "The Internationalization of Capital," **Journal of Economic Issues** 6 (March 1972). The multinational corporations are able to achieve their goal through their control of international capital movements, international capital production, and international government.

[39]Goldstein and Newman, p. 82.

[40]Cited in Sr. Caridad C. Guidote, **IDOC Project No. 9, In Search of Missions** (1974), pp. 110-111. It is important to note that these acts of aggression by the U.S. military and CIA are rarely fully discussed by American missiologists or missiological publications. Cf.: Paul Hopkins, **What is Next in Mission)** (Philadelphia: The Westminster Press, 1977)--no mention; Pierce Beaver, ed., **American Missions in Bicentennial Perspective** (Pasadena, Cal.: William Carey Library, 1977)--no mention; John T. Boberg and James

gering arms sales to less developed countries. It has been calculated that from 1970 to 1978 the worldwide arms trade has tripled. In 1978 the United States exported 40% of all arms sold abroad and the Soviet Union accounts for 28%.[41]

So far the state government has functioned to establish and assure the operation of American capitalist relationships in areas where such relationships have not been fully established or where they are unstable. This was true of the numerous U.S. Caribbean military interventions already cited. Since the end of World War II, the dominant concern of U.S. foreign policy has been the prevention of moves towards socialism by countries within the capitalist system. Thus, the interventions in Iran in 1953, in Guatemala in 1954, in Cuba in 1961, in the Dominican Republic in 1965 should be seen primarily as defensive efforts against the threat--real or perceived--that the nations in question would opt out of the international capitalist system. The same is true of the long and ultimately unsuccessful U.S. military involvement in Indochina and the intervention of the CIA in Chile which helped to overthrow the socialist government of Salvador Allende in 1973. Even though the role of the state in protecting the business interest of its citizens in other countries is clear from its foreign policy, one wonders what the foreign policy of the churches in the United States is.

This leads us to inquire about the role of ideology in the capitalist expansion, that is, speaking in Mannheim's sense, the role of ideas and views generated within a capitalist society to support and justify the system. In providing support for the system, one of its most important functions is to establish criteria for judging political activities. Thus, growing out of an economic process, the capitalist ideology provides a basis for unifying the economic and political realms of the system and for facilitating their joint operation. In order for capitalist expansion to be successful, it is necessary that basic capitalist institutions

---

A. Scherer, eds., **Mission in the 70's**--no mention; Gerald H. Anderson and Thomas F. Stransky, eds., **Mission Trends** (New York: Paulist Press, 1974), all issues--no mention; Arthur F. Glasser and Simon E. Smith, eds., **Missiology: An International Review**, since its inception in the 1970's, no mention; and so forth. The connival of American missiologists on these serious military and political involvements by the United States government in the internal affairs of other countries is tantamount to tacit support for the status quo.

[41] Goldstein and Neumann, pp. 82-83.

be created and maintained: the Labor market, private property, legal sanctions for economic contracts, and control of the work process by owners of capital. According to the ideology of capitalism, these institutions promote "economic freedom." So actions taken by the state to protect these "freedoms" or to facilitate its operation become synonymous with actions taken in order to preserve freedom and establish a decent society. Translated into the realm of foreign policy, the task of the capitalist state then becomes that of facilitating and protecting the international business activities of its nationals.

The keynote of the ideology of capitalist expansion during the post-World War II period has been anti-communism. Communism has been presented to the American people as an international conspiracy which has as its design the enslavement of all the peoples of the world and the consequent destruction of everything that they are taught to hold dear, from private family and religion to fredom of speech and the democratic process.[42] Such a threat must be fought at every step of the way. The real fact which the ideology does not emphasize, however, is that communism presents a systematic threat to the uninhibited operation of international capitalism.

Anti-communism is not the only form in which the expansionist ideology has been popularized. At an earlier time, especially during the colonial period, we saw how the British used the concept of mandated territory, protectorates, the white man's burden and Christianity as a rationale for an imperialist strategy. Apart from anti-communist slogans, there is the idea of "modern liberalism" which emphasizes the sentiment that it is the task of the rich, powerful United States to help the poor, backward countries of the world in their quest for development.[43] Economic advisory missions, foreign investments, the Peace Corps, missionaries and ultimately military involvement are all justified on this basis. But the statistics on U.S. profit from its overseas business activities expose the integrity of their aid to serious doubts. Concerning foreign aid, Paul G. Hoffman said in an article in **Fortune:**

During the last twenty-five years I have been working in the field called "foreign aid." . . . The words "foreign

---

[42] Robert Waelder, **Progress and Revolution** (New York: International University Press, 1970), pp. 299-307.

[43] Hopkins, pp. 90-95.

178

aid" led us to base vital policy decisions on what was considerably less than half a truth. Doesn't it badly distort reality to call something that creates large numbers of jobs for American workers "foreign aid"? Are actions that greatly increase our export earnings "foreign aid"? Is it "foreign aid" when we help to secure for ourselves new sources of essential raw materials? Is it "foreign aid" when we follow a course that could eventually lower the cost of goods and services Americans need every day? Above all, when we put our national security on the one solid footing it can ever really enjoy--while cutting the bill to the American taxpayer in the bargain--is it logical to term this "foreign aid"? Yet these are the kinds of benefits we have long been reaping from our relatively modest investment in helping other nations help themselves. We earned our first sizable dividends from that pioneering cooperative venture known as the Marshall Plan.[44]

This indicates that aid is not all charity, not just a simple giveaway to underdeveloped foreigners. To a large extent it is, as we can glean from Hoffman, an instrument of promoting, in this case, American domestic prosperity. Besides the domestic economic benefits, foreign aid provides its givers with powerful foreign aid policy instruments. For example, Chinweizu, a Nigerian journalist, describes in his book, **The West and the Rest of Us,** how this system works in the interest of the aid-giving government. He writes:

> Let us take a glimpse at what are called counterpart funds, and the uses to which they have normally been put and can be put.
> Into a local currency fund, said to be jointly controlled by the United States and the aid-receiving governments, are deposited the local currency proceeds from local sale of aid materials. Not convertible into dollars, money from this fund is used locally to pay for the overheads of the United States embassy, for CIA operations, for stockpiling raw materials, for building military bases and for making loans to American businessmen operating

---

[44] Paul G. Hoffman, "The Two Way Benefits of Foreign Aid," **Fortune,** March 1972, p. 118.

in the aid-receiving countries. Growing with the amount of aid given, this fund often becomes so large a part of the aid-receiver's active currency as to place in American hands enough economic power to dislocate the aid-recipient's economy, should it refuse to do America's bidding. For instance, in India at one time rupees controlled by the United States through counterpart funds amounted to half the rupees in circulation. And by 1973 United States counterpart funds in India were worth over $3 billion. If the power of that fund were exercised, America could dislocate India's economy. Given the mere existence of such economic power, the threat of using it is more than enough to make any government more "responsible," more "reasonable," more "moderate" in its reactions to United States policies.[45]

Foreign aid, therefore, is one of the ideological techniques by which the West attempts to preserve and protect the existing patterns of relationship within the world capitalist system. This is a world in which the prosperity of the European and North American industrialized countries is due to the capitalist evolution of their societies, based largely on the economic colonization of Africa, Asia and Latin America. Zwinglo Dias, a Latin American pastor from Brazil, in his article, "Evangelism Among Europe's Masses," draws our attention to the larger consequences of the ideological propaganda on the Western people when he says that the dominant ideology of these European societies tells the common man that "he is living in the best place in the world. His society is better organized and managed than any other. It enjoys power, knowledge and unlimited resources. It is a model for all the under-developed countries of the world. Its economic growth and its social achievements make it an indispensable partner if other countries are to develop."[46] This ideological sentiment, unconsciously generated by the industrialized countries, together with the socio-economic and political system that underpins them, has the tendency of upholding the status quo. To sharpen the focus, let us examine how "the system" operates in a typical African country like Kenya.

---

[45]Chinweizu, **The West and the Rest of Us** (New York: Random House, 1975), pp. 269-270.

[46]Zwinglio Dias, "Evangelism Among Europe's Masses," **IRM** 66 (October 1977): 262.

Kenya: A Paradise for Multinationals

In order to have an insight into the operation of Western capitalism in Africa, let us turn to Kenya as a typical example of an African country where Western capitalism has successfully attained maturity. The **IDOC Documentation Participation Project on Kenya,** [47] one of the most up-to-date and comprehensive accounts on the subject, will constitute our primary source of information. Kenya was a colony of Britain and the British monopolized all the profitable sectors of the Kenyan economy and culture. The Europeans (settler, diplomat, trader, missionary) acquired a monopoly on the high potential land in the highlands through the "white-highlands policy" by which the colonial government forcibly took over the best portions of Kenya's land and assigned these lands to Europeans. The missionaries acquired free of charge vast tracts of land under this policy. The Europeans also secured a monopoly over agricultural labor through the hut- and poll-tax system.

This tax system created an abundant labor supply for the benefit of the Europeans who owned the mines and farms and controlled the construction of roads, railways, ports and so on. The system involved imposing a high tax on migrant workers from the countryside who were desperate for additional sources of income to enable them to pay their tax and make ends meet. Jack Woddis' description of how the migrant labor system worked is instructive at this point:

> **First,** it [was] a migration almost over whelmingly of adult males, single men, or husbands unaccompanied by their wives and children, who have been left behind in the ruined countryside. **Secondly,** the migrants usually [took] up employment for a strictly limited duration--six months, a year, two years, but seldom longer. **Thirdly,** the migration [was] repeated again and again in the life of the individual peasant-worker, his career consisting of numerous short terms of employment alternating with periods at home in his village or the Reserve. **Fourthly,** whether he migrated from the countryside to a town or mining area within the same territory, or whether it [was] a question of "alien migration" across frontiers, it [was] on foot. **Fifthly,** it [was] frequently connected

---

[47] **IDOC Documentation No. 14: Uhuru and Harambee: Kenya in Search of Freedom and Unity** (1975).

with various forms of labor recruitment which sometimes tend[ed] to be disguised forms of forced labor. And **sixthly,** it [was] on such a scale and of such a character that it produce[d] a completely disproportioned population both in the towns and in the rural areas, aggravate[d] terribly the already acute agrarian crisis, and [led] to a total disharmony of the economy of the African territories most affected by it. From the standpoint of labor it [had] three further results; the constant change of personnel in employment which [arose] from this system [made] difficult the acquisition of labor skill, create[d] enormous difficulties for trade-union organization, and tend[ed] to depress wages.[48]

The 1955 East African Royal Commission on this hut and tax system confirmed that the system concerned mostly migrant workers who came to town with their families. "Their wages were calculated on the needs of a single man, and yet, even though many men had their families with them, this remained the basis on which wages are paid until the present day."

Commenting on this system, Basil Davidson, a specialist on African history, said:

> . . . urban wage earners still depend to some extent on their family food production in a more or less distant village. If you journey with African peasants going to town you may well be encumbered . . . with their piles of baggage; what they are likely to be carrying is not clothing or adornment, however, but food of one sort or another. The reason for this carrying of food to town is not a simple love of frugal living. It is rather a dislike of starvation. It arises from the happy colonial custom of calculating the wages of married urban African as though he were always a bachelor. . . .[49]

---

[48] Jack Woddis, "Migrant Labor," cited by Bernard Magubane, "The Evolution of the Class Structure in Africa," in **The Political Economy of Contemporary Africa,** ed. Peter C. W. Gutkind and Immanuel Wallerstein (London and Beverly Hills, Cal.: SAGE Publications, 1976), p. 182.

[49] Basil Davidson, "The Outlook for Africa," in **The Socialist Register** (London: Merlin Press, 1966), pp. 202-203.

These wages were insufficient for African urban workers, not only to feed, house, and clothe their families, but even for their own needs. According to a 1954 report of a Committee on African Wages, in Kenya, it was found that "approximately one half of the urban workers in Private Service, are in receipt of wages insufficient to provide for their basic, essential needs of health, decency and working efficiency."

Besides this system of migrant labor, which was created by the hut and poll-tax system, a Resident Labourers ordinance was introduced which converted the laborer into a kind of serf, bound to work for the white man for a minimum of 180 days a year.[50] Europeans also monopolized government services; engaged in the production of European-needed export foodstuffs at very low cost while imposing very high charges on imports for African consumption. European farmers also monopolized the cultivation of the most profitable crops and the most profitable markets. The European business-men in Kenya monopolized the transport industry by land, air and sea. As we have already noted, missionaries benefited from this colonial system. Hence they applied Christianity ideologically. They preached what they called a "purely spiritual gospel," but this gospel supported their own culture and helped Western capitalism take control of Kenya. This exploitation of the Kenyan people with its Western Christian justfication led to the Kenyan struggle for independence from European domination in the material as well as the spiritual sectors of life.[51]

On the attainment of independence, Kenya inherited a lopsided economy organized for the effective maintenance of the status quo. With very few exceptions, Europeans even today occupy the top of the income scale, while the Africans are at the bottom. This fact describes well the inherent inequality which Western capitalism fosters. The attainment of political independence marks the second stage in the development of Western capitalism in Kenya, with the capital for economic development generated almost solely from foreign investors.[52] In this stage, economic growth in Kenya (as the periphery) has largely continued to be controlled from the West (the center).

---

[50] **IDOC Documentation 14**, pp. 2-4.

[51] Ibid.

[53] Ibid., pp. 6-16.

Since the seventies, Kenya has become "a paradise for multinatonal corporations"[53] (the final stage of capitalism), which can spend more in advertising their products (£ 4 million a year) than the annual housing budget of the Kenyan government. As we have already noted, foreign investment takes away more capital than it puts in. In so doing the "center" under-develops the periphery."[54]

Kenya shows in the economic sphere an inequality of relationship between Europe and Africa. However, this unequal relationship existed and continues to exist in other than economic areas. Within the context of this unequal relationship and expressive of it is the attitude of many missionaries.

In some ways the attitude of the European missionary to the African is not different from the attitude of a European settler, diplomat or trader toward the African.[55] An example of this similarity of attitude is seen in the dominant/subordinate relationship obtaining in the social, economic and political realms in Kenya. This dominant/subordinate relationship is to some degree reflected in mission churches, particularly in the relationship between African clergy and European missionaries. There is a desire on the part of the African clergy to Africanize the Church. This desire shows that many African pastors are sensitive to the dominant-subordinate relationship and desire to undo it. This desire is clearly evient in the poem, "Africanization," written by a Kenyan seminary student, Dominic Mwasaru, who writes inter alia:

> Africanization!
> We want to see the church African!
> . . . We must have African bishops!
> . . . True we need them
> The African church should be in the
> hands of Africans themselves.
>
> Africanization! Africanize the church!
> That is a call for revolution--
> A revolution of church structures.[56]

---

[53] Ibid., p. 38.

[54] For a full discussion on the subject, see Walter Rodney, **How Europe Underdeveloped Africa** (Washington, D.C.: Howard University Press, 1974).

[55] Timothy Njoya, "Dynamics of Change in African Christianity" (Ph. D. dissertation, Princeton Theological Seminary, 1976), pp. 47-58.

[56] Dominic Mwasaru, "Africanization," **IRM** (April 1975): 121, 128.

This poem reflects a wider African desire not only to Africanize the church but also to free it from subjection to out-side control. This desire on the part of many African clergy is in accord with Mannheim's argument that the mentality of a dominated group is "utopian" and therefore critical of the domi-nant group which places them in a subordinate position. African clergy, in accord with Mannheim's thesis, seek for ways and means of destroying this system of domination in the hope of the realization of a new era free from the injustices of foreign institutions and domination. With the views of many Kenyan clergy in mind, we can examine the contemporary European missionary situation in order to locate where the African Christian or clergy belong in the overall picture and how he/she responds to the overall missionary system.

The Missionary Factor

Having looked at the geo-economic and political context of missionary sending and receiving countries, let us also examine the strength of the contemporary Western missionary situation which the moratorium call addresses. According to **Mission Hand-book: North American Protestant Ministries Overseas,**[57] there are at least 604 agencies doing mission work overseas. These agencies represent the overwhelming bulk of the personnel, funds and ef-fort of the North American Protestant Overseas endeavor.[58] Put in historical perspective, from the 1880's until 1945, missionary agencies ere founded at a rate of 30 to 40 per decade. The real impetus to establishing Protestant missionary organization from North America came after the Second World War, with over 100 being formed during the 1950's. Table 5 indicates that there has been upward increase in the number of agencies established.[59] The table shows the number of agencies founded per decade in this century.

---

[57]Robert Edward Dayton, ed., **Mission handbook: North American Protestant Ministries Overseas,** 11th ed. (Monrovia, Cal.: MARC, 1977).

[58]Ibid., p. 47.

[59]Ibid.

TABLE 5

NUMBER OF AGENCIES FOUNDED PER DECADE

Decade of Founding	Agencies Founded
1970-1979	110
1960-1969	84
1950-1959	103
1940-1949	70
1930-1939	46
1920-1929	42
1910-1919	38
1900-1909	27
Pre-1900	76

Related to the increase in the number of mission agencies is the corresponding increase in the number of Protestant missionaries abroad. The following table shows the steady increase in the overall number of missionaries from Western Europe and North America.[60]

1903	-	15,288
1911	-	21,307
1925	-	29,186
1952	-	35,533
1958	-	38,606
1963	-	42,952

Seen in the context of the United States, we observe that there has been an overall increase both in the number of missionaries recruited and sent and in the amount of income earned.[61] For example:

---

[60] "Missionary Statistics for the World including Africa," in **Map of the World's Religions**, 4th. ed. (Stuttgart, 1966).

[61] Eugene L. Smith, "Congress on the Church's Worldwide Mission," **IRM** 55 (1966): 457.

	Number of missionaries	Income in millions of dollars
in: 1960	27,039	$170.0
1968	32,087	$279.0
1976	35,458	$634.0

On the whole, the records show that the traditional missionary sending system is stronger than ever. The foreign missionary force has hit an all-time high and is still growing. There has been a steady increase in the total income of the agencies, from $170.0 millon in 1960 to $279.0 million in 1968, and $634.0 million in 1976. By way of additional perspective, the total income and contributions to 70 major U.S. and Canadian denominations in 1974 was approximately $5.5 billion, of which $1.1billion was designated for "benevolencies."[62] The same applies to the number of missionaries sent. It has grown from 27,039 in 1960 to 32,087 in 1968 and 35,458 in 1976.[63]

In the light of these figures, the numerical strength of these established institutional structures, over six hundred of them, their army of missionaries (about 40,000), their substantial wealth (about $5.5 billion), their geo-political location at the center of the world capitalist system, their global outreach, and so forth, one wonders what chances and choices Third World churches, e.g., in Africa, have to raise up a missionary agency that could participate effectively in the global missionary competition of the catholic church. How can the institutional power-gap, the wealth-gap, the numerical strength-gap, the global geo-polititical gap enhance "partnership in obedience," "mutuality in mission," "internationalizing mission," "ecumenical sharing of personnel," concepts that are formulated in missionary conferences? How can the glaring inequalities in the socio-economic world order be prophetically confronted by these missiological formulations? The 1973 Bangkok Assembly of the Commission on World Mission and Evangelism (CWME) of the World Council of Churches took this issue seriously when it called for "a mature relationship between churches."[64] In doing so it reviewed its earlier resolution

---

[62] Dayton, p. 57.

[63] Ibid.

[64] **Bangkok Assembly 1973** (New York: World Council of Churches, 1973), pp. 104-106.

at Whitby, Ontario, where the ideal of "older" and "younger" churches as mature partners was limited and interpreted to mean "absolute spiritual equality."[65]

In spite of Whitby's emphasis on partnership, we still find too much of a one-way traffic in the flow of missionaries from older churches in the West to younger churches in Asia, Africa and Latin America. The Bangkok Assembly recognized this phenomenon and bluntly stated that "Partnership in mission" remains an empty slogan. Even where autonomy and equal partnership have been achieved in a formal sense, the actual dynamics are such as to perpetuate relationships of domination and dependence.

As Rene Padilla, the Director of Ediciones Centeza in Buenos Aires, puts it:

> In actual fact, Whitby's call to partnership in obedience is still as relevant as when it was first issued. Many of its recommendations have not yet been implemented by a number of agencies involved in missionary work. Witness the growing numerical strength of North American Protestant Missions (almost wholly dependent on North America personnel, leadership, and finances) after World War II, and the persistent separation of "foreign missions" and "local churches" around the world. Witness the prevalence of policies and patterns of missionary work which assumes that the leadership of Christian missions lies in the hands of Western strategists and specialists. Witness the schools of "world mission" based in the West, with no participation of faculty members from the Third World. Witness, finally, the frequency with which an older church (or more often, a missionary board) in the West maintains a one-way relationship with a younger church (which may or may not be regarded as independent). As long as this situation endures, partnership is no more than a myth. [66]

---

[65] C. W. Ransom, ed., **Renewal and Advance** (London: Edinburgh House Press, 1948), pp. 176-184.

[66] C. Rene Padilla, "The Fullness of Mission," **Occasional Bulletin of Missionary Research Library** (January 1979): 7.

In the same vein, Edwin Luther Copeland, professor of Christian missions and world religions at Southern Baptist Theological Seminary, Wake Forest, North Carolina, comments: In spite of Whitby's statement, "do not older churches seem to assume without question that their own maturity qualifies them for partnership while they make their own judgments about the maturity of younger churches? If so, even this ideal trails clouds of paternalism with it."[68]

George Johnston, Dean of the Faculty of Religious Studies at McGill University, Montreal, Canada, spells out the problem of the implementation of conference resolutions which ignore the hard facts of socio-economic realities:

> The serious problems to which such questions refer (i.e. questions of inequities in world socio-religious and economic order) will not be solved by conferences of Christians that produce well-worded resolutions and little else. . . .[67]

In view of these dilemmas we have to consider the moratorium call by the All Africa Conference of Churches as part of a contemporary African response to the institutional power structure of Western missionary agencies in the context of neo-colonialism and multinational corporations and as a reaction to the ideological tendencies of Western missiological terminology which seems designed to preserve the traditional relationship between the center and the periphery. Granted that this could be so, we shall in the next chapter examine some aspects of the African (Third World) response to the Western missionary enterprise.

---

[67] Edwin L. Copeland, "Indigenous and More: Towards Authentic Self-hod," **Journal of Ecumenical Studies** 11 (Summer 1973): 501-503.

[68] George Johnston, "Should the Church Still Talk About Salvation)," **IRM** (1972): 52-53.

The Western Church has made the mistake of girding the Eastern David in Saul's armor and putting Saul's sword into his hands. Under these conditions the Church on the mission field has made a brave showing, but it is reasonable to expect that it will give a better account of itself by using its own familiar gear and weapons.

> J. Merle Davis, **New Buildings on Old foundations** (New York/London: IMC, 1947), p. 108.

The most difficult problem is the dichotomy between help from outside and growth from within. . . . Which honest church leader in the world would not admit that "help from outside" has eaten away the foundations of healthy self confidence and decent respectability in the younger churches and made them dependent miserably and even indecently on others? And yet which responsible and realistic church leader in the world of today will refuse all help from outside for the development of the work of God in the church he has been appointed to serve? . . . There is no easy answer. The only way out as I see it is in constant vigilance, utter selflessness, humility and frankness, depending on the mercy of God both on the side of the giver and on the side of the receiver.

> Hasan Dehqani al-Tafti, Anglican Bishop of Ispahan

Cited by Paul R. Gregory (General Secretary, Mission Division, United Church Board of World Mission, USA) in "Towards a UCBWM Stance on 'Moratorium,'" a personal statement.

There era of mission is not behind us. We have only begun, and now we can all be missionaries together.

> James McCord, **Princeton Theological Seminary Alumni News** (October 8, 1979).

CHAPTER VII

MORATORIUM IN THE CONTEMPORARY
SOCIO-ECONOMIC CONTEXT

The preceding discussion tends to indicate that the expansion of the economic, political and cultural imperialism of the West and the expansion of her missionary enterprise are closely related and interwoven. Mortimer Arias, the Methodist Bishop in Bolivia, puts it this way with reference to the Latin American situation: He submits that the work of the Western missionaries "was a civilizing and colonizing evangelization . . . more successful in transplanting culture than in transplanting the Gospel. Europeanization was the content and intent of Western evangelization."[1]

This observation leads us to speculate that the Western missionary enterprise may be part of Western imperialism which divides the world into two parts: the affluent West (the center of the world capitalist system) and the impoverished people of the Third World who belong to the periphery of the system. With the gap between the rich and the poor constantly widening and worsening to the disadvantage and detriment of the dominated and impoverished group, it is expected that the deteriorating situation could lead to a revolutionary tendency on the part of the oppressed against their oppressor as they seek to remedy the imbalance in their socio-economic and political realtions.[2]

We detect signs of this protest against captive relationship and economic exploitation in the moratorium call. An African advocate of the moratorium, a Presbyterian church leader from East Africa, the Reverend John Gatu, expressed the call as a rejection of their bondage to Western dependency and Western imperialistic attitude. He declared:

> We in the Third World must liberate ourselves from the bondage of Western dependency by refusing anything that renders impotent the development of our spiritual re-

---

[1] Mortimer Arias, "Contextual Evangelization in Latin America: Between Accommodation and Confrontation," **Occasional Bulletin of Missionary Research** (January 1978): 20-55.

[2] Robert McAfee Brown, **Theology in a New Key: Responding to Liberation Themes** (Philadelphia: The Westminster Press, 1978), pp. 102-130.

sources, which in turn, makes it impossible for the church in the Third World to engage in the mission of God in their own areas. The imperialistic attitude of the West . . . must be challenged.[3]

Gatu's call is also a call for authentic selfhood of the church in Africa. He tells his United States audience that the answer to Third World dependency is liberation and justice, not alms, because, as he puts it:

> We cannot build the church in Africa on alms given by overseas churches, nor are we serving the cause of the kingdom by turning all bishops, general secretaries, moderators, presidents, superintendents, into good enthusiastic beggars, by always singing the tune of poverty in the churches of the Third World. The need is commitment and a decision to go forward in faith. For Africa has money and personel. . . . Let mission be the mission of God in the world, not of the West to the Third World.[4]

Gatu's call is not only aimed at decolonizing the church in Africa in order to render them indigenous and relevant and protect them from European domination, it is also a protest against racial discrimination, which, according to him, supports the appointment of a European missionary to the legislative council in Kenya, and excommunicates an African from the church for becoming a member of a local political party. Gatu also protests against the Western cultural imperialism whereby missionaries set aside, despise and discredit the African religious beliefs and practices describing them as devil worship, magic, and superstition. In other words, Gatu's moratorium call is an appeal to restore the cultural integrity of the African and for authentic African religious beliefs and world view to be respected. [5]

---

[3]John Gatu, "Missionary Go Home," **IDOC No. 9: In Search of Missions** (1974): 70-72; see also Ruben Lores, "The Moratorium Issue and the Future of Mission," **IDOC 9**, pp. 53-56.

[4]Ibid.

[5]Ibid.

All in all, what comes through Gatu's call is not a rejection of the Christian message but a protest against racism, imperialistic domination and exploitation of Africa by the West.

In addition to Gatu's call, the 1971 Barbados meeting of anthropologists, sponsored by the World Council of Churches, also called for a moratorium on Western missionaries in Latin America. It was their considered judgment that missionary work was detrimental to the survival of the Indian cultures in Latin America, and that it also aided in the economic and human exploitation of the aboriginal population. They therefore recommended that all missionary work being conducted among the West Indians be stopped at once.[6]

Along with Gatu's call came other calls for a moratorium on foreign (i.e., Western and North American) missionaries. Emerito P. Nacpil, President of Union Theological Seminary near Manila, Philippines, told an august assembly of church leaders and missionaries gathered in Asia, Kuala Lumpur, Malaysia, in February, 1971:

> The missionary structure had performed magnificently the role of a successful midwife in helping to bring out into the light of day a new child, which is none other than the rise of Christian Community in the lands of the Third World. But now that the child is born, there is no longer any need for the midwife! It has also performed with love and sacrifice and patience and hard work the role of guardian and trustee over the growing life of the child. But now the child is grown-up. He is ready to enjoy his freedom as a son and to assume his rights and duties as an heir. The day of his independence and nativity has arrived. Therefore all guardians and trustees must now withdraw. Their last and final and most fitting act as guardians and trustees is to allow the son to claim his rightful freedom and to assume his responsibility in managing his own affairs and inheritance. . . . In other words, the most missionary service and a missionary under the present system can do today in Asia is to go home! And the most free, vital and daring act the

---

[6] Cited in Pius Wakatama, **Independence for Third World Churches** (Illinois: Inter Varsity Press, 1978), pp. 9-10.

younger churches can do today is to stop asking missionaries to come under the present system.[7]

Another call had come from India. Father Paul Verghese, a former associate general secretary of the World Council of Churches and new principal of an Orthodox Theological Seminary in India, said:

> Today it is economic imperialism or neo-colonialism that is the pattern of missions. Relief agencies and mission boards control the younger churches through purse strings. Foreign finances, ideas and personnel still dominate the younger churches and stifle their spontaneous growth. . . . So now I say, "The mission of the Church is the greatest enemy of the Gospel."[8]

And yet another call, this time from Latin America, from the dean of Union Theological Seminary in Bueonos Aires, Dr. José Miguez Bonino. He said:

> We can now see that we will either support the continuation of oppression or the struggle for liberation. We will support one or the other by the way we teach, worship, preach or use our money, speak or remain silent. There is no third possibility. . . . For us in the younger Churches integrity is of the essence. We cannot permit ourselves to forget integrity of our own responsibility before God and before men. We cannot for the love of our brethren or for the love of God let anybody or anything stand in the way of our taking on our own shoulders our responsibility. If in order to do that, we must say to you our friends, "Stay home," we will do so be-

---

[7] Emerito P. Nacpil, "Mission but not Missionaries," **IDOC No. 9: In Search of Missions**, pp. 78-80; see also Nacpil, "Mission but not Missionaries," **International Review of Mission** (1971): 356-362.

[8] Paul Verghese, cited by Gerald Anderson, "A Moratorium on Missionaries?" in **Mission Trends No. 1,** ed. Gerald Anderson and Thomas Stransky (New York: Paulist Press, 1974), p. 134. This article was originally published in **The Christian Century,** January 16, 1974.

cause before God we have this grave responsibility of our integrity.[9]

The reasons given by some of the other advocates from the Philippines and India are also worthy of note. They tend to reinforce Gatu's views. All of them belong on the side of those who occupy the "periphery" of the world capitalist system, and hence they share a common experience in relation to those who occupy the "center" of the capitalist system.[10]

The reasons which Nacpil advances for the withdrawal of missionaries are best expressed in his interview with many young people about what they see when they see a missionary:

> They tell me . . . they see green . . . the colour of the mighty dollar. They see white, the colour of Western imperialism and racism. They see an expert, the symbol of Western technology and gadgetry. They see the face of a master, the mirror of their servitude. They do not see the face of a suffering Christ but a benevolent monster which must be tamed because it can become a CIA agent which must be crushed. The young people in my own country have a name for missionaries and ecclesiastics. They call them "clerico-fascists." [11]

If this is how the present and future generations will see missionaries, Nacpil argues, then it follows, "that this image of the missionary cannot symbolize the authenticity of the Gospel and the universality of the church. Instead it can well be a symbol of the universality of Western imperialism among the rising generations of the Third World." [12]

---

[9] José Miguez Bonino, "The Present Crisis in Mission," **IDOC No. 9: In Search of Missions,** p. 76. This article was originally published in **Church Herald,** November 12, 1971.

[10] In contemporary parlance, Third World refers to the group of nations on the periphery of the capitalist system. They are economically less developed and less affluent than the West. They consider themselves injured by the West which has allegedly stunted their growth; cf. Robert Waelder, **Progress and Revolution** (New York: International University Press, 1970), pp. 341-348.

[11] Nacpil, **IDOC No. 9,** p. 8o.

[12] Ibid.

José Miguez Bonino's call for moratorium on missionaries is due to what he perceives as the crisis, the problem and the sickness of the missionary enterprise today. He argues:

> The real problem is that the alliance of missions and Western capitalistic expansion has distorted the Gospel beyond recognition and   evangelism, prayer, worship and personal devotions have been held captive to an individualistic, other worldly, success-crazy, legalistic destruction of the Gospel. . . .
> Consciously or unconsciously, and mostly unconsciously, the missionary enterprise has been related to the roots of expansion, the channels of penetration, the slogans, the cultural patterns of this process of expansion and domination. Christians in both the sending and receiving countries are increasingly aware of and concerned with this fact . . . of loss of confidence and crises in identity for many missionaries and national church leaders both here and overseas.[13]

Paul Verghese relates his call for mortorium to the control of the younger churches through the purse strings of relief agencies and mission boards. Foreign finances, he contends, "still dominate the younger churches and stifle their spontaneous growth."[14]

In the light of all these references, certain bold arguments for the advocates of moratorium emerge, namely that the overwhelming presence of missionaries dominates and distorts the image of the "younger" churches. Nacpil poses the problem of missionary domination thus:

> The missionary becomes the apostle of affluence, not sacrifice; cultural superiority, not Christian humanity; technological efficiency, not human identification; white supremacy, not human liberation and community. . . .
> [Therefore] I believe the present structure of modern missions is dead. And the first thing one ought to do

---

[13]Bonino, pp. 74, 76.

[14]Paul Verghese, "A Sacramental Humanism," **The Christian Century**, September 30, 1970, pp. 11, 18.

is to eulogize it and bury it, no matter how painful and expensive it is to bury the dead.[15]

The critics of economic imperialism of the foreign missionary system also protest the financial wrapping in which the Gospel is exported as a bait to the mission fields in the Thrid World. Bonino articulates this view sharply when he said:

> You have to learn to renounce resources as means of domination. In order to do this, you must learn to lose control over what you give. Our temptation is that of the poor--the temptation to sell ourselves. Your tempta- tion is that of the rich--to become masters. Both are sins against God and against men.[16]

Besides economic imperialsim, advocates of moratorium also protest against cultural imperialism. Gatu emphasized this. He protests against Racism and its manifestations in economic, political and ecclesiastical discrimination, its expression of superi- ority complex over Africans. He looks at Christianity in Africa in its historical dimension highlighting the missionary collabora- tions with colonialism and the missionary's distortion of African image. Gatu gives the impression that the African has not really forgiven the missionaries for their cultural genocide against the African.[17]

The moratorium question has not only operated in the realm of principle but has actually been in practice in a number of places. Towards the middle of 1968, the Methodist missionaries in Uruguay withdrew **en masse.** This moratorium, according to the President of the Methodist Church of Uruguay, The Reverend Luis Odell, "has affected only the presence and sending of per- sonnel. The mother church has continued to support our work financially. . . ."[18]

Another example of where a moratorium had been placed on foreign missionaries is in the national Presbyterian Church of

---

[15] Nacpil, **IDOC No. 9,** p. 79.

[16] Bonino, p. 78.

[17] Gatu, pp. 70-72.

[18] Luis E. Odell, "Reflections on the Total Withdrawal of Mission- aries in the Methodist Church of Uruguay," **International Review of Mission** (April 1975): 198-199.

Mexico. This was a negotiated agreement between the National Prsbyterian Church of Mexico and the three cooperating U.S. Mission boards of the United Presbyterian Church in the U.S.A., Presbyterian Church in the United States and the Reformed Church of America. They decided on a moratorium period for at least three years, 1971-73. This meant that "starting from January 1971 for at least three years the [Mexican] National Church would be without economic or personnel assistance from abroad except for reduced financial subsidy for the medical work and a few missionaries specialized in the Indian languages translation work."[19]

The Mexicans approved this moratorium plan because of their need to escape over-dependency on foreign aid which undermined their sense of selfhood and weakened the effectiveness of their witnessing for Christ. The foreign missionary personnel displaced qualified Mexicans from assuming leadership positions in the life of the Mexican Church. Therefore, by agreeing to the moratorium proposal they looked forward to having qualified Mexicans assume positions of responsibility in Mexican churches. The moratorium, according to the Mexicans, would assist them in dealing with "Yankee Imperialism" and in putting into proper perspective the issues of exploitation arising out of the business practices of North Americans. Such a move to dissociate themselves from Yankee imperialism and exploitation would make it possible, say the Mexicans, "for our church to enjoy greater acceptance as an integral part of the nation."[20]

At the expiration of the three years of moratorium trial, the leader of the national Presbyterian Church of Mexico said:

> On the whole the psotive points far outweigh the negative. Above all else, the moratorium has served to create a sense of responsibility throughout the Presbyterian Church of Mexico. It has helped local churches and presbyteries to acquire a new understanding of the wholeness of the church and to see the national aspect of our ministry and mission. . . . This has meant an increase of extension work, new projects and new congregations resulting from presbytery and local church initiative

---

[19] J. Gary Campbell, "Mexican Presbyterians' Adventure in Faith: A Case of Moratorium," **International Review of Mission** (1975): 200-209.

[20] Ibid.

198

and support. . . . growth in stewardship during these two and a half years. We now have greater economic support . . . from our churches and presbyteries for the denomination's publication, theological seminary and training schools.[21]

Other significant positive factors include the upsurge of natural leadership at the local and presbytery levels, greater lay initiative and participation in the work of the church and the transition from a state of "total dependence" in the Christian education program to a situation where the program functions "on the sole support of the Mexican Church."[22] On the negative side, says the leader of the Mexican Church, the church has not been able to adequately develop the Indian and medical ministries, nor has it been able to adequately finance the development of their library. He commented thus: "We probably made a mistake when we were making up the disengagement agreement with the U.S. churches not to have included some provision for a 'theological fund' to help us build up the seminary library and a scholarship fund for students."[23]

In his final summary of his evaluation of the moratorium experience which he described as an "adventure of faith." the Mexican Church leader said:

These three years of moratorium have been a good breathing spell, a helpful parenthesis. We are now open to new purposes which God may give us. My humble recommendation is that we should always be attentive to the work of the Holy Spirit, who moves in the midst of all situations in which we find ourselves in this world. To be the Church--the Body of Jesus Christ--is not to be isolated nor to be sufficient to oneself but to understand that we belong to one another, that we need each other, and that in fraternal and mutual dependence we must . . . place ourselves at the feet of Christ. . . .[24]

---

[21] Ibid., p. 205.

[22] Ibid., pp. 205-206.

[23] Ibid.

[24] Ibid., p. 209.

Other developments (compelled by circumstances) which amount to a moratorium situation in parts of Africa took place during the First World War (1914-18). At that time, Lutheran missionaries in the Usambara Mountains of Tanzania and Presbyterian missionaries in what is now Togo and Ghana had to return home to Germany. They left their churches in Africa to fend for themselvs. The Sudan Interior Mission had to leave their charges in Ethiopia during the Italian invasion. All these African churches not only survived this enforced "moratorium" but were strengthened by discovering their own self-reliance, by setting their own priorities and learning to take their place in the universal church.[25]

The cry against the Western churches became more urgent following the First World War which exposed the so-called "moral prestige and superiority of the West" as a pernicious, ideological myth, baneful in its outworkings for the whole world, East and West, South and North.[26] By 1928 during the Jerusalem meeting of the International Missionary Council (IMC), the colonial legacy and racist domination of the West were beginning to provoke bitter denunciations, rebellion and demands for justice and self-determination both from the younger churches in Asia and Africa and from their societies at large. Leaders of the younger churches were in the vanguard of the attack. It was during one of the discussions on the relationship between the "older" and younger churches that we hear the very first impressions of the concept of moratorium. It was mentioned by an Indian church leader, P. Oomman Philip, who during the 1928 Jerusalem meeting of the International Missionary Council (IMC) said:

> I sometimes think it will be a good thing for the growth of the indigenous churches in India if by some cataclysm, such as happened in China, this flow of men and money from the churches of the West may be arrested, even for a short time.[28]

Philip's suggestion was, however, rejected by the Jerusalem Council in favour of another new concept, "partnership." In spite of

---

[25] AACC brochure on Moratorium titled **A Strategy for Self Reliance;** also published in **International Review of Mission** (April 1975): 210.

[26] Cited by Jerald D. Gort, "Jerusalem 1928: Mission, Kingdom and Church," **International Review of Mission, Edinburgh to Melbourne,** pp. 280-281.

[28] Ibid., p. 282.

the rejection of Philip's suggestion, the challenges to Western churches and the denunciations of their accommodation to secular power have continued. In some sense their failure to come to grips with the hard realities of the social, economic and political exploitation of their governments and businessmen has produced the fresh call for moratorium today.

So since the 1910 missionary conference in Edinburgh, the issues culminating in the recent calls for moratorium have been central in the work of the ecumenical movement:[28] e.g., the World Council of Churches' study on institutionalism and unity, which was presented by the Commission on Faith and Order in 1961, called for increased theological investigation of the institutional factors that promote or hinder mission and unity and for a development of a theology of institutions. Also the emphasis by the Commission on World Mission and Evangelism (CWME) on "mission in six continents" and related program of Joint Action for Mission, the study of missionary structures of the congregations, the various studies on cultural identity and pluralism, the emphasis of the service and development structures of the Council on "appropriate technology" and the focus on human rights and social justice have all pointed towards the shared concern for issues of freedom and selfhood for the countries on the periphery of the world capitalist system. These issues are even more urgent today in the light of the increasing exposure of economic exploitation of the Western countries and the relative silence of most missionaries or even justification of these practices by some missionaries. The interplay of Western political and economic power with missionary enterprise and the colonization of the minds of men through cultural imperialism do not serve the ends of mission but constitute a hindrance to mission. To move from such patterns of alienation to selfhood and from imposed cultural homogeneity to pluralism requires a release from the chains of present missionary relationships characterized by personnel, propaganda, diplomacy, finance and organizational structures. We hear the demand for that release especially in the goals of moratorium as articulated by Burgess Carr while speaking on behalf of the All Africa Conference of Churches before the National Council of Churches Division of Overseas Ministries in the U.S.A. in January, 1975.

---

[28] See Documentations on "Moratorium," **International Review of Mission** 64 (April 1975): 210-217; **IDOC No. 9**, pp. 44-45.

Leave us alone for a while, so that we may be able to discover ourselves and you in Jesus Christ. When this has happened, you will be able to come to Africa and see churches renewed and empowered by the Holy Spirit to a new consciousness of what Christ means to them and their mission to others; you will see:

--Genuinely self supporting, self governing and self propagating churches making their full contribution to the whole church in the world;

--Churches that have found a new freedom to seek unity among themselves and

--Churches whose relationships with other churches are based upon equality under the Lordship of Jesus Christ . . .

These are the goals of Moratorium.[29]

Having reviewed the moratorium call from John Gatu (and other Third World advocates) and from Gatu's predecessors, we now turn to examine how the issue spread from Gatu to the World Council of Churches, All Africa Conference of Churches, and to the Lausanne International Congress on World Evangelization. The WCC was the first international ecumenical body to recognize the moratorium question as a crucial issue in contemporary missionary strategy. It was its joint committee meeting on Ecumenical Sharing of Personnel (ESP) held at Le Cenacle in 1971 that considered the issue at first. Later in July 1972 at Choully, Switzerland, the Task Force of the WCC on Ecumenical Sharing of Personnel (ESP) was again confronted with the moratorium proposal by African members of the group who opposed the ESP concept. In this proposal, the Africans spelled out the case for moratorium thus:

In this document the word moratorium is used to mean:
1. withdrawal of present and the discontinuation of future personnell sent into the service of receiving churches by foreign Church agencies;
2. discontinuation of money given to support churches and their institutions by the same sources;

---

[29] Burgess Carr, "The Mission of the Moratorium," **AACC Bulletin** 1 (January/March 1975): 19-20; see also **Occasional Bulletin of Missionary Research Library** (March/April 1975): 2-3.

3. provision of a reasonable length of time to allow for review, reflection and reassessment regarding the best use of money and personnel in response to the mission of God in our day and the searching for self-hood of the church in mission;

4. seeing anew the living Lord incarnated in the local situations and expressing that Lordship without foreign domination.[30]

The purposes of the moratorium, according to the African proposers, are:

A. To allow the receiving churches a time for critical questioning of the inherited structures and programs which may be cherished by some and yet are only relevant to a different age, and therefore remain a constant and unnecessary burden to the church;

B. To see and to struggle for that maturity which comes from the understanding of selfhood and self reliance without which ecumenism becomes an illusion and not a reality;

C. To give the sending churches the opportunity to question seriously the relevance of the expansionist missionary psychology which characterized the past and which still persists today, impoverishing the church by neglecting "witness in Jerusalem";

D. To encourage the churches in powerful nations to look objectively at the exploitative practices in which their countries are involved through trade, investment and aid in the Third World;

E. To give opportunity to receiving churches to prophetically challenge their governments, Christian councils and other institutions on the evils of over-dependence on foreign resources which hinder the necessary total liberation of man. . . .[31]

In terms of strategy, the African proponents of moratorium said:

---

[30] ESP Committee Meeting, Choully, July 1972, "Proposal on Moratorium"; see **IDOC 9: The Future of the Missionary Enterprise** (1974): 44-45.

[31] Ibid.

The moratorium is not a slamming of the door in the brothers' face; it is a dynamic process seeking a new way . . . to accomplish the freedom of the moratorium: experience says "do it totally at one time," lest the decisions be whittled away and the creative drive lost. . . .[32]

In view of the serious questions implied by the moratorium proposal, the matter comes up again at the WCC Bangkok Assembly of the Commission on World Mission and Evangelism in January 1973 as a response to the ESP Committee report on Partnership. It states:

The whole debate on the moratorium springs from our failure to relate to one another in a way which does not dehumanize. The moratorium would enable the reciving church to find its identity, set its own priorities and discover within its own fellowship the resources to carry out its authentic mission. It would also enable the sending church to rediscover its "identity in the context of contemporary situation." It is not proposed that the moratorium be applied in every country. . . . Missionary policy should be adapted to the particular circumstances in each area. . . . In devising new strategies for mission it is essential that all partners look together at the total challenge to mission.
    In some situations, however, the moratorium proposal, painful though it may be for both sides, may be the best means of resolving a present dilemma and advancing the mission of Christ.[33]

The recommendations arising from the moratorium debate at Bangkok are worthy of note, especially in anticipation of possible reactions from other mission agencies such as the Evangelical groups. The recommendations:

1. Call on the mission agencies, through its affiliated councils and churches, to restructure themselves in such a way as to provide for a mature relationship with the partner churches, and to involve the latter in the process of restructuring. Such involvement will

---

[32]Ibid.

[33]Ibid., pp. 82-83.

require drastic thinking and concrete steps by all partners concerned.

2. Urge all churches and mission agencies to review their bilateral relationships in the light of the fellowship of churches on the national and regional levels with a view to strengthening their ecumenical realtionships in mission.

3. Work with regional conferences, sponsored agencies and mission agencies to implement the internationalization of personnel on the regional level particularly in the field of theological education.

4. Seek to provide for the widest possible study and discussion of the call for moratorium as a possible strategy of mission in certain areas.[34]

The Bangkok recommendations underscored the need for mature relationships between the churches on the continents of Asia, Africa and Latin America and those in the Northern Hemisphere. The pressure and impression created by Bangkok was not for smashing relationships but rather for revising them, not for isolation but for better patterns of relationship. As Johannes Verkuyl, a Dutch missiologist, observed, "All attention at Bangkok was focused on one question: How can we by our inter-ecclesiastical relations become a better instrument for completing the uncompleted task of world mission"?[36]

Since Bangkok, there has been a series of ecumenical consultations dealing with a wide spectrum of moratorium issues. In January 1974 in Tagatay City, Philippines, counciliar representatives met to consider the ecumenical sharing of personnel for global Christian churches. The joint committee restated the basic sentiments at Bangkok to the effect that moratorium is to be a live option which is necessary and urgent in some situations. It is not applicable everywhere. If properly applied, "it could serve for the discovery of selfhood and for the reforming of structures of relationships for better co-operation among churches."[36]

---

[34] Ibid.

[35] Johannes Verkuyl, **Contemporary Missiology: An Introduction** (Grand Rapids, Mich.: William B. Eerdmans Publishing Co., 1978), p. 334.

[36] "Ecumenical Sharing of Personnel," report presented to the Commission on World Mission and Evangelism (CWME) of the World Council of Churches meeting in Basel, Switzerland, February 4-9, 1974; Ecumenical Sharing of Personnel meeting in Tagatay City, Philippines, January 21, 1974; see **IDOC 9**, pp. 34-39.

A year later, the Ecumenical Sharing of Personnel Committee held an ad hoc Consultation on Moratorium in Le Cenacle, Switzerland. There was a discussion about the ways and means and methods of disengagement, new ways of sharing personnel and possible consequences for the policy and grogram of the Commission on World Mission and Evangelism. The report of the ESP Committee stated that "Moratorium is not in contradiction to the basic understanding of Mission, rather it is inherent in the conception of mission."[37]

Another response to the moratorium question was by the Commission on World Mission and Evangelism (CWME) which met in Figueira da Foz, Portugal, in February 1974. They surveyed the post-Bangkok moratorium developments. After a careful deliberation on the issues at stake, they adopted a seven-point recommendation which could be regarded as an ecumenical position paper on Moratorium.

In a carefully worded statement, they referred to the Moratorium as "one way to create mature relationships of churches in mission." They also said, "We speak of a Moratorium for mission, not a moratorium of mission."[38]

Another outstanding Ecumenical/Evangelical conversation on the subject of moratorium took place at the Overseas Ministries Study Center, Ventnor, New Jersey, on May 13-17, 1974.[39] It was attended by some seventy-five participants representing a cross-section of the Third World people, missionaries, mission administrators, missiologists, Roman Catholics, conservatives, evangelicals, and mainline Protestant groups. It discussed some of the most basic issues of mission, including moratorium. We shall encounter some of the highlights of the meeting in due course.

So far we have traced the development of the moratorium debate, especially since its debut in the 1970's. We have listened to the call by the Barbados anthropologists, by Gatu, Verghese, Nacpil and Bonino. We have noted the ecumenical reac-

---

[37] ESP Interim Committee, "Report of the ESP Interim Committee Meeting," Le Cenacle, Geneva, Switzerland, January 1975, p. 6; see **IDOC 9**, p. 34.

[38] Commission on World Mission and Evangelism, "Recommendations on Ecumenical Sharing of Personnel," adopted by CWME in Figueira da Foz, Portugal, February 1975, p. 1; see **IDOC 9**, p. 35.

[39] The Report of the Ventnor Consultation is published in **IDOC 9: The Fortune of the Missionary Enterprise** (1974).

tions from the ESP committee meetings in Le Cenacle, Geneva, 1971; in Choully, Switzerland, 1972; in Bangkok, Thailand, 1973; in Tagatay City, Philippines, January 1974; and in Ventnor, New Jersey, May 1974. Finally, let us turn to the call as presented by the All African Conference of Churches (AACC) during its assembly at Lusaka on May 8-21, 1974.

The General Secretary of the AACC, by then Canon Burgess Carr, launched the moratorium call as a blueprint of the AACC. He declared:

> The African Church, as a vital part of the African Society, is called to the struggle of liberating the African people. The African Church, as part of the World Community, must also share in the redeeming work of Christ in our world. But our contribution must be African. The conribution of the African Church, however, cannot be adequately made in our world if the Church is not liberated and has not become truly national. To chieve this liberation, the church will have to bring a halt to the financial and man-power resources--the receiving of money and personnel--from its foreign relationships, be they in the Northern continents or foreign minority structures within Africa. Only then can the Church firmly assert itself in its mission to Africa and as part of the ecumenical world.
>
> Thus, as amatter of policy, and as the most viable means of giving the African Church the power to perform its mission in the African context, as well as to lead our governments and peoples in finding solutions to the economic and social dependency, our option has to be A MORATORIUM on the receiving of money and personnel.
>
> What does this mean to the structure and programmes of our churches today? What does it mean to our relationship with foreign mission boards and to the structure of those bodies and to sending churches? How can it be evolved in the situation of our individual churches? How does it affect the structure of the AACC itself?
>
> There is no doubt that the call for a Moratorium will be misinterpreted and opposed in many circles both within and without. But we recommend this option to the churches of Africa as the only potent means of coming to grips with being ourselves and remaining a respected group of the one Catholic Church.

The complete halt to receiving money and personnel will surely affect the structures and programmes of many of our churches today. Many church leaders will cease becoming professional fund raisers in foreign lands and come to face their true role in evangelizing and strengthening the Church at home. Surely election of this option may cause many existing structures of our churches to crumble. If they do, thanks to God, they should not have been established in the first place, and again it would be profound theology, for to be truly redeemed one must die and be reborn. What would emerge would indeed be African and be viably African. A Moratorium on funds and personnel from abroad will by necessity enforce the unifying drive of churches in Africa.

Should the Moratorium cause missionary sending agencies to crumble, the African Church would have performed a service in redeeming God's peoples in the Northern Hemisphere from a distorted view of the mission of the Church in the world. It is evident, however, that the enterprises of sending agencies will seek to manifest themselves in other ways. It is therefore vitally important that a strategy of implementation be carefully worked out. We call on the AACC to associate with member churches in evolving a strategy for each situation.

Such strategies should, in order to succeed, involve the development of awareness at the grass roots of the African Church. Only then will the church consciously develop authentic structures, orders and programmes based on the African values and priorities.[40]

This Lusaka declaration represents the deep feelings of the "ecumenical African Christians"; it served as a catalyst which caused the rumbling moratorium volcano to erupt. Lusaka created a new and most radical and dynamic awareness not felt at any previous meetings of the IMC.

---

[40] For full text of "Lusaka Declaration," see Verkuyl, pp. 334-335.

Responses: Ecumenical and Evangelical

Before we discuss the full implications of the call, given Mannheim's categories of ideology and utopia, let us review the responses to this call from the Western Ecumenicals and Evangelicals and also from their representatives in Africa and Asia. In this way we shall be able to deal with the issues raised in the responses as we come later to analyze the full implications of the call. We shall start with the Ecumenical response. But before that, we need to know who the Ecumenicals and Evangelicals are and what they represent. Thereafter we shall juxtapose an African ecumenical and an American evangelical in a live dialogue to capture some of the mood and emotions engendered by the moratorium debate. Having presented the responses, we shall apply Mannheim's categories to analyze both the call and its responses in order to further organize the arguments and explicate some of the problems and puzzles which have been raised by these Christian bodies.

The Christians related to the Ecumenical Movement [41] seek to foster unity and cooperation among Christian churches throughout the inhabited world. By extension they also press for greater understanding and cooperation between Christians and persons of other religions.

The ecumenical movement has developed along three lines marked particularly by international conferences. **The Life and Work movement** seeks practical cooperation of the churches for a stronger witness in the secular world. Their watchword is "doctrine divides, service unites." Through their influence, the ecumenical movement is usually considered to be strongly socially oriented. **The second arm** of the ecumenical movement is the **Faith and Order movement** which is designed to discuss the doctrinal divisions among the churches which Life and Work movement minimizes. It is directed to the theological search for unity among Christian churches and seeks to cure the scandal of Christian disunity which it considers an obstacle to Christian mission. **The third arm** of the ecumenical movement is **the International Missionary Council** (IMC), formed in 1921 following the historic international missionary conference which met in Edinburgh in 1910. The IMC organized and sponsored a series of ecumenical conferences on mission. In sum, the ecumenicals have a world-

---

[41] "The Ecumenical Movement," in **The Westminster Dictionary of Church History,** ed. Jerald C. Brauer (Philadelphia: The Westminster Press, n.d.), pp. 285-287.

wide vision of the church in the world. They press towards a greater expression of unity and cooperation among all Christians. In a sense they are considered liberals because of their concern also for the material well-being of the human condition.

On the other hand, **the Evangelicals**[42] refers to the group of Christians who affirm the exclusive sufficiency of Christ and His work for their salvation and the salvation of the sinful. They have a passion to preach the message of Christ's salvation to others--hence their special concern for missionary work. They stress the inerrancy and authority of theBible and are committed to the inspired Scripture as the divine rule of faith and practice. They stress the preaching of the Word over issues of social concern and insist on the need for individual religious experience. The Evangelicals, therefore, refer to those who stress evanglism, and personal religious experience, Biblical inerrancy and authority, human sinfulness and the necessity of a new birth. Their **raison d'être** has remained fellowship in the Gospel.

Let us examine briefly the place of these groups in Mannheim's categories of ideology and utopia. As we have already noted, Mannheim's concept of ideology basically refers to ways of thinking which express the interest and special outlook of a particular social group and which are conditioned and influenced by the socio-economic position of that group. He points out the distinction between conservative ideologies, such as Marx analyzed, and revolutionary, visionary utopia, such as Marx produced. In so doing, he extends the notion of socially conditioned and "interested" thinking to include the revolutionary tradition itself, and by implication every form of thought. So in his view, all "knowledge" expresses a relation between a style of social existence and a mode of intellectual production. As a result of this, Mannheim sees in ideological thinking the tendency of the ruling groups to become so intensively interest-bound to a situation that they are simply no longer able to see certain facts which would undermine their sense of domination. In other words, the ruling groups unconsciously generate views and values that legitimate and reinforce the existing order and protect them from competing groups.

Mannheim applies the concept of utopian thinking to reflect the opposite discovery, namely that certain oppressed groups are so strongly interested in the destruction and transformation of a given condition of society that they unwittingly see only those elements in the situation which tend to negate it. By their

---

[42]"The Evangelicals," in Brauer, pp. 316-318.

thinking they seek to change the situation that exists. The utopian mentality, according to Mannheim, is "the collective unconscious, guided by wishful representation in which the will to action hides certain aspects of reality. It turns its back on everything which would paralyze its desire to change things."[43] As the African proposers of the moratorium would put it: "To accomplish the freedom of the moratorium, experience says do it totally at one time. . . ."[44] Hence, even though they, the AACC, are heavily supported by foreign funds up to the tune of 80% of their budget, that does not alter their vision of a new order. As Mannheim has said, the utopian mentality is supremely concerned with the transformation of a given social condition that keeps them dependent and dominated. As a mentality that emerges from the temper of an oppressed class, the utopian tendency is conflictive, accusing, emotional, aggressive and provides a vision which serves as a horizon towards which the group struggles. They engage in a constant dialectic with the social context that keeps them oppressed.

These ideological and utopian categories shall provide us with conceptual tools to examine, evaluate and classify the mentality of the West, which for over a century has been at the helm of affairs in the missionary enterprise, and also that of the Africans who for more than a century as well have been overwhelmingly dependent and controlled through Western missionaries and money.

By belonging to the ruling group, the missionaries tend to manifest ideological thinking as a result of their social location and mental orientation vis-à-vis the Africans. The relationship of their views to their social position should not be regarded as that of strict determination; it is "not a mechanical cause-effect sequence," says Mannheim. It is a relationship of correspondence which is open, not deterministic.[45] This creates the possibility that there are likely to be those whose views do not strictly conform to their relative social and historical situation. Mannheim in this connection contends that only empirical investigation will show how strict is the correlation between life situation and

---

[43] Karl Mannheim, **Ideology and Utopia: An Introduction to the Sociology of Knowledge,** trans. Louis Wirth and Edward Shils (New York: Harcourt, Brace, 1954), p. 36.

[44] **IDOC 9,** p. 45.

[45] Mannheim, p. 239.

211

thought process, or what scope exists for variations in the correlation.

On this score we would expect differences of opinion between the Western ecumenicals and evangelicals on the moratorium issue, in spite of the fact that they are the same people sharing the same world views and generally belonging to the same socio-economic class. Likewise, we can account for the rejection of the moratorium call by some African church leaders by examining the life situations under which they declared their objection.

For a closer inquiry into the ecumenical responses, let us examine the views of Ruben Lores and Paul Hopkins, whose ideas on the subject of moratorium could be said to represent the ecumenical position.

Lores is a seasoned and thoughtful missionary and former Rector of Seminario Biblico Latinamericano, San Jose, Costa Rica. He sees the call for moratorium more as a symptom than a disease. He contends that it is the disease and not the symptom that the moratorim points to. Hence he speaks of the moratorium as the quest for identity and selfhood for which the missionary presence is a hindrance and from which freedom is sought. It is a search for a new image of the church, and an insistence to let the church be the symbol of the universality of the Gospel and not the missionary. It is a plea against any acts of dehumanization of the weak by the strong.[46]

Lores considers the call to apply to both the evangelicals and the ecumenical missionary agencies regardless of their style of relationship. He calls for a total revision of the theological and ideological conceptions that have undergirded the missionary movement since its inception. He protests the presence of foreign missionaries in the mission fields as an onerous blessing from which deliverance was expected. In effect Lores says ". . . We should call for an end to the foreign missionary enterprise much in the same way and for the similar reasons that we have called for an end of the era of colonialism." Lores is skeptical of the effectiveness of the present structures which he calls "Christian corporations" with all their vestige of the colonial era, their aggressive mentality and their spirit of capitalism which is quite remarkable for their lack of a theology of poverty."[47]

---

[46] Lores, pp. 53-57.

[47] Ibid., p. 56.

Paul Hopkins in his response indicates a good grasp of the moratorium issue. He serves the United Presbyterian Church-U.S.A. in her overseas mission endeavor, especially in Africa. He writes from personal knowledge and long involvement in the missionary effort in Africa. Among his latest wirtings on the subject of mission is his book titled **What Next in Mission?** [48] The gist of this book bears directly on the issue of moratorium. Unlike other North American and European missiologists, Evangelicals and Ecumenists, he perceives the problem in mission through the lenses of Third World Church leaders who are calling out for changes and renewal in the present patterns of missionary endeavour. He understands the issues to be basically conflicting mores--affluence versus poverty--and conflicting objectives--imperialism versus self-determination. "We have failed our membership. We talk about partnership, yet we try to hold on to the strings. We have been told for years that this continuing colonial attitude is no longer acceptable and yet we do nothing about it."[49]

In the light of these perspectives, Hopkins rightly diagnoses Gatu's call as "the cry of a man who is **desperate:** 'If you can't hear us, get out!' This isn't a rational statement, it is a cry of despair engendered by **our** refusal to listen."[50] What then is the moratorium all about? According to Hopkins:

> It is that the overseas church tends to see us as attempting to hold on to an outdated system of missionary endeavor, of trying to maintain control of their lives through our people and dollars, of refusing to assist them in developing their selfhood because we want to keep them dependent on us.[51]

> It is the need to change totally our missionary system . . . because evangelization belongs to every church in every nation not just to the church in the West.[52]

---

[48] Paul A Hopkins, **What Next in Mission?** (Philadelphia: The Westminster Press, 1977).

[49] Paul Hopkins, "A Conciliar Protestant Mission Board Perspective," **IDOC 9,** pp. 18-19.

[50] Ibid.

[51] Paul Hopkins, "What is the Call to Moratorium and How Should We Respond?.," **Concern** (November 1974): 13-14.

[52] Ibid.

Hopkins locates the heart of the problem in the system, i.e., the mission boards and their staff that make the policies that keep the system intact long after it has served its purpose. For example, he contends, "We have managed to restructure our own church to serve six continents mission . . . without seeking advice from sister churches. The new structure is incomprehensible to the leders of overseas churches."[53]

In sum, Hopkins calls not only for changes in attitudes and straegy and paradigm, but also for a look beyond the religious frontier to the economic and actual living conditions of the people, the Christians in the Third World-- in Africa--whose hunger and anger the Christians in the West must reckon with. He quotes with approval the ESP Committee Meeting Report that "Moratorium [should be] understood to be a process of liberation from captive relationship."[54] Their cry is that of a powerless and oppressed group, demanding a hearing from their masters. It is a product of their historical and cultural experience as those who have been unequally yoked to more powerful and more aggressive partners. They are asking their privileged and powerful partners to help them affirm their selfhood. They are asking for help to become self-reliant. They have become ashamed of their prolonged dependency and are eager to become self-supporting and self-governing and self-propagating. They are aware of their economic, financial, political and technological limitations. Hence their demand is not for cutting off relationships with their more privi-leged Christian partners but for a changed relationship.

Given Lores' and Hopkins' views, we would say that the ecumenical response to the moratorium call is favourable. Nonethe-less, we have to recognize that some of the ecumenicals have in practice interpreted moratorium as a retreat in mission rather than a renewal and reconcilliation in mission. This misinterpreta-tion seems to underscore the need for a theoretical framework to enable some of the ecumenicals understand the full implica-tions and dynamics of the moratorium. One indication in this direc-tion is the understanding of the moratorium call as characteristic of utopian mentality, with its tendency to have grossly inadequate means for the achievement of their desired ends. This is clearly seen by the fact that while the AACC was agitating for a mora-torium, it was at the same time seeking $500,000 in grant and loans from U.S. mission boards to help construct a new head-

---

[53] Ibid.

[54] Ibid.

214

quarters.[55] In this connection, no one can consider the call for a moratorium rational. Let us consider the response of the evangelical group as well.

Having looked at two representative views of the ecumenical responses to the moratorium, it is now necessary to look at Evangelical Christian responses. The Lausanne gathering of the International Congress on World Evangelization in July 1974 can be seen as the first place where Evangelical Christians publicly and consciously confronted the issue of Moratorium. Billy Graham, who delivered the opening address, said unequivocally that a moratorium on the sending of missionaries should be rejected by evangelicals. Until then the evangelicals had paid no serious attention to the early calls for moratorium. Even the Evangelical mission leaders who met at Green Lake, Wisconsin, in 1971 to discuss the best model for church-mission relations and structure did not consider the possibility of withdrawing or reducing the number of their missionaries to be a viable device for solving church-mission tension.

In **The Evangelical Response to Bangkok** and **Official Reference Volume of the International Congress on World Evangelization,** Lausanne, Switzerland, there are no direct references to moratorium, but there was criticism of "Salvation Today," the theme of the 1973 Bangkok WCC Conference where the issues related to the moratorium were recognized and affirmed. For instance, Susumu Uda[56] of Japan Christian Theological Seminary, in his paper on "Biblical Authority and Evangelism" (published in the **Official Reference Volume of the International Congress on World Evangelism**), remarked that the Bangkok Conference on "Salvation Today" revealed a crisis-situation within the WCC-related churches. He argued that the Christian elements were being swallowed up. The evangelicals at Lausanne considered the issue a conciliar concern and none of their business. Nonetheless, John Gatu, who figured on the list of "conveners" of the Lausanne Congress kept the discussion alive especially with his East African colleagues. Eventually the drafters of the "Lausanne Covenant" broke the evangelical silence in the section on "The Urgency of the Evangelistic Task." Although the term "Moratorium" was not

[55] Cited by Peter Wagner, "Colour the Moratorium Gray," **International Review of Mission** (April 1975): 167.

[56] Susumu Uda, "Biblical Authority and Evangelism," in **Let the Earth Hear His Voice,** ed. J. D. Douglas (Minnesota: World Wide Publications, 1975), pp. 86-87.

used, the congress approved a "convenant" statement that declares:

> A reduction of foreign missionaries and money in an evangelized country may sometimes be necessary to facilitate the national church's growth in self-reliance and to release resources for unevangelized areas. Missionaries should flow even more freely and to all six continents in a spirit of humble service.[57]

With this lead from Lausanne, the evangelicals began to participate in the moratorium debate and their voices began to be heard in theological and church journals. Their initial responses were basically negative especially among the North American evangelicals. Following their initial emotional responses, they later approached the issue more objectively. We shall consider the views of Peter C. Wagner and Bryant Hicks as typical of the Western evangelical stance on the moratorium. Thereafter we shall evaluate the evangelical contribution to the debate using Mannheim's categories. We shall also refer to some contradictions in evangelical missionary thinking which can only be resolved using Mannheim's categories.

Donald McGavran in his reaction to the WCC Bangkok theme on "Salvation Today" said in **The Evangelical Response to Bangkok:**

> It is highly significant that while the mission aim of the World Council of Churches, and indeed of all churches of Christ is "to further the proclamation of the Gospel to all men that they may believe and be saved," all the advanced publications concerning this meeting indicate that the World Council is making a massive effort to re-interpret the classic meaning of that aim so that "being saved" will come to mean having more food, more justice, more clothes, more freedom, more production, less disease, more peace, more brotherhood, in short, more this-worldly improvements.
>
> . . . Advance WCC materials insist (on Old Testament grounds) that "Salvation" has primarily to do with the current life of flesh and blood, hunger and satisfaction, manufacturing and distributing, freedom and wholeness

---

[57]Ibid., p. 6.

in this world. . . . We hope and pray that as the meeting takes place, better counsels will prevail. . . .

Evangelicals will maintain, on the basis of the total Biblical record . . . that Salvation means a change in status of the soul, the essential person is achieved through faith in Jesus Christ alone, and results in abundant life in this world.[58]

These samples of the Evangelical posture are indicative of their lack of strong emphasis and involvement on social and political issues. With reference to the actual moratorium question, Peter Wagner,[59] an influential missionary scholar of the evangelical persuasion, has responded forcefully to the moratorium debate. According to him, "I myself shouted a hasty 'no' along with many others" when the call for a "Moratorium of missionaries" went up from some Christian leaders from such platforms as the World Council of Churches Assembly in Bangkok. Later Wagner responded with "yes and no." In general, Wagner raised the typical evangelical questions concerning the crucial theological and missiological issues about the ultimate, unique and universal significance of the Lordship of Jesus Christ and the question of the unevangeized parts of the world. He was critical of "a churchman such as Burgess Car" who, while advocating the crumbling of the missionary-sending agencies and a ban on Western missionaries, was at the same time asking for funds from the Western Mission Churches. This posture, according to Wagner, suggested that the proponents of moratorium were saying, "We need your dollar and marks and pounds, but not your people."[60]

Wagner was the first to boldly spell out the occasions in which there was a need for a moratorium on missionary work. In this connection he recognized the cultural, theological, ecclesiastical and missiological pitfalls in the Western missionary enterprise. His arguments in this connection sounded like those of the advocates of moratorium, but differed radically from theirs in that he applied them only with reference to the Great Commission. With regard to Western cultural chauvinism, Wagner contends, "We need a moratorium on missionaries who continue to

---

[58] Donald McGavran, "Salvation Today," in **The Evangelical Response to Bangkok,** ed. Ralph Winter (Pasadena, Cal.: William Carey Library, 1973), pp. 27-28.

[59] Wagner, p. 167.

[60] Ibid., p. 174.

extend Western cultural chauvinism." He suggests, "We need a moratorium on missionaries who continue to indulge in theological and ethical imperialism." He recommends, "We need a moratorium on missionaries who are dedicated to paternalistic interchurch aid. . . ."[61] In sum, we could say that Wagner advocates a type of selective moratorium, not a total moratorium. As he puts it: "The moratorium issue has surfaced at an opportune moment in history. . . . It is time to prune the dead and fruitless branches from the missionary enterprise and graft in new vital branches through which the power of Jesus Christ will flow unimpeded producing abundant fruit for life eternal."[62]

Wagner's response is brilliant but not satisfactory. It ignores the radical demand of the moratorium that calls for a change of the "one way traffic" of doing mission. His analogy of a missionary tree that needs trimming and pruning and grafting of new branches rather than a cutting down of the entire tree and planting an entirely new one betrays the ideological orientation of his response.

Another view of moratorium is expressed by Bryant Hicks, an Associate Professor of Missions and World Religions at Southern Baptist Theological Seminary, Louisville, Kentucky. He argues "why we still need more missionaries despite the moratorium development."[63] He contends that moratorium could "promote the domestication of the churches in their respective cultures . . ., ignore the multitudes of unreached peoples particularly in those areas where the church comprises only a small percentage of the total population. Hence a moratorium in the face of the increasing internalization of mission especially when it seems to be ready to burst from bud, appears almost anachronistic." Hicks argues for a better church-mission relationship and advances reasons why missionaries "should flow ever more freely from and to all six continents in a spirit of humble service."[64] He contends that, given certain preconditions with regard to foreign mission fields, the deployment of labourers from abroad should be a matter that calls for careful consideration, prayer and planning. Hicks

---

[61] Ibid., p. 176.

[62] Ibid.

[63] W. Bryant Hicks, "Why We Still Need More Missionaries," **Review and Expositor: The Impact of the Third World on Missions, A Baptist Theological Journal** 74 (Spring 1977): 219-228.

[64] Ibid.

suggests that expatriate personnel are very much like fertilizer; when properly spread, it causes plants to flourish; if applied in too great a quantity, it can injure or kill. Therefore, he recommends that: 1) the receiving association should be heavily involved in all decisions about placement of missionary personnel for they understand the local setting in ways that are beyond the grasp of the outsiders; 2) the receiving associations should be the ones to set their own direction with colabourers from overseas offering themselves as requested; 3) missionaries must avoid the development of a proprietary attitude towards an assignment or a place of labor; 4) the need for more missionaries lies in the continuing activity of God as Holy Spirit by which persons affirm themselves to have been called to enter into transnational setting to share Christ; 5) another reason for increasing missionary personnel is that they "serve wherever they are, by their mere presence as a constant symbolic reminder of the urgency of thrusting the gospel out to the yet unreached peoples."[65]

Hicks then outlined what he says should be the true marks of a missionary today. The western missionary must not let legitimate political, social and survival needs crowd out the legitimate needs to be made whole at the inner core of life through new life in Christ. Today's missionaries should be humble and like Christ assume the role of a servant. They must "labour and pray towards the assumption of initiative by the local Christians in everything. They will have to be teachers and trainers to the end that they will lead the people to the freedom to discover truth as the Holy Spirit enlightens their study of the Bible." Hicks' position is an optimistic and evangelical one. His view supports the traditional sending missionary system which the moratorium considers inadequate and anachronistic. At best, his response to the moratorium call for change is negative and his arguments in support of the traditional missionary system are ideological.

Having reviewed typical evangelical arguments on the moratorium, we can now make some critical analyses of their views. Harvie Conn, a Professor of Missions at Westminster Thelogical Seminary in Philadelphia, offers us a critical review of the evangelical stance on the moratorium debate. He points out that the evangelicals have not dealt with the heart of the

---

[65]Ibid.

matter.[66] He asks what the evangelicals have said in regard to the institutional and structural questions posed by the moratorium.

> . . . Can the evangelicals canonise the historical forms of mission societies as Sodalities, and make a normative generalization out of a historical particularity? Will the over 3,400 missionaries being sent to the Third World by at least 209 mission agencies continue to use the old mission/order structure pattern? If so, how do they escape paternalism and colonialistic control from Wheaton or Pasadena or Philadelphia?[67]

In other words, Conn argues that the evangelicals have not answered the question of how Christians can express their identity in structural relations. "Will the evangelicals' protective impulses for western ecclesiastical and paraecclesiastical agencies lead them into a new defense of status quo, or will their Biblical impulses for the world church lead them to a new investigation of how the whole people of God could be together?" Furthermore, Conn asks: "Can the evangelicals not consider the moratorium to be raising a radical communication question, i.e. how can the gospel be communicated from one culture to another in its pure form, without a foreign cultural embellishment or coating?"[68] Cast in the poetic words of Bishop Frederico Pagura, a Costa Rican Church leader, the question reads thus:

> Does not the moratorium call missionaries to go home if they are not able to separate the eternal word of God from the cultural molds in which we try to teach it? Does not the moratorium call on missionaries to go home if their allegiance to the nation of their origin is stronger than their loyalty and obedience to Christ?

---

[66]Harvie Conn, "The Moratorium Message to Evangelicals," **Issues for Christian Leaders, Briefs From Westminster Theological Seminary** (January 1977): 1-3.

[67]Ibid.

[68]Ibid., p. 3.

Does not the call for moratorium ask us to give up our culture for God's Christ and His Kingdom?[69]

In order to have a better grasp of the Ecumenical and Evangelical perspectives on moratorium, let us listen to the tone and temper of some part of a dialogue between an African ecumenical, Thomas Leeuw, and an American evangelical, Gerald Anderson, as they try to explicate and communicate their views during a panel discussion on the subject of moratorium.[70]

Anderson citing a direct quote from Gatu, comments that:

John Gatu does not have the support of his people in proposing the call for moratorium.

Leeuw replies:

Yes, but you must understand what he [Gatu] meant. He was not saying: I have little support for my position at home, therefore, do not take me seriously. He is saying: I am a leader of the church, and while not everyone will understand what I am saying or agree with it, I am in a position to raise consciousness; as a leader, I must try to help my people define the problem and set goals. The point of the issue is not to take a nose-count of African Christians. It is to hear what Gatu is saying, and so affirm it or reject it.

Anderson is criticized by Ruben Lores. Lores says:

What I hear being said here is that it is very difficult for Americans to really hear what is being said. Jerry Anderson, for instance, has said that Gatu's call for a moratorium is simplistic. Perhaps it is simplistic from a Western, academic, American point of view. But come to Asia, to Africa, or to Latin America, and it is not simplistic at all. Jerry also affirms Christians participating in the struggle to change social and economic inequities, but he sees it as something apart from the

---

[69] Bishop F. Pagura, ". . . Missionary Go Home," quoted by Lores, pp. 55-57; cited in part by Conn, p. 3.

[70] "Panel Discussion on Moratorium," **IDOC 9**, pp. 65-66.

preaching of the Gospel. Peter sees these as two different things as well. It is hard for Americans generally
not to think in terms of "evangelism," on the one hand,
and "social action" on the other. But to the emerging
people of Africa, Asia, and Latin America who are struggling with oppressive situations, there is no dichotomy.
The developing theology of liberation asserts that there
is no distinction between preaching the Gospel and putting it into action in society. So it is difficult for Westerners who have been in a habit of controlling the process to really give up that control. Americans and Europeans keep talking about new strategies and establishing
new channels to deal with Asia, Africa and Latin America. I think it is important for Americans and Europeans
to see, to dialogue, to listen without trying to create
a new design for us . . . without even trying to **help**
create the new process or movement. It is time that
moratorium is taken seriously. While it will not be the
same in every situation, while it will differ between Asia,
Africa and Latin America it is important that you listen,
and listen seriously.

Anderson responds to the panel members:

I have a question for Tom Leeuw. When you said a moment ago that there is no middle ground, that one either
has to be for or against moratorium, were you suggesting
that anyone who has reservations about the general kind
of moratorium that John Gatu calls for is thereby a part
of the oppressor system?

Leeuw replies:

Yes, if you begin to speak at cross purposes, whenever
the moratorium question is brought up, if you refuse to
discuss it on Gatu's terms and insist on discussing it on
your own terms. We must not forget the historical fact
of the collaboration between the missionaries and the
imperialists, and the likelihood that the church will therefore be in danger of standing out as a sign of the extension of imperialism. This is why it is important that missionaries listen when Africans speak. Missionaries are
so closely associated with the oppressors that it is difficult for them to extricate themselves without help.

Anderson asks in response:

> But do you want missionaries and fellow Christians who
> share a common concern to be quiet, or do you want
> them to engage in dialogue with you?

Leeuw replies:

> I think that there are times when they ought to be quiet.
> This is one time when they have to be quiet and listen.
> Listening is also a very strong means of communication.

Anderson then asks:

> But after the listening, do you welcome responsible dia-
> logue?

Leeuw responds:

> Yes, I do. Now I have a question for you. In your sec-
> tion on tribal religions, you talk about your aversion to
> the American civil religion, and you refer to the White
> House. Dont't you think then that America has a place
> where missionaries ought to be working? Don't you think
> you have a mission in America?

Anderson reacts saying:

> Precisely. It is "both/and" mission. It is both universal
> and particular. One of my concerns for America is in
> the area of theological education. So much of it goes
> on with the presupposition that everything of importance
> in church history and theological construction has hap-
> pened somewhere between Heidelberg and Berkeley, which
> simply reveals a North Atlantic tribalism.

Leeuw comments:

> It seems to me that when you become familiar with the
> whole phenomena of the Social Gospel in America, you
> realize that the whole problem for America is itself.
> There is another sense in which you can speak about
> American tribal religion. Race is deeply interwoven with
> economic and political privilege in this country. The

churches themselves are, in some sense, repositories of tribal religion, in terms of where they are located, what kind of industries they are supporting, and where the people who are in the churches belong economically and politically. I think that if you are going to talk about a global mission of the church, these are the barriers that are being transported abroad. American missions create the same divisions wherever you go.

Anderson replies:

I heartily affirm what you are saying, and I would welcome you as a missionary to us. In fact, in the kind of honesty and insights you have brought here, you have indeed been in mission to us.

Leeuw says:

My point is that America needs to take her missionaries unto herself for a while and reflect on her own shortcomings, leaving us free to deal with ours.

Anderson rejoins:

But you must not cut us off from you.

Leeuw replies:

Moratorium is not a cutting off of relationships. It calls for **changed** relationships.

African Response

In considering African Ecumenical and Evangelical responses, we find a further twist in the moratorium question. Some African church leaders tend to oppose the moratorium. Some of these church leaders belong to the ecumenical and evangelical groups in Africa. We need to underscore the fact that these groups with their national church councils or continental associations such as the All Africa Conference of Churches (AACC) or the Association of Evangelicals of Africa and Madagascar (AEAM) are created and to a large extent maintained by Western mission

agencies. They are, in some respects, ecumenical bodies for promoting the sense and reality of self-affirmation and self-reliance.
But these goals are still in the process of being fully realized.
In spite of this, some of the leaders of these groups tend to
interpret the moratorium call as a cutting off of relationship
rather than a call for changed relationship. Let us examine some
of these responses further.

The reactions from both the Evangelicals and Ecumenicals
in Africa to the call by the AACC for the withdrawal of foreign
missionaries and mission funds has been widespread but not uniform. Some of the churches and church organizations have opposed
it and some have accepted it. The secretaries of the National
Christian Council of Kenya, Tanzania, Malawi, Zambia and Uganda
have issued statements criticizing the moratorium. Since Lusaka,
several key leaders of the AACC, including some officials of the
AACC executive committee, have openly opposed the moratorium.[71] The evangelical Lutheran Church of Tanzania issued
an official statement in which they dissociated themselves from
the Lusaka Declaration. They said:

> While confirming the call of the AACC that the churches
> in Africa make a systematic effort towards self-reliance
> in finance and manpower, we the churches of Tanzania
> would like to dissociate ourselves from the recent call
> of the AACC for a moratorium and we feel very strongly
> that such an action is not appropriate.[72]

Their rejection of the moratorium is in keeping with the stand
of the Lutheran World Federation Commission on Church Co-operation which opposed the idea of a moratorium during their conference in Australia in May 1975. Nevertheless, they affirmed
the legitimacy of the struggle for self-reliance and self-identity,
but considered the moratorium proposal to contradict ideas of
interdependence, partnership and togetherness in mission.

The negative reactions have not been limited to the
organizations. There have also been a good number of African
church leaders who felt that way. For instance, Byang H. Kato

---

[71] Carr, "The Mission of the Moratorium, **Occasional Bulletin of Missionary Research Library,** pp. 2-3; see also Emilio Castro, "Structures for
Mission," **IRM** (October 1973): 397-398.

[72] "Evaluation of 'Moratorium' Urged in 'Local Situations,'" **Lutheran World Federation News Service,** May 28, 1975, pp. 1-2.

objected to the call for moratorium. He argued "it is merely an emotional appeal without adequate consideration of the ramifications involved--Moratorium is unbiblical and unnecessary."[73] Paul Hopkins, the Africa Liaison for the Presbyterian Church U.S.A., was one of the members of a U.S. team which travelled to Africa in February/March 1975 in order to have personal dialogue with leaders of African churches regarding the moratorium proposal. He found the African church leaders well disposed to discuss the issue. Reporting on the outcome of his trip, Hopkins said:

> With only one exception, nobody we talked with supported the idea as stated at Lusaka and apparently none of them had voted for it . . . . Many of them opposed the idea in principle; others felt that it was too harshly stated; still others felt that it was premature. . . . The one church that supported the idea is in a unique position. . . . It is a church in South Africa with a comparatively strong economic base. . . .
>
> I came out from these moratorium discussions with the feeling that the churches of Africa which came into being as a result of western missionary work have a deep symbiotic relationship to our churches and that the meaning of that relationship will not come easily.[74]

Some of the African churches have answered "yes and no" to the moratorium question. The executive committee of the Ethiopan Evangelical Church, Mekane Yesus' (ECMY) stance is a case in point. According to them, "there is no other answer for the ECMY than a NO in principle to the call for moratorium," including concrete steps to become less dependent on foreign sources. For them, the identity of the ECMY as a church in Ethiopia should be fostered at all levels in all facets of the life of the ECMY. The committee further said: "All planning for new projects of programs should from now on be done within the framework of socialist Ethiopia and be consistent with the goal

---

[73]Byang H. Kato, **Theological Pitfalls in Africa** (Kenya: Evangel Publishing House, 1975), p. 167.

[74]Paul Hopkins, "Moratorium: The Future of the Mission of the Church in Africa," paper presented at the Overseas Ministries Study Center, Ventnor, New Jersey, May 2, 1975, pp. 3-5.

of self-reliance."[75] These resolutions seem to sound more of "yes" than of "no" to the moratorium question.

The moratorium question, especially since Lusaka, has continued to provoke much discussion and soul-searching among African churches. As we have already shown, some have said no to it, others say yes and no. There are also those who agree with the proposal. One is The United Congregational Church of South Africa. One of their strongest points in voting for moratorium is because of its potential political significance for Blacks in South Africa. They contend that the whites undertake missionary activity as a matter of political expediency to keep the black man dominated and dependent. They insist that even though heavy odds are against them, yet they prefer to remain as "Prisoners of Hope."[76]

At a consultation on mission convened by the Board of Global Ministries of the United Methodist Church, Bishop Calvaltro of Angola called for a radical restructuring of the missionary enterprise so that the old traditional image of the missionary, with is paternalistic approach to the African people, must stop. He further said, almost in the spirit of Lusaka,

> What we need today is partnership not paternalism. Concepts such as these: missions, churches in the Third World, and Fourth World, mother churches etc. must cease to exist.[77]

The Third World published reactions have been very slight. Besides the **AACC** Bulletin which monitors developments on the moratorium debate, there seems to be no other missionary journal in Africa by Africans which has carried articles on the moratorium debate. So it is difficult to assess the total reaction of the African churches based on published materials. Most of the published materials we have on the subject are carried by Western missionary journals. It is interesting to note that all national and regional church councils in the Africa countries who oppose the moratorium are "supported overwhelmingly by Western

---

[75] Gudina Tumsa and Paul E. Hoffman, "The Moratorium Debate and the Evangelical Church Mekane Yesus (ECMY)" (August 1975), pp. 1-3.

[76] John Thorne, "Prisoners of Hope," **AACC Bulletin** 9 (1976): 38-40.

[77] J. M. Carvalho, "The Dawning of Partnership," **AACC Bulletin** 9 (1976): 41-44.

financing." [78] Therefore, for them to support the moratorium call will be suicidal to the institution which they represent. Besides we need to be aware of the reports from Western missionary officials who went to Africa to monitor the views of leaders of African churches who are on their payroll. Their tendency to select partner voices who are most, likely to say what they would like to hear cannot be ruled out. Besides, we need to recognize the dangers involved in soliciting reactions from people who have been and still are beneficiaries of the Western pattern of relationship and stand to benefit most if these patterns remain essentially unchanged. In the light of these observations, we could understand the responses from the secretaries of the National Council of Churches in Kenya, Tanzania, Malawi, Zambia and Uganda who oppose the moratorium call.

We should also note Paul Hopkins' report on his tour of Africa in the wake of the Lusaka declaration. He said: "Apparently none of them [i.e., African church leaders] voted for it . . . nobody we talked with supported the idea. . . ." Hopkins' field report to those who sponsored their trip to Africa does not seem to square with his personal views on the subject.[79] Other Western agencies also made trips to Africa in the wake of the moratorium call. Some of them seem to recognize the dangers inherent in the responses of those on their payroll. Hence they went beyond their field reports to examine their own procedures, policies, and relationships with churches in Africa (or the Third World) with a view to eliminating practices which:

--retain basic decision-making power in the West alone;
--discourage contextual expressions of the Christian faith and life;
--unabalance the relationship as to make any real patnership impossible;
--or fail to maximize the local potential for Christian mission.[80]

---

[78] Consult files on National Christian Council of Kenya or Nigeria at Africa Department, Programm Agency, United Presbyterian Church USA, 475 Riverside Drive, New York, New York. See the files for financial support of staffs of the National Christian Council of Kenya.

[79] Hopkins, "Moratorium: The Future of the Mission of the Church in Africa," pp. 2-3; see also Hopkins, **What Next in Mission?**

[80] Eugene Stockwell, **Guidelines: Directions of Change in Overseas Relationships** (New York: United Church Board for World Missions, June 3, 1975), pp. 1-4.

Asian Response

There is also an Asian response to the moratorium theme.[81] For the Christian Conference of Asia, the issue of moratorium has generated some lively awareness and concern of the critical need for reflection on missionary stragegies and priorities in Asia today. Asia, as the Conference noted, is part of the Third World which has been a victim of "centuries of [Western] esploitation in colonial days" and whose people and resources are still being exploited today.[82] This awareness of oppression and explitation at all levels (socio-economic and religious) has led them to choose a Liberation theme, "Let My People Go," as the charter for action in fulfilling their missionary task in present-day Asia. In describing Asian responsibility in mission under the Liberation theme, "Let My People Go," the Conference said:

> Our Asian history, as part of the people of God called in Christ, makes it difficult for us to express our responsibility in mission. We have been "receiving" churches, and in many ways we still are. The word "mission" denotes to us something foreign, something which came to us in western missionaries and resources, something we received and responded to, rather than our calling which requires of us both response and responsibility. The missionary movement has come to us as something western, something which brings in its company the values of western society as if these values are the values of the Christian faith. With it, our ways of life have become western and our cultural roots have been loosened. Because it has been western, the missionary movement has been carried out with tremendous material resources, leaving unexamined the question whether those resources are really necessary for our participation in the mission of God. We often feel dependent in consequence, and act in a dependence which inhibits our imagination to see ways in which mission can proceed with our given scarcity of such resources. Even missionaries are mainly western because western resources are necessary for mis-

---

[81] Harvey Perkins, Harry Daniel and Asal Simandjuntak, "Let My People Go," in **Mission Trends No. 3, Third-World Theologies,** ed. Gerald H. Anderson and Thomas F. Stransky (New York: Paulist Press, 1976), pp. 192-210.

[82] Ibid., p. 194.

sionaries to be sent. Our poverty becomes what disqual-
ifies us from participating in mission. "Let my people
go."[83]

In the light of these concerns, the issue of moratorium
became a stimulating one on the agenda of the CCA. It led them
to face "anew and radically, questions of priorities in mission."
The Conference, while not endorsing the radical strategy proposed
by the Lusaka declaration, supported the vital issues of selfhood
and self-reliance raised by the Lusaka Assembly. As they put it:

> . . . the issues raised by the African call for moratorium
> are real. We have raised them as we share our concern
> with you in this matter. But moratorium is a matter for
> each or any Asian church in its relationship with Western
> churches and ecumenical agencies. Our task is to draw
> attention to the context which makes the option for mora-
> torium important.[84]

What could be said about the response of the Christian Conference in Asia on moratorium is that they are "moderates" while
the Africans are "radicals." Their goals are the same with that
of the AACC, given their social location, collective aspiration
and temporal orientation, within the context of world mission.
Both have a vision of a new order free from oppression and domination from the West and are seeking for ways and means to
realize their aspiration. The CCA's search for new patterns of
relationship is underscored by their awareness that their traditional priorities have been determined by others and have been
developed in styles which are inherently dependent on personnel
and resources from outside the Asian region. Hence they contend
"our action on new priorities must spring from our initiative,
reflect our agendas, implement our decisions. As we seek to
review our understanding of the priorities of mission in the future,

---

[83] Ibid., p. 195. In view of the stress on the socio-economic and
political context by the Asian Christian thinkers, they are now being censur-
ed by some Evangelicals as producing indigenous heresies. As Saphir P. Athyal
said in "Asian Theologies Betray Overenthusiasm for Context," **Christianity
Today**, September 1977, "The danger of several Asian Christian thinkers is
their over-enthusiasm in preferring the 'context' to the hard core of Christianity, namely the historical Christ and the Gospel, as seen in the 'text'."

[84] Ibid., p. 208.

we need to relate our review to the question of greater reliance on our own resources. . . ."[85] In the light of this assertion, we could say that the CCA does not support the existing (traditional) pattern of world missionary enterprise dominated by the West. They too are seeking for release from over-dependence on the West. Their search for self-identity does not lead them into mystical withdrawal from the existing situation. Rather they have taken practical steps to reverse their subordinate status to the West. They opt for selective moratorium[86] as an alternative to the more radical demand from Lusaka. All the same, we can categorize their response as "utopian" in Mannheim's sense since they are critical of, and seek to transform or change the traditional order of doing mission in Asia.

Implications of the Moratorium Call

Having examined the call and its responses, let us attempt a comprehensive interpretation of their implications given Mannheim's categories of ideology and utopia. So far we have tried to employ the concept of ideology not in the Marxian sense of an idea which masks interests, but in Mannheim's sense of ideas related to the perspective of a social group. It is from this perspective idea that Mannheim developed his famous antinomy of ideology-utopia. He related ideology to the perspective of a ruling group who tend to support the status quo and utopia to a dominated or subordinated group who seek to destroy the existing conditions.

By this approach, we would expect all Western missionaries, both Evangelicals and Ecumenicals, to support the traditional missionary methods. But from our analysis of the perspectives of the Evangelicals and the Ecumenicals, we observed a difference in their perspectives even though they share the same socio-economic location. For example, with reference to issues

---

[85] Ibid., pp. 200-201.

[86] Ibid., p. 208. See also Gerald H. Anderson, ed., **Asian Voices in Christian Theology** (Maryknoll, New York: Orbis Books, 1976; Douglas J. Elwood, ed., **What Asian Christians Are Thinking: A Theological Source Book** (Quezon City, Philippines: New Day Publishers, 1977); Choan-Seng Song, **Christian Mission in Reconstruction: An Asian Attempt** (Maryknoll, New York: Orbis Books, 1977).

like **"Salvation Today"** [87] which the Ecumenicals insist has primarily to do with current life of flesh and blood, hunger and satisfaction, manufacturing and distributing, freedom and wholeness in this world, that is with socio-political and economic issues of the contemporary world, the Evangelicals maintain that Salvation means a change in status of the individual soul, achieved through faith in Jesus Christ alone, and results in abundant life in this world.

These different approaches to a common problem tend to indicate that while the Ecumenicals will like to be directly involved with the hard realities of socio-economic issues of contemporary life, the Evangelicals tend to lack such strong emphasis and involvement on socio-economic and political issues. [88]

One implication of these tendencies is that Western capitalistic business societies with their expansionist orientation tend to give more support to the Evangelicals who lean towards letting the socio-economic conditions remain as they are, with occasional repairs in the condition rather than a replacement of the situation. In contrast, many capitalist business enterprises tend to withhold support from the Ecumenicals who tend to question

---

[87] Manuel J. Gaxiola, "Salvation Today: A Critical Report," in **The Evangelical Response to Bangkok**, ed. Ralph Winter, pp. 61-77; see also John V. Taylor, "Bangkok 1972-1973," **IRM Edinburgh to Melbourne** (n.d.), pp. 365-370.

[88] Arthur P. Johnston, "The WCC's Impact on the Future of Missions," **Evangelical Missions Quarterly** 12 (1976): 77-78. Johnston criticises the Ecumenicals (WCC) for their increased social concern and neglect of the Scriptures. He warns: "Evangelization has not only acquired the dimension of social concern, but the WCC understanding of salvation is distorted from that of the Scriptures . . ." For details on Evangelical low profile on liberation movements, see Ralph Winter, ed., **Evangelical Response to Bangkok**; "The Frankfurt Declaration," in Peter Beyerhaus, **Mission: Which Way? Humanization or Redemption?**, trans. Margaret Clarkson (Grand Rapids, Mich.: Zondervan, 1971), pp. 107-119. For a detailed analysis of Western critique on liberation movements, see Robert McFee Brown, **Theology in a New Key** (Philadelphia: Westminster Press, 1978), pp. 102-129. Brown analyzes the whole spectrum of Western critiques of liberation theologies (movements) under an eightfold sequence of critiques, namely: defensive critiques, total rejection critiques, oversimplified critiques, pseudo-issue critiques, reductionist critiques (p. 102). We find some elements of these critiques in the Western (especially Evangelical) responses to the moratorium which is a movement of liberation from Western domination.

existing socio-economic arrangements in the world economic order and who even go so far as to support liberation movements which struggle for socio-economic justice.[89] Peter Wagner, an American of the Evangelical persuasion and a lecturer at the Fuller Seminary School of World Mission in Pasadena, California, talks about the call for a moratorium as "a Smoke Screen." He says that the mainline denominations are losing the support of their American local church members because of their increased involvement in worldwide social and political action, while the "Evangelicals" are gaining more support because "they keep the vertical dimension . . . prominent." He declares:

> It is a well-known fact that the missionary budgets in most mainline denominations have been drastically reduced over the past few years. It is also known that the denominational budget reductions do not necessarily reflect lowered income on the local parish level, rather such a growing reluctance of local churches to entrust their denominational agencies with the disbursement of their missionary funds. Many local churches . . . are increasing support of faith missions such as Sudan Interior Missions or Wycliffe Bible Translators. Some are investing in missiological research at institutions such as the Fuller Seminary School of World Mission. . . .
>
> The reason for this significant shift is largely the trend among U.S. denominational agencies to decrease involvement in evangelization and church planting and increase involvement in worldwide social and political

---

[89] Bishop Stephen Neill remarked during a private consultation on April 14-15, 1978, of North American evangelical mission executives at the Overseas Ministries Study Center in Ventnor, New Jersey, that the World Council of Churches (WCC) was losing the support of Western donors because of their support forliberation movements. The topic discussed during the consultation was "The Africanization of the Church: Lessons for Christian Mission." Study papers for the meeting were prepared by Professor Andrew Walls of the University of Aberdeen, Scotland, and Professor David Bosch of the University of Pretoria, South Africa. It has to be observed that Western Christians, especially in North America, were very critical of the WCC support in food and medicine to the freedom fighters in Zimbabwe-Rhodesia. One rarely comes across a similar spate of criticism by American Christians against their government who provide Ian Smith a million dollars' worth of ammunition to destroy the so-called "Marxists and Maoists."

action. Many local parishes, however, do not feel that this is the best way for missionary funds to be spent. . . . Biblical mission must keep the vertical dimension (reconciliation of lost men and women to God) prominent. . . .[90]

One indication of the preceding observation about the Evangelicals is that they seem to be favored by the business community. This is reflected in the increase of funds they are receiving and in the number of missionaries they are able to recruit, as shown in the tables below.[91] The tables also show the decline in funds and in number of missionaries in agencies related to the Ecumenical persuasion who show greater concern for issues of socio-economic justice.

TABLE 6

ASSOCIATION INCOME

Association	1960 Income (Millions)	1968 Income (Millions)	1976 Income (Millions)
DOM-ICCCUSA	$ 92.0	$149.2	$137.4
EFMA	27.0	60.0	150.4
IFMA	15.4	32.7	70.6
FOM	3.3	6.3	13.2
CCC-CWC	4.6	23.1	9.2
Unaffiliated	41.2	74.3	274.0
Total Reported	$170.0	$279.0	$634.0

DOM-NCCCUSA: Division of Overseas Ministries-National Council of Churches of Christ in U.S.A. (Ecumenical).

EFMA: Evangelical Foreign Mission Association (Evangelical).

---

[90] Wagner, p. 170.

[91] Edward R. Dayton, "Current Trends in North American Protestant Ministries Overseas," **Occasional Bulletin of Missionary Research Library** 1 (April 1977): 6.

IFMA: Interdenominational Foreign Missions Association (Evangelical).

FOM: Fellowship of Missions (Evangelical).

CCC-CWC: Canadian Council of Churches-Commission on World Concern.

TABLE 7

ASSOCIATION MISSIONARY PERSONNEL OVERSEAS

Association	1960 Missionary Personnel	1968 Missionary Personnel	1976 Missionary Personnel
DOM-NCCCUSA	10,244	10,042	5,010
EFMA	5,744	7,369	7,347
IFMA	5,343	6,206	6,101
TAM-ICCC	877	1,128	153+
CCC-CWC	530	1,873	329
Unaffiliated	6,662	11,351	15,917
Total	27,039	32,087	35,458

TAM-ICCC: The Associated Missions - International Council of Christian Churches.

In the diagram below,[92] the EFMA in 1975 increased significantly in both missionaries and income, whereas the IFMA increased slightly in missionaries and significantly in income. DOM-NCCCUSA, while increasing slightly in income, decreased significantly in the number of missionaries. It is important to note the income shown is not the income of the associations, but is the total income of its member agencies.

---

[92] Edward R. Dayton, ed., **Mission Handbook: North American Protestant Ministries Overseas,** 11th ed. (Monrovia, Cal.: MARC, 1977), p. 61.

MISSIONARIES IN MAJOR MISSION ASSOCIATIONS

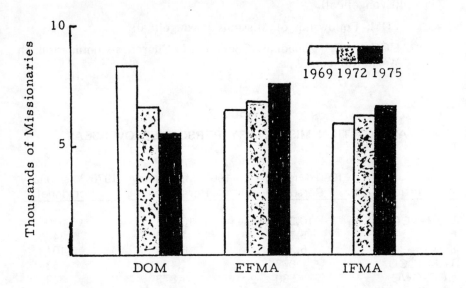

Not only are Ecumenicals losing support, but they aggravate the loss by criticizing the multinational corporations which support the capitalist system. In assessing the activities of multinational companies, the Ecumenicals during the 1975 fifth Assembly of the World Council of Churches Conference in Nairobi, Kenya, criticized the multinationals for creating problems such as:

> vast accumulation of untold wealth, and power; stimulation of 'empty consumerism'; sales of products which are sometimes lethal and often ill designed to meet basic needs of the masses; deflection of research from serving the people; manipulation of wage and price structures; exercise of undue political influence and interference in internal affairs of states; reinforcement of imperialist patterns of ownership and control influence over mass media; use of wealth to promote corruption, bribery and squandering of scarce resources.[93]

[93] Quoted by S. L. Parmar, "A Third World Perspective on the International Economic Order and the Role of Transnational Corporations in it," Consultation Paper No. 3 (Geneva: World Council of Churches, n.d.), pp. 21-22.

However, the Evangelicals viewed the issue differently. Arthur P. Johnston, a professor of missions and evangelism at Trinity Evangelical Divinity School, Deerfield, Illinois, who attended the fifth Assembly of the World Council at Nairobi, Kenya, criticized the Council for making funds available for "liberation movements" in Africa, the United States and South Africa, and these funds, he claims, "are needed to create loyalties to Marxist or Maoist forces so often spearheading these revolutions." Concerning the criticisms levied on the multinationals by the World Council, Johnston said:

> Transnational companies receive abusive criticism in the plenary Assembly. While evangelicals are not unaware of the abuses of certain international businesses, the entire . . . report leaves the clear impression that the answer to the world's economic and social problems begins with eduation that leads to revolution and the destruction of capitalism as the root of all evil. Wittingly or unwittingly, the WCC is promoting Maoism and Marxism, totalitarian systems based upon class dialectic and controlled economic systems. Cardinal Biblical doctrines of sin, the nature of man, salvation of the soul and eschatology have not been introduced into their philosophy of education.[94]

Given these postures on socio-economic issues, we detect utopian tendencies among the Ecumenicals and ideological tendencies among the Evangelicals. This evidence goes further to explain, to some extent, the posture of the agencies towards the moratorium call, i.e., the Ecumenicals tended to be more sympathetic than the Evangelicals on the issue. While the general tendencies remain, certain anomalies arise both in Africa and in Europe in the matter of responses to the moratorium.

Not all African church leaders support the call for moratorium. There are those African church leaders who are on the payroll of the Western mission agencies, who tend to argue for the preservation of the traditional system of doing mission since supporting a radical change like the moratorium would be a threat to their job security. However, there are exceptions to the rule as well.

---

[94] Johnston, p. 85.

Some of the advocates of moratorium are also on the payroll of Western mission agencies. Therefore the correspondences between social location and mental production are not perfect, but we have to recognize that, as Mannheim exclaims, the correspondence is not one of strict determination. So in actual life situation, we find not only anomalies but some exceptions to the rule. For example, even though Karl Marx was an advocate for the proletariat, he himself was not a member of the proletariat.

Another way to analyze the moratorium call as utopian is to employ Robert Waelder's views. He believes that the utopian tendency includes an appraisal of two aspirations: first, the dialectic of freedom and equality, and second, the contradiction of applying inadequate means to solve immense problems.[95] We shall focus our attention on the moratorium as it is expressed in the Lusaka declaration using Waelder's insights.

The declaration asserts that the African church is part of the world community and demands a share in the missionary work of Christ in the world. The Lusaka declaration draws attention to the African demand for equality and seeks recognition from the Western missionary agencies who from the outset of the Euro-Afro missionary endeavour have completely dominated the missionary enterprise. By the call, the Africans are saying to the West that they too have a part to play in the missionary enterprise. They want liberation from their dependency. In other words, the Africans are seeking autonomy to self-direct themselves in the missionary task rather than be controlled and directed from the West. By claiming to be part of the global ministry of Christ, Africans are contending for equality not only in opportunity to carry out mission but also for the rights and privileges attached to that office. Seen in this way, the moratorium call could be interpreted as an appraisal of the dialectic of freedom and equality in mission.

According to Robert Waelder, these terms--freedom and equality--are reconcilable and may be identical if liberty or freedom means liberation from restraints imposed by a common master. For example, for slaves liberty and equality mean the same thing. They become opposites once liberty is applied "to their relation among themselves; for where there is liberty in interpersonal relations, a pecking order quickly emerges, whereas equality means the absence of such a hierarchy."[96]

---

95 Waelder, pp. 50-53.

96 Ibid.

Since we are considering the moratorium call as utopian, we shall consider freedom and equality as referring to liberation from external restraints and therefore as being identical. Calls for freedom and equality have throughout history been expressions of utopian desires. We can show this by examining how the call for moratorium compares with similar declarations by Protestant Reformers and the Anabaptists, and how similar sentiments informed the French, English and American revolutions.

The "equality" we shall be referring to is not equality of persons but "the principle of equal treatment as applied to associated entities or groups, that are thought to require similar consideration without regard to number of persons which the group may include." [97] The claim to equality does not assert that the things compared are wholly alike, but that they are alike in certain respects and for certain purposes. This principle of "equality" is a relevant criterion of criticism of religious or social hierarchy. The principle of "liberty" or "freedom" by same token serves the same purpose for community's unity. [98]

The Protestant reformers asserted the equality of Christian believers as a means of overthrowing the special position of the papacy and the priesthood. Luther considered all people equally capable of spiritual life, repentance, and hence salvation. They differed in worldly function, but could lead equally holy lives in any calling. To drive his point home, Luther said:

> It is pure invention that popes, bishops, priests and monks are to be called the "spiritual estate"; princes, lords, artisans and farmers the "temporal estate." . . . There is really no difference . . . except that of office and work, but not of "estate." . . . Again, it is intolerable that in the canon law so much importance is attached to the freedom, life, property of the clergy. . . . Why are your life and limb, property and honour so free, and mine not? . . . If a priest is killed, the land is laid under interdict--Why not when a peasant is killed? Whence comes this great distinction between those who are

---

[97] "Equality," in **Dictionary of the History of Ideas,** ed. Philip Weiner (New York: Charles Scribner's Sons, 1973), p. 138.

[98] Reinhold Niebuhr, **Pious and Secular America** (New York: Charles Scribner's Sons, 1958), see chapter on "Liberty and Equality," pp. 61-77.

equally Christians? Only from human laws and inventions.[99]

In these lines, written by Luther in 1520, he anticipated the overthrow of the traditional priesthood in order to establish a spiritual equality of believers. This overthrow was part of rebellion against the ecclesiastical system. But the Anabaptists, religious radicals, went even further than Luther in their understanding of the equality of believers, which for them meant not only an equality of laity with ecclesiastics, but an equality of poor and simple men with the learned and well-to-do. They insisted on a direct, mystical and personal revelation from God, which need not be mediated through any sophisticated exegesis of scripture. Calvin also took a radical stand on the question of equality. He protested the inequalities created by the church between the laity and the clergy. In fact, he went further than Luther in equating the laity with the clergy. He rejected the institution of bishops and the hierarchic ordering of the clergy themselves. He further reduced the office of priest to that of pastor or minister.[100] By his reform, Calvin strongly contributed to the republican tradition and ideas and the Anabaptists greatly influenced the English Puritan revolution of 1688. The two centuries following the English Revolution were in fact the classic period for the consideration of equality in human society. It was during this period that the interlocking triad of Liberty, Equality, and Fraternity was invented. By the fact of the French Revolution, according to Reinhold Niebuhr, "the mold of organic aristocratic civilization" was shattered and France became the symbol of the new day of liberty and fraternity. The American Revolution of 1776 also had a similar message of equality, though in a narrower sense, since the Blacks and Indians were excluded.

The central idea in these Revolutions which were destined to change the course of human history was aimed at the abolition of inequality of privilege which was always proportioned to prestige and function. These revolutions were against the rulers or domiant class because their prestige, power an privilege, particularly privilege, tended to be inordinate. This is why, according

---

[99] Martin Luther, "Three Treaties to the Christian Nobility" (1520), in G. L. Abernethy, **The Idea of Equality: An Anthology** (Richmond, Va., 1959), pp. 14-19.

[100] "Equality," in Weiner, p. 142.

to Niebuhr, "equality must remain a regulative principle of justice, and [why] equalitarianism the ideology of the poor."[101]

Still another element of utopian mentality refers to the imbalance between means and ends. We find this imbalance reflected in the relationship between the countries in the "center" and those on the periphery. Consequently, when the periphery challenges the center, it is obvious that it has not got enough force or funds to effectively challenge the center. Yet it does, and this is what makes it utopian: visionary, imaginative, and a contradiction. But while moratorium could be a contradiction to a Western missionary, to John Gatu and the AACC, it is a bold and imaginative vision of a new order. It is true that the AACC lacks the funds to run its secretariat; it has to depend on the West for funds, yet by its utopian mentality, it seeks to challenge and change the situation of dependency overnight. It is in this sense guided by its vision of a new order and the will to action which hides certain aspects of reality from them, such as its lack of funds. This type of utopian mentality is well illustrated by Mussolini's aspiration to establish Italy as a world power, to restore the Roman Empire. Yet Italy was too narrow a power base for such an ambitious project.[102]

As we have already shown, Mannheim identified utopian mentality among the "chiliastic religions,"[103] that is, the radical religious movement of the late Middle Ages which expected the coming of the new age of the Spirit, an ecstatic age in which the contradictions of life, imposed mainly by domination and institutions, would be overcome. This movement sometimes encouraged people to revolt. Because of their utopian orientation they suffered persecution and death at the hands of the established authorities, both secular and religious. Rosemary Reuther has shown in her book, **The Radical Kingdom,** that the revolutionary mindset of the Anabaptists had its origin in Jewish apocalypticism in the centuries preceding the Christian era and that it has been mediated to Western culture through the apocalyptical elements in New Testament literature.[104] As a reminder, the Jewish apoc-

---

[101] Niebuhr, pp. 62-63.

[102] Benito Mussolini, "Fascism," in **Classical Philosophical Questions,** ed. James A. Gould, 3rd ed. (Columbus, Ohio: Charles E. Merrill Co., 1979), pp. 565-572.

[103] Mannheim, pp. 201-206.

[104] Rosemary Reuther, **The Radical Kingdom: The Western Experience of Messianic Hope** (New York: Paulist Press, 1970), pp. 4-8.

alyptic consciousness was created among the faithful believers who read the ancient messianic promises made to Israel under the pressure of political occupation and cultural oppression. Since the prolonged occupation of Israel threatened the survival of Jewish independence and tended to undermine its traditional values, some of the Jews began to form resistance groups inspired by their belief that the injustices of the existing order cried to heaven for vengeance. They reasoned that God could not remain silent. We find elements of utopian tendency in this apocalyptic consciousness. This consciousness sees the existing order as evil, and therefore reasons that it deserves to be destroyed. Its hope is that a new order will emerge free from the injustices of the old order. Seen in the light of the preceding discussion, we conclude that the moratorium call is utopian.

Concluding Comments

Having reviewed the moratorium call from Africa (and the Third World) and the responses from the West, we shall now summarize the ways in which we consider the European mission outlook to be ideological and the African (Third World) mission outlook to be utopian.

Viewing the position of the West in the context of "World Mission," [105] we find that they occupy a dominant position and are powerful and rich, both in missionaries and in money. According to our theory their mentality is supposed to reflect ideological tendencies, i.e., tendencies which unconsciously generate teachings or symbols, views and values which legitimate their power, defend their privileges and protect them against those who challenge their privileged position. This ideological thinking of the dominant group seeks to maintain the existing social order. However, their thinking, according to Mannheim, is situationally transcendent in

---

[105] John V. Taylor, **For All the World: The Christian Mission in the Modern Age,** Christian Foundation Series, no. 12 (London: Hodder & Stoughton, 1966). The terms "World" and "Mission" in pre-World War II had special connotation in Taylor's book. "World" meant the world of "far away places and strange sounding names," not the "total world" which includes also the so-called Christian world of the West. "Mission" was not conceived as the total mission of God through Christ and His church to all people in all their needs, but the specific activity by which Western churches express their missionary obedience in the traditional mission fields of non-Western countries.

242

that it is rooted in the past in so far as the past lives on in the present. Hence, in their thinking the dominant group does not see certain facts which undermine their sense of domination.

We detect elements of this type of thinking in Western missions. One of the issues that has caused this tendency to narrowness of vision to come to the fore is the challenge to their dominance in world missions by the dominated ones who called for a moratorium on Western missionaries and money. The responses to this challenge from the West, especially from the Evangelical wing of the mission agencies, reflect elements of ideological mentality. They do not see the issue as one of radically changing the traditional one-way traffic in world mission nor of eulogising it and then burying it such that a completely new system could emerge. Rather they think in terms of "pruning the dead and fruitless branches from the missionary enterprise and grafting in new vital branches through which the power of Jesus will flow unimpeded producing abundant fruit for life eternal. [106] Another Evangelical respondent speaks in terms of adjustment of missionary personnel to the needs of the system, by properly applying the Western missionary as "fertilizer" in a way that does not injure or kill such that the traditional missionary system is kept alive through the flow of Western missionaries to all six continents in a spirit of humble service.[107] Others from the West see the call in part as "misleading and confusing, a negative term that generates poor public relations, turns away [Western] mission workers and donors and engenders frustration, bitterness, and impasse between younger and older members of the family of God."[108] There are also those who see the moratorium call as pathological, as due to a maladjustment to the demands of the missionary system. Hence they consider it as dysfunctional to the Wesern missionary establishment and, therefore, look for solutions in terms of organizational restructuring which attempts to adjust the past to fit the present since the past no longer fits the expec-

[106] Wagner, p. 176.

[107] Hicks, pp. 219-228.

[108] Louis J. Juzbetak, "Two Centuries of Cultural Adaptation in American Church Action: Praise, Censure, or Challenge," in **American Missions in Bicentennial Perspective**, ed. R. Pierce Beaver (Pasadena, Cal.: William Carey Library, 1977), pp. 348-349.

tations of the future.[109] This restructuring approach is to some extent reflected in the position of Western Ecumenicals.

As a generalization from the preceding observation, we could say in Mannheim's language that the stand of the West to the moratorium question is ideological since it tends to support the maintenance of the traditional system in doing mission, and interprets deviations from the system as requiring administrative or organizational adjustments to achieve the goals of the system rather than a dismantling of the system for a new one.

Africa (and the Third World) occupy a subordinate position in the world mission. Thus, according to Mannheim, their mode of thinking is most likely to be utopian in the sense that they would seek to change the situation that keeps them in subjection. Mannheim also describes the utopian mentality as situationally transcendent. It is unreal with respect to the existing social conditions, unreal not in the metaphysical sense, but in terms of the socio-economic structure, the political organization and culture which actually exist in that moment of history. The utopian mood is one born out of an extreme sense of alienation, in which the alienated people see no possibility of bettering their condition within the existing system. Their hope for a change lies in a dream for a total overthrow of the present system and its reconstruction on a radically new basis. According to Mannheim, the hopes are not mere dream; the group does not withdraw from the scene and seek to make its peace with the ruling group in mystical meditation and thereby let the social, political and economic order remain as they are. Rather they attempt to take action by uncompromisingly challenging the system as oppressive and inadequate in the hope of effecting a change. In so doing they become so strongly interested in the destruction and transformation of a given condition of society that they unwittingly see only those elements in the situation which tend to negate it. Hence they are aggressive and critical of the system and their mental attitude is oriented towards a new order which does not exist in the present situation. Consequently, their thought is never a rational diagnosis of the situation; it is rather guided by wishful representation and the will to action, which hides certain aspects of reality. Utopian thought tends to reject anything and everything which tends to paralyze its desire to change things. Hence, as the African advocates say, "to accomplish the freedom of the moratorium, experience says do it totally at one time lest the

---

[109] Margrethe B. J. Brown, "Restructuring as a Response to a New Era in Mission," *IRM* (1972): 374-388.

decisions be whittled away and the creative drive lost."[110] And even though they want to do it all at once, they forget that they are still heavily dependent financially and in fact need the help of the dominant group whose assistance they are calling off. The point seems to be that what the African advocates of the moratorium seem to be rejecting is the paternalistic attitude that accompanies the help they receive. And paternalism, as Louis Luzbetak, former president of the American Society of Missiology, puts it, is neither true charity nor true virtue, but rather it is "charity" and compassion that humiliates and makes the beneficiary dependent on the donor.[111] This sense of humiliation is at heart of what the African advocates seek to change at all costs. And even though African churches need aid, it is genuine aid which they need. Dominic Mwasaru, a Kenyan student at the Peramiho Seminary in Tanzania, expresses it thus:

> Genuine aid is not mere charity to a beggar.
> It is lending a hand to a struggling fellow-man.
> It is helping a fellowman to stand up on his own feet.
> Genuine aid is a pledge of freedom.
> It shatters the fetters of dependence and inferiority.
> It inspires self-confidence and creativity.
> It humanizes men dehumanized by poverty and disease.
> Such aid is an expression of true love.
> That is the type of aid we need.[112]

The utopian mentality also has the tendency to release some social impulses characterized by attempts at secession from the existing system in order to create new ones. This was true of most of the African independent churches. We find the same sentiments among the African advocates of the moratorium who say, "leave us alone to find our own identity. . . . We want to be genuinely self-supporting, self-governing and self-propagating. . . . We want our relationship with other [meaning Western] churches to be based upon equality under the Lordship of Jesus Christ."[113]

------

[110] ESP Committee Meeting, "Proposal on Moratorium," **IDOC 9**, p. 44.

[111] Luzbetak, p. 336.

[112] Dominic Mwasaru, "Africanization," **IRM** (April 1975): 125.

[113] Carr, "The Mission of the Moratorium," **Occasional Bulletin of Missionary Research Library**, p. 9.

African attitudes in the existing situation of "world mission" show their awareness of occupying a subordinate position and their desire to no longer adjust the existing practices and organizational requirements so that the system remains. Rather they seem to be concerned with change from the alienating practices of the dominant group; they contend with both what is and what is in the process of becoming. Their problem is not solved by administrative adjustment but by a radical re-organization of missionary relationships on totally new principles of social life.

In sum, the criterion of distinction between European missionary mentality which we have described as ideological and African missionary orientation which bears utopian tendencies concerns a very complex process of adjustment to the existing order. The African utopian mentality as situationally transcendent is necessarily poorly adjusted in the existing socio-economic and cultural order. It is rather adapted to a future order. By the same token, the European ideological mentality, as equally situationally transcendent, tends to glory in its past which no longer corresponds to the existing social situation. This fact prevents its proper adjustment to the extant order.

CONCLUSION

In the preceding chapters we have attempted to show that the moratorium call indicates the presence of conflict[1] within the Euro-Afro cross-cultural missionary organization. We shall now conclude our study by showing that the moratorium "conflict" has been functional to the cross-cultural missionary enterprise. This type of conflict is "interest conflict,"[2] that is, conflict generated by a felt disequilibrium in the allocation of authority within the missionary organization. It is not a "value conflict,"[3] that is, conflict that has to do with a doctrinal or theological

---

[1] Conflict is used here as the clash of differing points of view. About a century ago Karl Marx used the word "conflict" to describe the violent clash of irreconcilable interests, loyalties or opinions. Today the term is used to describe more moderate differences of opinion or values. Some scholars prefer to use the term "social tension" than "conflict." For others the term "conflict" refers to disputes, contests, competitions, as well as to more formidable types of social antagonism. The differences among these terms refer to differences of intensity. For our purpose we are using the term simply as a relationship involving two sets of individuals or groups with a desire on the part of both contestants to attain what is available only to one. The form that the moratorium conflict has taken in this respect is that of something like a parliamentary debate. For further elaboration, see Lewis Coser, **The Functions of Social Conflict** (New York: The Free Press, 1956), pp. 33-38; see George Simmel, **Conflict and the Web of Group Affiliations** (New York: The Free Press, 1955), p. 13. This book is one of the most provocative analyses of conflict as a factor in group formation. For instance, Simmel writes: "If every interaction among men is a sociation, conflict . . . must certainly be considered as sociation. . . . Conflict is . . . designed to resolve divergent dualisms; it is a way of achieving some kind of unity. . . ." Cf. R. E. Park and E. W. Burgess, **Introduction to the Science of Sociology** (Chicago: University of Chicago Press, 1921), p. 574. They treat conflict as well as competition as "forms of interaction." in contrast, a number of scholars see conflict as a dissociative process, for example, G. A. Lundberg, **The Foundations of Sociology** (New York: The Macmillan Co., 1939), p. 275. Lundberg argues that conflict is characterized by a suspension of communication between opposing parties.

[2] Gerald E. Bates, "Mission and Cross Cultural Conflict," **Missiology: An International Review** 5 (April 1977): 197.

[3] Ibid.

issue. It is not even a conflict between Christians and pagans. It is an internal conflict between two Christian groups in "imperative cordinated association," that is, an association within which "some positions are entrusted with a right to exercise control over other positions. . . ."[4] Our use of the term conflict here refers to the clash of differing points of view which has erupted from the African group who desire to attain the power and privilege available only to the European group. In this case, the conflict is not only an "interest conflict" but a social conflict.

Since we must define as accurately as possible the sources of a conflict situation in order to understand it, we have employed Karl Mannheim's sociology of knowledge which seeks through an historical sociological method of research to determine the existential origin of ideas. This is an investigation through description and structural analysis of the ways in which social relationships, in fact, influence thought. In the light of this, we have examined the socio-historical origins of both the proponents ofmoratorim and the opoonents of moratorium. We have shown, usig Mannheim's categories of ideology and utopia, that the encounter between Africa and Europa produced a European dominant class and a Arican dominated, deprived, discontented and dependent class. Consequently, Mannheim referred to the thinking of the dominant class as "ideological" and that of the dominated class as "utopian."

The ideological thinking of the dominant class is characteristic of the ruling European group. In their thinking they unconsciously tend to maintain, protect and defend the status quo.

The dominated and discontented African group with its utopian mentality is critical of the existing patterns of relationship. It considers the existing system to be inadequate, faulty and outdated; it seeks to destroy it, even though it lacks the means to do so, in the hope that in a new era, a changed pattern of relationship will emerge.

In terms of missionary values and ideals, the ideological tendency of the ruling group tends to apply ultimate reference

---

[4]Ralph Dahrendorf, **Class and Class Conflict in Industrial Society** (Stanford, Cal.: Stanford University Press, 1959), p. 165.

[5]Karl Mannheim, **Ideology and Utopia: An Introduction to the Sociology of Knowledge,** trans. Louis Writh and Edward Shils (New York: Harcourt, Brace, 1954), p. 243.

for their justification. Hence the use of such terms as universality, internationalizing, mutuality, Biblical mandate, great commission and the like. These terms abound in the Western missionary vocabulary. This tendency to engage in high-level abstraction creates a functional gap between theory and practice, between principles and praxis.

The deprived, dependent and discontented African group adopts the utopian model of the interpretation of ideals and values of mission. This implies judgment on mission in terms of its ideals and its unrealized standards. It is not interested in abstract, universalistic and psychological terminologies, but represents a radical criticism of specific historical situations. It seeks for union of theory and practice in social action in its bid to alter the existing authority structure. That is why it is important to analyse the Lusaka declaration and all the other calls for moratorium in the context of power relations in the contemporary missionary and socio-economic world order, not from the classical world of the Bible.

In considering definitions of health and pathology in the missionary enterprise, the dominant European group interprets their problems in institutional or organizational contexts to mean system imbalance, social disorganization which is seen as lack of or breakdown in social organization, weakened social control, inadequate institutionalization of goals, inadequate means to achieve systems goals or inadequate socialization. To deal with these problems, it generally adopts an administrative procedure. Such a procedure seeks to restructure [6] and adjust the existing patterns of relationship to conform with institutional goals. It attempts to achieve this through a more efficient institutionalization of the values to ensure the adjustment of individuals to organizational needs. Essentially, the dominant group equates health with conformity to dominant values.

The deprived and dependent group, with its utopian mentality, sees its problem in the control and exploitation by the ruling and dominant group. Its resentment is that it is excluded from the exercise of authority; it is not allowed to realize its individual or group aspiration to self-direct its affairs nor to participate fully in decision-making processes. Hence it seeks to disrupt and possibly transform the existing patterns of relationship. Its goal is to achieve a revolutionary change in the order

---

[6] Margrethe B. J. Brown, "Restructuring as a Response to a New Era in Mission," **IRM** (1972): 375-388.

of relationships that keep these people in a subordinate status. Its concept of health is seen in its utopian vision which it seeks to realize. This vision, as a reaction to the existing conditions, is both a "denunciation of what is and an annunciation of what is not yet, but will be; it is the forecast of a different order of things, a new society."[7] **The emphasis of moratorium is on changed relationships, not on cessation of relationships.**

Thus far, we have examined the sources of the conflict in Euro-Afro, cross-cultural missionary structures and seen them as due chiefly to the relations of authority within the cross-cultural missionary organization. Other causes include:[8] the appointment of only white missionaries to key positions in mission fields; economic differentials between white missionaries and local ministers are also a source of "interest conflict." The situation of cultural dissonance is also a potential source of interest conflict. This occurs where representatives of the affluent and industrialized West rub shoulders with Third World members in mission conferences, councils and committee meetings. For the Third World members, there seem to be a kind of vague, uneasy relationships which render such meetings as a potential source of conflict which may seize on almost any kind of issue for its expression. As a conflict of perspectives, the moratorium call contributes to the maintenance of group boundaries and prevents the withdrawal of members from the group association. It strengthens group consciousness and awareness of separateness, thus establishing the identity of groups within the system.

Lewis Coser, in his reinterpretation of George Simmel's concept of conflict, shows that conflicts contribute to the maintenance of group boundaries and the adjustment and adaptation of social relationships.[9] Since we consider the Afro-Euro cross-cultural missionary enterprise as an imperatively coordinated group, we conclude that the conflict arising from it is an internal social conflict since it concerns the goals, values, interests and the basic assumptions upon which the relationship of the parties in mission is based. Such conflicts, according to Coser, are positively functional, for the social group. "It makes possible the

---

[7] Gustavo Gutierrez, **A Theology of Liberation: History, Politics and Salvation,** trans. and ed. Sr. Caridad Inda and John Eagleson (New York: Orbis Books, 1973), p. 233.

[8] Bates, p. 198.

[9] Coser, pp. 33-38.

readjustment of norms and power relations within the group and in accordance with the felt needs of its sub-groups."[10] Coser sees internal conflicts as means of equilibrating social relations or readjustment of rival claims. The capacity of an internal conflict to tear apart the group structure depends to a large extent on the nature of the group structure within which the conflict arises. Closely knit groups such as the institutional Euro-Afro missionary group, with its high frequency of interaction in men and money and high personality involvement of the members, have a tendency to suppress conflict through well-worded conference resolutions. In closely knit groups, according to Coser, feelings of hostility therefore tend to accumulate and hence intensify.[11] If conflict breaks out in such a group that has consistently tried to prevent its expression, it usually has far-reaching consequences. This seems to be true of the moratorium call. Its advocates did not only deal with immediate issues which led to the call but aired all the accumulated grievances which were denied expression previously. Hence the issues raised referred to conquest, colonization, domination, partition of Africa, slave trade, slave labor and the like.[12] Also because of the total personality involvement of the group members, there seems to be a full mobilization of all sentiments in the conduct of the debate as could be observed from the preceding live dialogue.

Since the moratorium call erupted in the 70's a host of national and international and interconfessional missionary conferences have been summoned to review the future of the missionary enterprise and examine the grievances of the advocates of moratorium. These conferences have helped a great deal to revitalize the essential aims of mission, to review missionary principles and practices and to revamp missionary enthusiasm. In this sense the moratorium call contributes to the emergence of new norms (mature relationship, mutuality in mission, internationalizing mission, etc.) which aim at strengthening the missionary service and the proclamation of the gospel. Hence the conflict generated by the moratorium call provides a mechanism for the adjustment of missionary principles and norms to new conditions. It also helps not only to create new norms but to modify

---

[10] Ibid., p. 154.

[11] Ibid., pp. 151-153.

[12] John Gatu, "Call for Africanization of the Church in Africa," **AACC Assembly,** 1972.

old ones in order to assure their continuance under changed conditions. The moratorium call and the debate it generated have
served as a means for ascertaining the relative strengths of the
interest groups within the missionary structure. In this way the
call has shown how vital the Third World is to the existence of
the Western missionary agencies and therefore draws attention to
the need for continual readjustment of the balance of power
within the missionary enterprise.

PERSONAL STATEMENT ON THE MORATORIUM

No one who is concerned about the mission of God in Jesus Christ to the world can afford to be neutral on the issue of moratorium. As one who is both a product of western Christian mission and a student of Christian missionary history, I feel persuaded to make some personal remarks on the basis of my Christian belief and commitment and on the strength of the literature on missions which I have been privileged to read.

One of the issues that has bothered me about western Christian mission in Africa is: Why is Africa still so dependent on western metropolis after over a century of missionary enterprise in Africa? Ogbu U. Kalu, a Nigerian church historian, poses the question this way: "Why are the churches in Africa . . . still needing to climb on someone else's shoulders to watch the parade?"[1] Kalu argues that Africa's problem is not genetic nor the product of a nonviable environment. The African environment, as we have shown in Chapter III, was economically viable until his encounter with the West which consequently led to his exploitation and political enslavement, processes which not only destroyed the native's base civilization but also ensured that he might never be free from dependency on the West. Africa consequently became dominated by Western Europe. With regard to the churches in the context of this domination, Kalu writes: "The end products were churches which could not stand on their feet, and a relationship which made aid the glutinous agent for the maintenance of a dependent relationship. Finance has always been power."[2]

In view of the preceding observation about the socio-economic location of Africa in the context of western mission, we could surmise why the call for a moratorium seems to reflect such an intense desire on the part of the churches in Africa to break the vicious aid relationship in order to become self-supporting, self-governing and self-propagating. The call seems to manifest the mentality of a lower class or subordinate group perspective; it focuses on socio-political and economic inequities and injustices; the advocates tend to believe in acquiring political power as a means of changing and improving the existing patterns

---

[1] Ogbu U. Kalu, "The Peter Pan Syndrome: Aid and Selfhood of the Church in Africa," **Missiology** 3 (January 3, 1975): 15-16.

[2] Ibid., p. 18.

of relationship which keep them dependent and dominated. Hence their struggle for socio-economic justice and for a greater measure of political power to check the growing affluence of the northern hemisphere acquired at the expense of the increasing poverty and penury of the southern hemisphere. With this picture in mind, I consider the moratorium call as the challenge of the Third World to the affluent "First World." Rene Padilla, the Ecuadorian Baptist, conveys this view when he says:

> The challenge of the Third World is thus a challenge to the affluent--to their values and ideals, their ambitions and standards, their assumptions and life style. And the response to that challenge cannot be merely in terms of charitable activities and aid programs; it has to be in terms of a redistribution of wealth which would meet the demand of social justice.[3]

The call for moratorium stresses the need for educating public opinion in the rich and powerful countries of the North to prepare them to accept and encourage a more equitable distribution of the world's resources and a genuine partnership in trade and investment possibilities. Such attempts to educate Western public opinion will awaken in them the consciousness of their "European ideology" which conquered non-European races and people, forcibly incorporated them into their cultural institutions and offered them an economic system that benefited chiefly the European market and expanded mainly European industries. Their ideology presents to the European public the viewpoint that human history and development justify European aggression on non-European countries. This ideology of "superior mentality" is deeply woven into their language, their values, their institutions, their symbols, their culture, and even their religion. The moratorium call, with its utopian mentality and orientation, challenges European ideology in order to enable both parties to face the reality about themselves and others. In this sense, the moratorium is a reaction against the distorted view of mission which presents cross-cultural Christian mission as the right and priviledge of only the rich and powerful nations and not the obligation of all Christian people everywhere who are called, chosen and sent. This aspect of the moratorium call emphasizes the need for self-

---

[3]Rene Padialla, "The Fullness of Mission," **Occasional Bulletin of Missionary Research Library** (January 1979): 10.

reliance and self-identity. This view is underscored by Ruth M. Harris and patricia J. Patterson, of the staff of the World Division of the Board of Global Ministries of the United Methodist Church, U.S.A., who, writing about the attitude of the U.S. mission agencies towards the clamour for self-determination and self-direction in mission by the "younger churches" in Asia, Africa and Latin America, declare:

> Our temptation as mission agencies is to analyze and debate their selfhood, but the selfhood question demands that we as U.S. churches and missionaries look at our own identity. Who are we that our selfhood has impinged on the sacred space that is the selfhood of our brothers and sisters? Why does our missionary vocation frequently seem to be in contradiction to that of other people who are in mission? The call to moratorium demands we step back and examine before God and our fellow Christians our own identity and integrity as people in mission.[4]

Reporting on the same issue for the British response to "no entry signs for Western missionaries" and "The Future Role of Western Missionary Bodies in the Christian World Mission," Ronald K. Orchard, general secretary of the conference of missionary societies in Britain and Ireland, referred to the need for each church to express its proper selfhood in its particular area. He declares: "Churches in Britain also have to give an account of their existence. . . . We need help to know how to be bearers of Christian mission in Britain. We need the help of our fellow Christians from Asia, Africa, Latin America and the Pacific if our answers are to be the right ones. . . . Help must be without impinging their responsible selfhood. . . ."[5]

The call also aims at giving the Western sending churches the opportunity to question seriously the business practices and procedures of their home governments, banks and multinational corporations in the Third World. In so doing, the call draws the attention of Western missionaries to the tendency of neglecting "witness in Jerusalem," i.e., the West itself. This neglect is caus-

---

[4] Ruth M. Harris and Patricia J. Patterson, "People in Mission: Towards Selfhood and Solidarity," **IRM** (April 1975): 137.

· Ronald K. Orchard, "The Future Role of Western Missionary Bodies in the Christian World Mission," **IRM** (1966): 258-259.

ing the growth in numbers of European neo-pagans[6] and the diminution of spiritual capital in the West. Stephen Neill points to this loss of spiritual vitality in the West when he laments the disappearance of the old European systems of religion and culture and the desiccation of the human spirit as a result in which men are not merely not religious, but can see no reason why they should concern themselves with anything beyond the world of the senses.[7] George W. Peters in his essay on "Missions in Cultural Perspective" seems to sharpen this Western dilemma when he said:

> Christendom has failed to a considerable degree to be the light of the world, the salt of the earth, the conscience of society, the prophetic voice among the nations, a model of society, and in many ways to create an effective counter culture. Believers have often permitted themselves to be molded by the forces of this world and to be slaves rather than liberators.[8]

In the light of some of these observations about "Christian West," we find that the moratorium call is pointing to a conception of "World Mission" in which the West also should be seen as a mission field. The call therefore deprecates the equalization of Wesern mission with world mission.

The moratorium also calls attention to a seemingly neglected area of missionary activity which limits and blunts the revolutionary impulse of the Gospel from challenging the principalities and powers of this world. These powers spend more money in manufacturing and distributing instruments of human destruction than in alleviating human suffering. They engage in destabilising popularly elected governments in other countries, replacing them with fascist rulers who do their bidding.[9] Rather

---

[6]W. A. Visser t'Hooft, "Evangelism Among Europe's Neo-Pagans," **IRM** (October 1977): 349-360.

[7]Stephen Neill, **A History of Christian Missions** (Middlesex: Penguin Books, 1964), pp. 564-565.

[8]George W. Peters, "Missions in Cultural Perspective," **Bibliotheca Sacra** 136 (July-September 1979): 204.

[9]Noam Chomsky and Edward S. Herman, **The Washington Connection and Third World Fascism**, vol. 1 (Boston: South End Press, 1979). This volume is a shattering and devastating critique of U.S. foreign policy in the Third World. It presents with overwhelming documentation the awesome facts of "the

than confront and condemn these principalities and powers, mission tends to take the broad and easy way of going only to the poor peasants in the Third World, to "Turkish labourers in Germany"; "Racetrack dwellers in the United States"; "Highrise dwellers in Singapore"; "Moslem farmers in Bangladesh"[10] and such powerless victims of the western capitalism. Missionaries and mission agencies seem to be afraid to say to "David," "Thou art the Man."

To confront the global task of Christian mission (in the years ahead) there must be a total mobilization of all missionary forces and resources everywhere in the world. There is need for "mission together." James McCord, President of Princeton

---

U.S.-sponsored neo-colonial world, the nature of the client states and the processes and rationales that the ideological institutions have employed to defend and justify the proliferating terror" (Preface, pp. x-xi). Every American Christian missionary to the Third World should read this book to see what his/her counterparts in the state and secular (CIA) "missionary" are doing in the Third World. See also Philip Agee, **Inside the Company, CIA Diary** (Middlesex: Penguin Books, 1975). The author of this book worked for the CIA for twelve years in three different countries. He began by accepting the "Company's" views and aims, but as time went by he came to see it as a bureaucracy designed **not** to help those in whose countries it works, but simply as an arm of American interests. (See Appendix 5.)

Lately, on Friday, February I, the **New York Times** bore the stunning news of the Carter Administration proposal to use journalists, clergymen (i.e., missionaries) or academics as intelligence agents (that is, as spies) in covert operations in other countries.

David Millwood, **The Poverty Makers** (Geneva: World Council of Churches, 1977), pp. 1-4; Fidel Castro Ruz, **Address to the Thirty-fourth Session, General Assembly of the United Nations,** New York, October 12, 1979. Castro draws the attention of the world body to the alternative value of the annual $300 billion spent on military around the world. He argues that with $300 billion one could build 600,000 schools, with a capacity for 400 million children; or 60 million comfortable homes for 300 million people or 30,000 hospitals with 18 million beds; or 20,000 factories with jobs for 20 million workers, or an irrigation system that could water 150 million hectares of land, which with appropriate technology could feed a billion people (p. 56). For a low-key but important reference to the same problem, see Paul A. Hopkins, **What Next in Mission?** (Philadelphia: The Westminster Press, 1977), pp. 93-105.

[10] Edward R. Dayton and Peter C. Wagner, eds., **Unreached Peoples' 79** (Illinois: David C. Cook Publishing Co., 1979).

Theological Seminary, expresses it thus: "The era of mission is not behind us. We have only begun, and now we can all be missionaries together."[11] This implies that mission in this decade should involve East and West, North and South, rich and poor, young and old, black and white, and men and women working together, not as groups brought together in contractual relations, but as a new community of love, bound by ties that must be experienced as fulfilling rather than as limiting; a voluntary community in which inter-personal relations are experienced chiefly as liberating rather than as restricting and in which people think of themselves as members of one of the other in the intimate way in which the parts of the body belong to one another, not only as interdependent on one another but also as inter-connected to a common faith, a common calling and a common goal in manifesting the Divine to the human and in bringing the principalities and powers of this world into subjection to the Lordship of Jesus Christ. To accomplish this grand objective, the sea of differences between the races, the classes, the sexes, the nations should be greatly minimized. As James E. K. Aggrey of Ghana once put it, rather crudely,

> . . . Let the white folks bring their gold, their great banks, their big buildings, their marvelous achievements in science and technology to the manger, that will not be enough. Let the Chinese and the Japanese and the Indians bring their frankincense of ceremony to the manger, that will not be enough. The African must be allowed to step in with their myrrh of child-like faith, then the gifts will be complete. . . . [12]

In the light of this need to crystalise a unity of purpose out of a diversity of gifts, each group, each culture, should be allowed to bring his unique gifts and endowment to the manger and to the service of the Child-King.

To this end, the goal of missionary enterprise in the 80's which the moratorium points to is the liberation of all people from subjection to earthly principalities and powers which not only exploit and dehumanize the underprivileged people, but also

---

[11]James McCord, "President's Message," **Princeton Theological Seminary Alumni News** (October 8, 1979).

[12]James E. K. Aggrey, cited in Byang Kato, **Theological Pitfalls in Africa** (Kenya: Evangel Publishing House, 1975), p. 133.

delude and deceive those who take refuge in them. The idea of mission together radicalizes the need for a greater integration of social concern and evangelism. It stresses the task of mission to include both proclamation and service, both principle and praxis, both spiritual and physical concern. It is a mission which calls for a sensitivity to human values and a concern to work for the conversion and transformation of both persons and the socio-economic systems in which they live. Samuel Escobar, the general secretary of the Intervarsity Christian Fellowship of Canada, in his article on "The Search for Freedom, Justice and Fulfillment" states the matter thus:

> The First and Powerful answer to the social and political needs of men--to the search for freedom, justice and fulfillment--is given by Jesus in his own work and in the church. Jesus takes seriously the problems of property and power relationships, which are essentially the problems that cause social and political maladjustment and injustice.
>
> Jesus creates a new people, a new community, where social problems are dealt with under the Lordship of Christ. . . . In this community there is a new attitude to money and property . . . a new attitude to power and its exercise. It is a community where human barriers and prejudices have been overcome under Christ's rule. It is a community ready to suffer for Justice. . . .[13]

In the light of this goal, the task of mission is no longer the question of choice between "Liberation, Development and Evangelism." These are not exclusive alternatives; they are in fact complementary imperatives of mission, as Emilio Castro declares:

> In carrying out God's mission, we cannot opt permanently for one aspect of mission or another, be it liberation, development, humanization, or evangelization. These are all essential, integral parts of the mission entrusted to us and cannot be set against one another without becoming, simply, caricatures of what they really are. Indeed, they exist as parts only, and can only be discovered or

---

[13] Samuel Escobar, "The Search for Freedom, Justice and Fulfillment," **Engage/Social Action: Evangelism/Social Action, Either/Or** (November 1974): 34-35.

recognized separately within the framework of their interrelatedness.[14]

On the whole, the moratorium call, rather than be interpreted as anti-mission or anti-West, should be understood as dramatising the need for a more prophetic, holistic, authentic and contextualized missionary endeavour which testifies to its existence and relevance, not only through the quantity of missionary literature produced, amount of money raised and number of missionaries recruited, but also through its preparedness to suffer for justice in order to demonstrate the force of its conviction in its belief in the Gospel as capable of challenging and transforming both the powers that oppress and dehumanize and the victims of oppression and dehumanization.

---

[14]Emilio Castro, "Liberation, Development, Evangelism: Must We Choose in Mission?," **Occasional Bulletin of Missionary Research Library** 2 (1978): 88.

APPENDIX 1

Excerpt from the Demand of the Third World as Presented by
Fidel Castro, President of the Council of State and of the
Council of Ministers of the Republic ofCuba,
on Behalf of the Non-Aligned Nations
United Nations General Assembly
October 12, 1979

The developing countries demand that the countries that
have created inflation and that stimulate it through their policies
adopt the necessary measures now to control it and thus put an
end to the aggravation of the unequal exchange between our
countries.

The developing countries demand--and will continue their
struggle to achieve this--that the industrial products of their in-
cipient economies be given access to the markets of the developed countries to put an end to the vicious protectionism which
has been reintroduced in the international economy and which
threatens to lead us once again into a murderous economic war.
They demand that, without deceptive falsehoods, generalized and
non-reciprocal tariff preferences be applied, so that the young
industries of the developing countries may develop without being
crushed in the world market by the superior technological
resources of the developed countries.

The non-aligned countries consider that the negotiations
about to be concluded on the law of the sea should not be used--
as certain developed countries seek to use them--in order to
ratify and endorse the existing imbalance as regards sea resources,
but should serve as a vehicle for equitable redress. The Conference on the Law of the Sea has once again brought out and
stressed the arrogance and imperialist determination of some
countries which, placing their technological possibilities before
the spirit of understanding and accommodation requested by the
developing nations, threaten to take unilateral action in carrying
out deep-sea mining operations.

The foreign debts of the developing countries have now
reached $335 billion. It is estimated that about $40 billion a year
go to servicing that foreign debt--and that is more than 20 per
cent of their exports. Moreover, the average per capita income

in the developed countries is now 14 times that in the under-developed countries. This surely is an untenable situation.

The developing countries need the establishment of a new system of financing through which they would receive the necessary financial resources to ensure the continuous and independent development of their economies. These financing methods should be long range and low-interest. These financial resources should be completely at the disposal of the developing countries, to enable them to establish priority systems in their own economies and in accordance with their own plans for industrial development and to prevent those funds from being absorbed, as they are today, by transnational corporations which use alleged financial contributions for development to aggravate the distortions of their economies and to reap maximum profits from the exploitation of the developing nations' own resources.

The developing countries--and, on their behalf, the Movement of Non-Aligned Nations--demand that a substantial portion of the immense resources now being squandered on the arms race be diverted for development which in turn would contribute to reducing the danger of war and to helping to improve the international situation.

Expressing the position of all the developing countries, the non-aligned countries call for the establishment of a new international monetary system which will put an end to the disastrous fluctuations to which the main currencies used in the international economy--especially the United States dollar--are subject today. The financial disorder also hits the developing countries and the latter hope that, when the outlines of the new international monetary system are drawn up, they--as the majority of the countries in the international community, representing as they do more than one and a half billion men and women--may be given a voice in the decision-making process.

To sum up: unequal exchange is ruining and impoverishing our peoples and must cease. Inflation, which is being exported to us, is impoverishing our peoples and must cease. Protectionism impoverishes our peoples and must cease. The existing imbalance in the exploitation of sea resources is abusive and must be abolished. The financial resources received by the developing countries are insufficient and must be increased. Arms expenditures are irrational. They must cease and the funds thus released be used to finance development. The international monetary system prevailing today is bankrupt and should be replaced. The debts of the least developed countries and of those in a disadvantageous position are burdens impossible to bear and to which no solution can be found and they should be cancelled. Indebtedness oppresses the rest of the developing countries economically and should be relieved. The wide economic gap between the developed countries and the countries seeking development, instead of diminishing is being widened, and should be closed and eliminated. These then are the demands of the underdeveloped countries.

APPENDIX 2

SOME U.S. THOUGHTS ABOUT "MORATORIUM"

Eugene L. Stockwell
(Secretary of the Division of Overseas Ministries
of the National Council of Churches, U.S.A.)

The word "moratorium" has come into prominence in the past two years symbolizing a concept whereby "sending" churches might, under certain clearly specified conditions, refrain from sending missionaries and funds to a particular "receiving" church or geographic area for a determined period of time. The initiative for such a step might be taken by either church or agreed upon jointly. At the 1972 meeting of the World Council of Churches' Committee on the Ecumenical Sharing of Personnel the moratorium debate was a central concern, and at the Bangkok "Salvation Today" Conference in early 1973 again it surfaced as a matter of considerable interest and discussion.

Section III of the "Salvation Today" Conference, on the theme "Churches Renewed in Missions," analyzed a variety of possible new patterns of interrelationship between churches and said:

"We have also examined more radical solutions, such as the recent proposal for a moratorium in the sending of funds and personnel for a set period of time. The whole debate on the moratorium springs from our failure to relate to one another in a way which does not dehumanize. The moratorium would enable the receiving church to find its identity, set its own priorities and discover within its own fellowship the resources to carry out its authentic mission. It would also enable the sending church to rediscover its identity in the context of the contemporary situation.

It is not proposed that the moratorium be applied in every country. Missionary policy should be adapted to the particular circumstances in each area. In some parts of the world other alternatives to bilateralism should be considered. In devising new strategies for mission it is essential that all partners look together at the total challenge to mission. Churches which have been preoccupied with their bilateral relationships may find new areas for common action.

In some situations, however, the moratorium proposal, painful though it may be for both sides, may be the best means of resolving a present dilemma and advancing the mission of Christ."

Judgments vary considerably about the wisdom and viability of the moratorium proposals. It is important to keep certain considerations clearly in mind as the debate proceeds:

1. The moratorium, in the minds of its advocates, is a means to contribute to the furtherance of God's mission on earth, not a way to counteract or inhibit God's mission as expressed in interchurch relationships. It is all too easy for traditional sending churches to see in the moratorium proposals a step that diminishes or even terminates mission in a given area. No responsible proponent of the moratorium concept has any such intent in mind. If the moratorium idea is worth considering, it is precisely because it may contribute to a more faithful mission under God.

2. The moratorium is not meant to terminate relationships between churches, but rather it aims at a change in relationships which presumably will in time lead to improved relationships between churches in different areas of the world Christian community. Proponents of the moratorium suggest that relationships between two churches in different parts of the world do not depend exclusively on the provision of personnel and funds by one church to the other. Were relationships depend exclusively on such provisions they would be extremely precarious at best. Many churches enter into relationships in a variety of ways where no funds or personnel are given by one church to another: relationships of prayer, mutual thought, relationships within the World Council of Churches fellowship, relationships established by lay persons of one church who travel and enter into ties with another church, and many more.

3. The moratorium is designed, hopefully, to bring both churches involved into a new sense of their own identity and integrity. The Bangkok document points out that the moratorium may be painful. The pain involved may be very real, requiring as the moratorium does considerable readjustment in the use of persons and resources, but the pain may be a worthwhile price to obtain the greater gain of a genuine sense of new identity, a release from an undue dependency relationship and an ex-

perience of integrity born of careful use of personnel and resources available.

If in truth the moratorium is aimed at fostering mission rather than restricting it, at improved relationships rather than traditionally dependent relationships, and at new experiences of identity and integrity, there would seem to be much to commend it. The reality we face, however, is that at least in the United States, where many traditionally sending churches are based, there is to date little discussion or acceptance of the moratorium idea. Indeed, in some churches and missions much thought is directed to ways in which the U.S. missionary force abroad may be greatly increased. The purpose of this article is to analyze some aspects of this reaity.

1. One argument frequently advanced against the moratorium concept is that the universal church needs the reality and symbolism of the presence of persons from many countries to be at work in all countries. The missionary, it is argued, should be present in our midst to remind us of the transnational character of the church and of the universality of the gospel. It is further argued that in a shrinking world in which international realities impact us all it would be foolhardy for a church to live and act on a purely national level without the presence of persons from other nations integrally related to its life. The same line of argument fits well with the "mission to six continents" idea that missionaries from traditionally "receiving" churches should be sent to the traditionally "sending" countries, so that particularly in North America and Europe there would be a strong presence of persons from other lands who as missionaries would bring new dimensions of understanding of the gospel to those accustomed to send but not to receive.

One need not disagree with the principles stated, but these principles do not really deal with the moratorium proposal. The moratorium is not designed to attack the universality of the church, nor to terminate the movement of persons across national borders in the name of Christ, nor certainly to suggest that interpreters of the gospel from traditionally receiving areas should not come to North America and Europe. The moratorium rather seeks to take seriously certain patterns of relationship which over the years have militated against the universality of the church, and which have created patterns of dependency that have restricted the gospel's full expression in too many places. Talk about the universality of the church should not obscure the fact that often the gospel has been carried from one nation to another wrapped in a cultural form which continuing generations of missionaries and gifts of funds tend to solidify or perpetuate. The moratorium might be one way (neither the only nor the infallible way) to break out of the cultural forms in which the gospel has been received to make possible a more profound identification of the gospel with the realities, issues and conflicts of the land in which it seeks to take ever more significant root.

2. Another argument which counters the moratorium proposal is that those who propose it--generally individuals in traditionally receiving countries--are not really representative of the church leadership in the countries where they speak. Is it not true, we are told, that many requests still come for more missionaries, and more funds, so that though isolated voices may call for a moratorium they are but a few voices in the wilderness? Usually this line of inquiry is topped of with the affirmation that if the churches to which we send missionaries and funds clearly say with one voice that they do not wish missionaries and funds the sending church will gladly honor their wishes.

There are many problems with this line of argument. One is that in the sending countries we must be cautious in assuming to decide what voices we will listen to, and particular care is appropriate if we find ourselves listening approvingly only to those voices who agree that we should simply continue doing what we have been doing for the past hundred years! It is quite true that there is ample diversity of thought in North America and Europe as well. The wisdom of the moratorium will not therefore be decided by adding up the lists of proponents and opponents to see which list is longer. A more critical question is to inquire whether the sending churches have created receiving churches in their own image, that is, churches which are, and almost always have been, dependent churches so they have little or no possibility of breaking out of their dependency relationship and little incentive to try such a painful process. Many leaders of sending churches decry the dependent relationships we have fostered over many years but argue at the same time that we must continue insofar as possible to meet the requests for more personnel and funds that will only prolong the dependenca. It is understandable that such leaders are reluctant, having been tagged as imperialists for so long, to risk a new charge of imperialism by taking a unilateral decision to cut off the provision of personnel and funds to a receiving church. Everyone would surely agree that ample dialogue should precede any implementation of the moratorium proposal, but if the representatives of sending churches assume at the outset of the dialogue that they can only respond creatively if the receiving church is in substantial agreement in favor of the moratorium, the chance of finding new patterns is slim indeed. Even if the moratorium isnot the most desirable answer for a given situation, as may well be the case, the issues that the moratorium proposal raises are worth analyzing in order that dependency patterns may be seen for what they are and radically new types of relationships might be explored. Sending churches have an especially important responsibility not to delude themselves into continuation of traditional patterns just because others who benefit most from those patterns urge their continuance.

3. A third argument against the moratorium proposal hinges on the fact that churches in many sending nations, particularly in the United States, are becoming increasingly isolationist in spirit, program and giving. The moratorium is seen to be a move which might simply expedite such isolationism. It is not unusual to hear a United States local church leader say, when the moratorium is discussed, that "if they don't want our people and money over there that is alright with us, we have plenty of places to use both here." Isolationism from the rest of the world, with its many and various roots, is a problem in the United States, and one would not want to encourage it within the church. The danger of strengthening isolationism is not so much a result of the moratorium itself as it is of the way in which the underlying meaning and purposes of the moratorium are interpreted. In the Bangkok discussions of the moratorium one of the notes repeatedly sounded was that if, as a result of moratorium, sending churches had no place to send personnel or funds for a time (an unlikely prospect!) they might give much new thought to the places where people and funds could be used within their own nation to attack ancient structures of injustice, to seek a more human society at home, and to press for a much more profound analysis of the way in which our nation deals in its foreign policy with the rest of the world. It is at this point that the sending church may be encouraged to face up to its own identity and integrity. Sending churches often have a self-image of generosity which is dependent upon their ability to give to others. If the moratorium, as to a particular area of the world, eliminates the possibility of such generosity, the sending church involved may have to rethink the image and hopefully seek out some new ways to participate creatively in an international world. One such way might be participation in much needed developmental education programs in the United States and in efforts to influence United States foreign policy towards more humane purposes. If by chance the moratorium would encourage such new concern for interna-

tional responsibility, isolationism would be avoided and potentially new pressures for just international relationships might emerge.

The moratorium proposal is no panacea that will automatically get us out of old patterns. But it may be one important step to consider among others. There is a danger that in the United States the moratorium, with all its possibilities for potential good, will be shunted aside too quickly. Some conservative evangelical constituencies both inside and outside the historic churches urge that U.S. churches send more missionaries, apparently the more the better. Such thinking dismisses the moratorium concept out of hand. Established sending patterns are difficult to break and to many the moratorium seems to be too radical an option at this moment of history, so sending churches tend to shrink from raising the moratorium question with their related receiving churches.

There may be another factor which reduces the need to consider the moratorium, namely, that in denomination after denomination in the United States resources for world mission are declining so precipitously that personnel and resources available which might be sent are fewer and fewer. In other words, events and financial facts may be forcing a moratorium of sorts quite apart from any carefully thought out decision that a moratorium may be desirable. Whatever the reasons, which might militate against serious and careful consideration of the moratorium proposal, there is enough potential in the concept that United States church sending agencies should give it far more attention than they have seemed to do thus far. The moratorium debate may well be an opportunity God provides the church for a more faithful understanding of mission at this juncture of history.

APPENDIX 3

THE U.S. STAKE IN AFRICA

Africa

AREA: 11.7 million square miles, more than three times as big as U.S.

POPULATION: Nearly 400 million. 1 in every 10 of world's people.

TOTAL OUTPUT: About $115 billion a year, a tiny fraction of that of U.S. Income per capita of less than $300 is at bottom of world scale.

Africa's resources include:
1. DIAMONDS--almost all of world's reserves
2. CHROMIUM--nearly all of free world's reserves
3. COBALT--90 percent
4. COCOA--65 percent of world production
5. GOLD--half of world reserves
6. PLATINUM--40 percent of reserves
7. URANIUM--nearly a third of free-world reserves
8. BAUXITE--more than a fourth
9. COFFEE--25 percent of output
10. COPPER--20 percent of world reserves
11. NATURAL GAS--12 percent
12. PETROLEUM--8 percent of world reserves

The U.S. Stake in Africa

Trade with Africa accounts for only a small fraction of U.S. exports and imports--13 billion dollars out of a total of 203 billion in world trade. But for some strategic materials, Africa accounts for a significant proportion of U.S. imports:

* 100 percent of industrial diamonds
* 58 percent of uranium
* 48 percent of cocoa
* 44 percent of manganese used in producing steel
* 40 percent of antimony to harden softer metals
* 39 percent of platinum
* 36 percent of cobalt for jet engines and high-strength alloys

270

* 33 percent of petroleum
* 30 percent of beryl used in weapons and nuclear reactors
* 23 percent of chromite used in making armor plate, jet engines, gun barrels
* 21 percent of columbium-tantalum for heat-resisting alloys in missiles and rockets
* 21 percent of coffee

Actually, small as it was, U.S. trade with Africa climbed sharply in 1975 nearly tripling the 4.7 billion level of 1973.

Even more significant rapid growth of U.S. investment on the continent--to nearly 4 billion dollars in 1975--compared with 1.8 billion in 1966.

SOURCE. Eleanor Goldstein and Joseph Newman, eds. **What Citizens Need to Know About World Affairs** (Washington, D.C.: U.S. News and World Report, 1978), pp. 138-139.

APPENDIX 4

U.S. MILITARY INVASIONS

The following is part of a list of American invasions of other countries and the purposes for such actions published by the Committee on Foreign Affairs of the U.S. House of Representatives. Only actions of uniformed services were reported; in all, the Committee identified 165 interventions between 1798 and 1970.

U.S. Congress, House, Committee on Foreign Affairs, "Background Information on the Use of United States Armed Forces in Foreign Countries," 91st Congress, 2nd Session (1970).

1899-1901 Philippine Islands: To protect American interests following the war with Spain, and to conquer the islands by defeating the Filipinos in their war for independence.

1900 China: A permanent legation guard was maintained in Peking, and was strengthened at times as troubles threatened. It was still there in 1934.

1901 Columbia (State of Panama): To protect American property on the Isthmus and to keep transit lines open during serious revolutionary disturbances.

1902 Columbia; State of Panama.

1903 Honduras: To protect the American consulate and the steamship wharf at Puerto Cortes during a period of revolutionary activity.

1903 Dominican Republic: To protect American interests in the city of Santo Domingo during a revolutionary outbreak.

1903 Syria.

1903-14 Panama: To protect American interests and lives during and following the revolution for independence from Columbia over construction of the (Panama) Canal. With brief intermissions, United States Marines were stationed on the Isthmus from 1903 to 1914, to guard American interests.

1904 Dominican Republic: To protect American interests in Puerto Plata and Sosua and Santo Domingo City during revolutionary fighting.

1904-5 Korea; Morocco; Panama; Korea.

1906-9 Cuba: Intervention to restore order, protect foreigners, and establish a stable government after serious revolutionary activity.

1907-11 Honduras; Nicaragua; Honduras

1911 China: Approaching stages of the nationalist revolution.

1912 Honduras: Small force landed to prevent seizure by the government of an American-owned railroad at Puerto Cortez. Forces withdrawn after the United States disapproved the action.

1912 Panama; Cuba; Turkey.

1912 China: To protect Americans and American interests during revolutionary activity.

1912-41 China: In 1927, the United States had 5,670 troops ashore in China and 44 naval vessels in its waters. In 1933 we had 3,027 armed men ashore. All this protective action was in general terms based on treaties with China ranging from 1858 to 1901.

1912-25 Nicaragua: To protect American interests during an attempted revolution. A small force serving as a legation guard and as a promoter of peace and governmental stability remained until 1925.

1913-14 Mexico; Haiti.

1914 Dominican Republic: During a revolutionary movement, United States naval forces by gunfire stopped the bombardment of Puerto Plata, and by threat of force maintained Santo Domingo City as a neutral zone.

1914-17 Mexico.

1915-34 Haiti: To maintain order during a period of chronic and threatened insurrection.

273

1916-24 Dominican Republic: To maintain order during a period of chronic and threatened insurrection.

1917-18 Europe: World War I. Fully declared.

1917-22 Cuba: To protect American interests during an insurrection and subsequent unsettled conditions.

1918-20 Panama; Mexico.

1918-20 Soviet Russia: Marines were landed at and near Vladivostok in June and July. In August the project expanded. Then 7,000 men were landed in Vladivostok and remained until January 1920, as part of an allied occupation force. In September 1918, 5,000 American troops joined the allied intervention force at Archangel, suffered 500 casualties and remained until June 1919. All these operations were to offset effects of the Bolsheviki revolution in Russia and were partly supported by Czarist or Kerensky elements.

1919 Honduras: A landing force was sent ashore to maintain order in a neutral zone during an attempted revolution.

1920-22 Russia (Siberia); China; Guatemala; Panama-Costa Rica; Turkey.

1924 Honduras: To protect American lives and interests during election hostilities.

1924-25 China.

1925 Honduras: To protect foreigners at La Ceiba during a political upheaval.

1925 Panama: Strikes and rent riots led to the landing of about 600 American troops to keep order and protect American interests.

1926-33 Nicaragua: The coup d'etat of General Chamorro aroused revolutionary activities leading to the landing of American marines to protect the interests of the United States. United States forces came and went, but seem not to have left the country entirely until 1933. Their work included activity against the outlaw leader Sandino in 1928.

1926-27 China.

1933 Cuba: During a revolution against President Gerardo Machada naval forces demonstrated but no landing was made.

1940 Newfoundland, Bermuda, St. Lucia, Bahamas, Jamaica, Antigua, Trinidad, and British Guiana: Troops were sent to guard air and naval bases obtained by negotiation with Great Britain.

1941 Greenland: Taken under protection of the United States in April.

1941 Netherlands (Dutch Guiana): In November the president ordered American troops to occupy Dutch Guiana.

1941 Iceland; Germany.

1941-45 Germany, Italy, Japan, etc. World War II. Fully declared.

1950-53 Korea.

(1953 Iran: CIA-sponsored coup overthrew popular government, installed Shah as ruler.)

(1954 Guatemala: CIA-sponsored coup overthrew popular Arbenz government and installed pro-U.S. ruler.)

1958 Lebanon.

(1961 Cuba: Bay of Pigs invasion organized by CIA to overthrow revolutionary government.)

1963 Cuba: (Missile crisis, naval blockade).

1962-7(5) Laos: From October 1962 until (1975) the United States played a role of military support in Laos.

1961-197(5) War in Vietnam.

(1964 Brazil: CIA-supported coup overthrew elected Goulart government, installed dictatorship.)

1965 Dominican Republic: Intervention to protect lives and proberty during a Dominican revolt. More troops were sent as the U.S.

feared the revolutionary forces were coming increasingly under Communist control.

(1965 Indonesia: CIA-sponsored coup overthrew government, installed military regime.)

(1967 Greece: CIA-sponsored coup overthrew democratic government, installed "colonels" regime.)

1970 Cambodia: U.S. troops were ordered into Cambodia. The object of the attack, which lasted from April 30 to June 30, was to ensure the continuing safe withdrawal of American forces from South Vietnam and to assist the program of Vietnamization.

(1972-1975 Cambodia: Support of military government.)

(1973 Chile: CIA-supported coup overthrew elected government, installed military regime.)

(1975-76 Portugal, Angola: Support of right-wing factions.)

APPENDIX 5

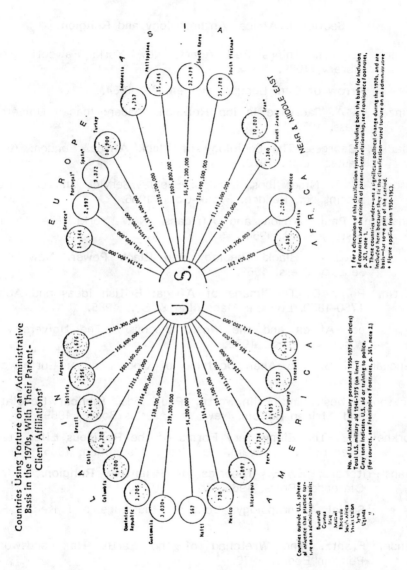

SOURCE: Noam Chomsky and Edward S. Herman, <u>The Washington Connection and Third World Fascism</u>, vol. 1 (Boston: South End Press, 1979).

277

SELECTED BIBLIOGRAPHY

Section I: Africa, Anthropology and Religion

Achebe, Chinua. **Things Fall Apart.** New York: Fawcett World Library, 1959.

--- **Arrow of God.** London: Heinemann, 1964.

Arinze, F. A. **Sacrifice in Ibo Religion.** Ibadan: Ibadan University Press, 1970.

Baladier, Georges. **The Sociology of Black Africa.** London: Andre Deutsch Ltd., 1970.

Basden, G. T. **Niger Ibos.** London: Seebley/Service and Co., Ltd.; reprint ed., London: Frank-Cass, 1966.

Bohannan, Paul. **Africa and Africans.** New York: The Natural History Press, 1964.

Cone, James H. **Black Theology and Black Power.** New York: Seabury Press, 1969.

Curtin, Philip D. **The Image of Africa: British Ideas and Action 1780–1850.** London: Macmillan & Co., 1965.

---, ed. **Africa and the West.** Wisconsin: The University of Wisconsin Press, 1972.

Danquah, J. B. **The Akan Doctrine of God.** London: Lutterworth Press, 1944.

Dickson, Kwesi, and Ellingworth, Paul, eds. **Biblical Revelation and African Beliefs.** New York: Orbis Books, 1969.

Durkheim, E. **The Elementary Forms of the Religious Life.** Translated by J. W. Swain. New York: Macmillan, 1965.

Evans-Pritchard, E. E. **Theories of Primitive Religion.** Oxford: Clarendon Press, 1965.

--- **Social Anthropology.** London: Routledge and Kegan Paul Ltd., 1972.

Fanon, Frantz. **The Wretched of the Earth.** Hammondsworth: Penguin Books, 1970.

Forde, D. I., ed. **African Worlds.** Oxford: Clarendon Press, 1954.

Forde, D., and Jones, G. I. **The Ibo and Ibibio-Speaking Peoples of South-Eastern Nigeria.** London: Oxford University Press for the International African Institute, 1950.

Fortes, Meyer. **Oedipus and Job in West African Religion.** London: Oxford University Press, 1959.

Frazer, J. G. **The Golden Bough.** 1 vol., abridged. New York: The Macmillan Co., 1928.

Green, M. Margaret. **Igbo Village Affair.** London: Sidgwick and Jackson, 1947.

Hunter, Guy. **The New Societies of Tropical Africa.** New York: Frederick A. Praeger, 1962.

Idowu, E. B. **Olodumare: God in Yoruba Belief.** London: Longmans, 1962.

Ilogu, Edmund. **Christianity and Igbo Culture.** Leiden: E. J. Brill, 1974.

Isichei, Elizabeth. **A History of the Igbo People.** London: Macmillan Press Ltd., 1976.

Malinowski, B. **Magic, Science, and Religion and Other Essays.** New York: The Free Press, 1948.

Mbiti, John S. **African Religions and Philosophy.** London: Heinemann, 1969.

--- **Concepts of God in Africa.** London: S.P.C.K., 1971.

--- **New Testament Eschatology in an African Context.** London: Oxford University Press, 1971.

Middleton, John, ed. **Black Africa, Its Peoples and Their Cultures Today.** London: Macmillan & Co., 1970.

Moore, Jane Ann, ed. **Cry Joy, Cry Sorrow.** New York: Friendship Press, 1971.

Murdock, G. P. **Africa: Its People and their Cultural History.** New York: McGraw-Hill Book Company, 1959.

Nadel, S. F. **Nupe Religion.** London: Routledge and Kegan Paul, 1954.

Neal, Marie Augusta. **A Sociology of Letting Go.** New York: Paulist Press, 1977.

Norbeck, Edward. **Religion in Primitive Society.** Evanston, Ill.: Harper & Row, 1961.

Nsugbe, Philip O. **Ohaffia: A Matrilineal Ibo People.** Oxford: Clarendon Press, 1974.

Nzimiro, Ikenna. **Studies in Ibo Political Systems: Chieftaincy and Politics in Four Nigerian States.** London: Frank Cass, 1972.

Parrinder, E. G. **West African Religion.** 2nd ed. London: The Epworth Press, 1961.

--- **African Traditional Religion.** 2nd ed. London: The Epworth Press, 1962.

--- **Religion in Africa.** London: The Epworth Press, 1969.

P'Bitek, Okot. **African Religions in Western Scholarship.** Nairobi: East African Literature Bureau, 1971.

Peel, J. D. Y. **Aladura, A Religious Movement Among the Yoruba.** London: Oxford University Press, 1968.

Ranger, T. O., and Kimambo, I., eds. **The Historical Study of African Religions.** Berkeley and Los Angeles: University of California Press, 1972.

Ray, Benjamin. **African Religions, Symbols, Rituals and Community.** Englewood Cliffs, N.J.: Prentice-Hall, Inc., 1976.

Shorter, Aylward. **African Culture and the Christian Church: An Introduction to Social and Pastoral Anthropology.** Maryknoll, N.Y.: Orbis Books, 1974.

--- **African Christian Theology.** New York: Orbis Books, 1979.

Smith, E. W., ed. **African Ideas of God.** London: Edinburg Press, 1961.

Sundkler, B. G. M. **Bantu Prophets in South Africa.** London: Oxford University Press, 1961.

Talbot, P. A. **The Peoples of Southern Nigeria.** 4 vols. London: Oxford University Press, 1926.

--- **Some Nigerian Fertility Cults.** London: Oxford University Press, 1927; reprint ed., London: Frank-Cass, 1967.

Temples, P. **Bantu Philosophy.** Paris: E.T., 1959.

Tylor, E. B. **Primitive Cultures.** 2 vols. American ed. New York: Henry Holt and Co., first published in 1871.

Uchendu, Victor C. **The Igbo of Southeast Nigeria.** New York: Holt, Rinehart and Winston, 1965.

Van Gennep, Arnold. **The Rites of Passage.** Chicago: The University of Chicago Press, 1960.

Vogt, Evon Z., and Lessa, W. A., eds. **Reader in Comparative Religion.** New York: Harper & Row, 1965.

Wilson, Monica. **Religion and the Transformation of Society: A Study in Social Change in Africa.** Cambridge: Cambridge University Press, 1971.

Section II. Christian Mission: The Encounter and Crisis of Christianity with Other Cultures and Religions (with special attention to Africa)

Ahlstrom, Sidney. **A Religious History of American People.** New Haven: Yale University Press, 1972.

Ajayi, J. F. A. **Christian Mission in Nigeria. 1841–1891.** London: Longmans, 1965.

Allen, Ronald. **The Spontaneous Expansion of the Church.** Grand Rapids, Mich.: Eerdmans, 1962 (first published in 1927).

Anderson, Gerald H., and Stransky, Thomas S., eds. **Mission Trends.** Nos. 1, 2 and 3. New York: Paulist Press, 1974.

Appia-Kubi, Kofi, and Torres, Sergio. **Africa Theology En-Route.** Maryknoll, N.Y.: Orbis Books, 1979.

Assmann, Hugo. **Theology for a Nomad Church.** Maryknoll, N.Y.: Orbis Books, 1976.

Ayandele, E. A. **The Missionary Impact on Modern Nigeria.** London: Longmans, 1966.

Baeta, C. G., ed. **Christianity in Tropical Africa.** London: Exford University press for the International African Institute, 1968.

Barret, D. B. **Schism and Renewal in Africa: An Analysis of 6000 Contemporary Religious Movements.** London: Oxford University Press 1960.

Barret, D.B. ed. **African Initiative in Religion.** Nairobi. East African Publishing House, 1971.

Beaver, R. Pierce. **Ecumenical Beginnings in Protestant World Missions: A History of Comity.** New York: Thomas Nelson and Sons, 1962.

--- **The Missionary Between the Times.** Garden City, N.Y.: Doubleday Co., 1968.

--- ed. **American Missions in Bicentennial Perspective** Pasadena, Cal.: William Carey Library, 1977.

Beetham, T. A. **Christianityand the New Africa.** London: Pall Mall Press, Ltd., 1967.

Berg, Johannes van den. **Constrained by Jesus'Love: An Inquiry Into the Motives of the Missionary Awakening in Great Britain in the Period Between 1698 and 1815.** Kampen: J. H. Kok, 1956.

Berman, Edward H. **African Reactions to Missionary Education.** New York: Teachers Press, 1975.

Beyerhaus, Peter. **Missions: Which Way? Humanization or Redemption.** Michigan: Zondervan Press, 1971.

Bigo, Pierre. **The Church and the Third World Revolution.** Maryknoll, N.Y.: Orbis Books, 1978.

Blauw, Johannes. **The Missionary Nature of the Church: A Survey of the Biblical Theology of Missions.** Translated by W. L. Holiday. New York: McGraw-Hill Book Company, 1962.

Bouquet, Allan Coates. **The Christian Faith and Non-Christian Religions.** New York: Harper Brothers, 1958.

Buhlmann, Walbert. **The Coming of the Third Church. An Analysis of the Present and Future of the Church.** Maryknoll, N.Y.: Orbis Books, 1977.

--- **The Mission on Trial.** Maryknoll, N.Y.: Orbis Books, 1979.

Cervin, Russell A. **Mission in Ferment.** Chicago: Covenant Press, 1977.

Coggins W., and Frizen, E. L., Jr., eds. **Evangelical Missions Tomorrow.** Pasadena, Cal.: William Carey Library, 1977.

Cooke, Gerald. **As Christians Face Rival Religions.** New York: Association Press, 1962.

282

Costas, Orlando. **The Church and Its Mission: A Shattering Critique From the Third World.** Wheaton: Tyndale House, 1974.

Davis, J. G. **Christians, Politics and Violent Revolutions.** Maryknoll, N.Y.: Orbis Books, 1978.

Dennis, James S. **Christian Missions and Social Progress.** 3 vols. New York: Revell, 1897.

Desai, Ram, ed. **Christianity as Seen by Africans.** Denver: Allan Swallow, 1962.

Dike, K. O. **Origins of the Niger Mission 1841-1891.** Ibadan: Ibadan University Press, 1957.

Doge, Ralph. **The Unpopular Missionary.** Westwood, N.J.: Revell, 1964.

Douglas, J. D. **Let the Earth Hear His Voice.** Minneapolis: World Wide Publishers, 1975.

Ekechi, F. K. **Missionary Enterprise and Rivalry in Igbo Land. 1857-1914.** London: Frank Cass, 1971.

Fife, Eric S., and Glasser, Arthur F. **Missions in Crisis.** Chicago: Inter Varsity press, 1961.

Goodall, Norman. **Christian Missions and Social Ferment.** London: Epworth Press, 1964.

Green, Michael. **Evangelism in Early Church.** Grand Rapids, Mich.: William B. Eerdmans Publishing Co., 1970.

Grimley, John B., and Robinson, G. E. **Church Growth in Central and Southern Nigeria.** Grand Rapids, Mich.: William B. Eerdmans Publishing Co., 196.

Groves, C. P. **The Planting of Christianity in Africa.** Vol. 2. London: Lutterworth Press, 1954.

Guttierrez, Gustavo. **A Theology of Liberation.** Translated and edited by Sister Caridad Inda and John Eagleson. New York: Orbis Books, 1973.

Harnack, Adolf. **What is Christianity?** Translated by Thomas Bailey Saunders. New York and Evanston: Harper and Row Publishers, 1957.

Hastings, Andrian. **Church and Mission in Modern Africa.** London: Fordham University Press, 1967.

Hastings, Andrian. **African Christianity.** New York: Seabury Press, 1976.

Hocking, William Ernest. **Living Religions and a World Faith.** London: Allen and Unwin, 1940.

Holme, L. R. **The Extinction of the Christian Churches in North Africa.** Reprint ed., New York: Burt Franklin, 1969 (originally published 1898).

Horner, N. A., ed. **Protestant Crosscurrent in Mission.** Nashville: Abingdon Press, 1968.

Idowu, E. B. **Towards Indigenous Church.** London: Oxford University Press, 1965

Kalu, Ogbu U. **Divided People of God: Church Union Movement in Nigeria. 1867-1966.** New York: Nok Publishers, 1978.

Kane, J. Herbert. **Winds of Change in the Christian Mission.** Chicago: Moody Press, 1973.

Kato, Byang. **Theological Pitfalls in Africa.** Kenya: Evangel Publishing House, 1975.

Kent, John. "The History of Christian Missions in the Modern Era." In **Pelican Guide to Modern Theology.** Vol. 2: **Historical Theology.** Baltimore: Penguin Books, 1961.

Kitagawa, D. **Race Relations and Christian Mission.** New York: Friendship Press, 1964.

Kraft, Charles H. **Christianity in Culture.** Maryknoll, N.Y.: Orbis Books, 1979.

Kramer, Hendrick. **Religion and the Christian Faith.** Philadelphia: Westminster Press, 1956.

Lamott, W. C. **Revolution in Missions.** New York: Macmillan, 1954.

Latourette, K. S. **A History of the Expansion of Christianity.** Vol. 4. New York: Harper and Brothers, 1941.

Leber, Charles T. **The Church Must Win! The Place, Power and Promise of the Christian Church in the Conflict of Our Time.** New York: Fleming H. Revell Co., 1944.

Leeuwen, Arend Th. Van. **Christianity in World History--The Meeting of the Faith of East and West.** London: Edinburgh House Press, 1966.

284

Little, Franklin H. **The Origins of Sectarian Protestantism: A Study of the Anabaptist View of the Church.** New York: Macmillan Co., 1964.

McAfee, Cleland B. **The Foreign Missionary Enterprise and its Sincere Critics.** New York: Fleming H. Revell Co., n.d.

McGavran, Donald A., ed. **Crucial Issues in Missions Tomorrow.** Chicago: Moody Press, 1972.

Mobley, Harris W. **The Ghanaians' Image of the Missionary.** Leiden: E. J. Brill, 1970.

Mouw, Richard. **Political Evenglism.** Grand Rapids, Mich.: Eerdmans, 1973.

Murphree, M. W. **Christianity and the Shona.** London: The Alblone Press; New York: Humanities Press Inc., 1969.

Nduka, Otonti. **Western Education and Nigerian Cultural Background.** Ibadan: Oxford University Press, 1964.

Neill, Stephen. **Creative Tension.** London: Edinburgh House, 1959.

--- **Christian Faith and Other Faith: The Christian Dialogue with Other Religions.** New York: Oxford University Press, 1964.

--- **History of Christian Mission.** Middlesex: Penguin Books, 1964.

--- **Colonialism and Christian Mission.** New York: McGraw-Hill, 1966.

--- **Call to Mission.** Philadelphia. Fortress Press, 1970.

Newbigin, J. E. Leslie. **The Household of God.** London: SCM Press, 1953.

--- **A Faith for this One World?** New York: Harper & Row Publishers Inc., 1962.

Ngugi, James. **A Grain of Wheat.** London: Heinemann, 1967.

--- **The River Between.** African Writers Series. London: Heinemann, 1968.

Niebuhr, H. Richard. **Social Sources of Denominationalism.** New York: Henry Holt, 1929.

--- **Christ and Culture.** New York: Harper and Row, 1951.

Oliver, Roland. **The Missionary Factor in East Africa.** London: Longmans, 1952.

Panikkar, K. M. **Asia and Western Dominance.** New York: Collier Books, 1969.

Parsons, R. T. **Churches and Ghana Society, 1918–1955.** Leiden: E. J. Brill.

Paton, David. **Christian Missions and the Judgment of God.** London: SCM Press, 1953.

Peel, J. D. Y. **Aladura: A Religious Movement Among the Yorubas.** London: Oxford University Press, 1968.

Rossel, Jacques. **Mission in a Dynamic Society.** London: SCM Press, Ltd., 1968.

Rotberg, Robert I. **Christian Missions and the Creation of Northern Nigeria.** London: Oxford University Press, 1965.

Ruether, Rosemary. **The Radical Kingdom.** New York: Paulist Press, 1970.

Sawyer, Harry. **Creative Evangelism: Towards a New Christian Encounter with Africa.** London: Lutterworth Press, 1968.

Scherer, James A. **Missionary, Go Home.** Englewood Cliffs, N.J.: Prentice-Hall, Inc., 1964.

Sklar, Richard. **Power in an Emergent African Nation.** Princeton: Princeton University Press, 1963.

Smock, Audrey. **Ibo Politics: The Role of Ethnic Unions in Eastern Nigeria.** Cambridge, Mass., 1977.

Stock, Eugene. **History of the Church Missionary Society: Its Environment, Its Men, Its Work.** Vol. 1. London: CMS, 1899.

Stott, John R. W. **Christian Mission in the Modern World.** Downers Grove, Ill.: Inter Varsity Press, 1975.

Sundkler, B. G. M. **Bantu Prophets in South Africa.** London: Oxford University Press, 1961.

--- **The Christian Ministry in Africa.** London: SCM Press, 1962.

Taylor, J. V. **The Growth of the Church in Buganda.** London: SCM Press, 1963.

Temu, A. J. **British Protestant Missions.** London: Longmans, 1972.

Tillich, Paul. **The Protestant Era.** Chicago: University of Chicago Press, 1948.

--- **Christianity and the Encounter of the World Religions.** New York: Columbia University Press, 1964.

--- **Systematic Theology.** Vol. 1. Chicago: University of Chicago Press, 1973.

Todd, John Murray. **African Mission: A History of the Society of African Missions.** London: Burns and Oates, 1962.

Toynbee, Arnold. **Christianity Among Religions of the World.** New York: Charles Scribner's Sons, 1957.

Trimingham, J. S. **The Christian Church and Islam in West Africa.** London: SCM Press, 1956.

Troeltsch, Ernest. **Protestantism and Progress, A Historical Study of the Relation of Protestantism and the Modern World.** Boston: Beacon Press, 1958.

Turner, H. S. **African Independent Church.** 2 vols. Oxford: Clarendon Press, 1967.

--- **Profiles of Change: African Society and Colonial Rule.** London: Cambridge University Press, 1971.

Varg, Paul A. **Missionaries, Chinese, and Diplomats.** Cambridge: Harvard University press, 1960.

Vicedon, George F., ed. **Christ and the Younger Churches.** London: SPCK, 1972.

Wagner, Peter C., ed. **Church-Mission Tensions Today.** Chicago: Moody Press, 1972.

Wakatama, Pius. **Independence for Third World Churches.** Downers Grove, Ill.: Inter Varsity Press, 1976.

Warren, Max. **The Missionary Movement from Great Britain in Modern History.** London: SCM Press, 1965.

Welbourn, F. B., and Ogot, B. A. **A Place to Feel at Home: A Study of Two Independent Churches in Western Kenya.** London: Oxford University Press, 1966.

Wieser, Thomas, ed. **Planning for Mission.** New York: U.S. Conference for the World Council of Churches, 1966.

Williamson, George S. **Akan Religion and the Christian Faith.**
Accra: Ghana University Press, 1965.

Wilmore, Gayrand. **Black Religion and Black Radicalism: An Examination of the Black Experience in Religion.** New York: Doubleday, 1973.

Wong, James, et al. **Missions From the Third World World.** Singapore: Church Growth Study Center, 1973.

Section III: Religion in Economic and Socio-Historical Context

Bellah, Robert N. **Beyond Belief: Essays on Religion in a Post Traditional World.** New York: Harper and Row, 1970.

--- **The Broken Covenant: American Civil Religion on Trial.** New York: Seaburg Press, 1975.

Benett, John C. **Christianity and Communism.** London: SCM Press, 1949.

Berger, Peter. **The Sacred Canopy.** Garden City, N.Y.: Doubleday and Co. Inc., 1969.

Berger, P., and Luckmann, T. **The Social Construction of Reality.** New York: Doubleday, 1964.

Brown, Radcliffe, and Ford, D. **African Systems of Kinship and Marriage.** London: Oxford University Press, 1950.

Brown, Robert M. **The Spirit of Protestantism.** New York: Oxford University Press, 1965.

--- **Theology in a New Key.** Philadelphia: Westminster Press, 1965.

Brunner, Emil. **Christianity and Civilization.** 2 vols. New York: Scharles Scribner's Sons, 1949.

Burrow, J. W. **Evolution and Society: A Study in Victorian Social Theory.** Cambridge. The University Press, 1966.

Buswell, J. O. III. **Contextualization: Theory, Tradition and Method in Theology and Mission.** Edited by David Hesselgrave. Grand Rapids, Mich.: Baker Book House, 1978.

Coats, William R. **God in Public: Political Theology Beyond Niebuhr.** Grand Rapids, Mich.: Eerdmans, 1974.

288

Cone, James H. **A Black Theology of Liberation.** New York: J. Lippincott & Co., 1970.

Coser, Lewis. **Masters of Sociological Thought.** New York: Harcourt Brace Jovanovich, 1977.

Cox, Harvey. **The Secular City.** New York: The Macmillan Company, 1966.

Curtis, James E., and Petras, John W., eds. **The Sociology of Knowledge: A Reader.** New York: Praeger Publishers, 1970.

Daly, Mary. **Beyond God the Father: Towards a Philosophy of Women's Liberation.** Boston: Beacon Press, Inc., 1973.

Davies, J. G. **Christians, Politics and Violent Revolution.** Maryknoll, N.Y.: Orbis Books, 1976.

Dayton, Edward R., ed. **Mission Handbook: North American Protestant Ministries Overseas.** 11th ed. Monrovia, Cal.: Missions Advanced Research and Communication Center, 1977.

Dougall, J. W. C. **Christians and the African Revolution.** Edinburgh: St. Andrews Press, 1963.

Freire, Paulo. **Pedagogy of the Oppressed.** Translated by Myra B. Ramos. New York: Herder and Herder, 1970.

Garaudy, R. **The Christian Marxist Dialogue.** New York: Free Press, 1968.

Hegel, G. W. F. **Reason in History: A General Introduction to the Philosophy of History.** Translated by Robert Hartman. Indianapolis: Bobbs-Merrill, 1953.

Heilbroner, Robert. **The Limits of American Capitalism.** New York: Free Press, 1970.

--- **Between Capitalism and Socialism.** New York: Free Press, 1971.

Herberg, Will. **Protestant, Catholic, Jew.** New York: Doubleday, 1960.

Johnson, Ernest F., and Ackerman, J. E. **The Church as Employer, Money Raiser, and Investor.** New York: Harper and Row, 1959.

Johnson, Robert A., et al. **Critical Issues in Modern Religion.** Englewood Cliffs, N.J.: Prentice-Hall, 1973.

Lantinari, Vittorio. **The Religions of the Oppressed.** Translated by Lisa Sergio. New York: New American Library, 1965.

Lenski, Gerhard. **The Religious Factor: A Sociological Study of Religion's Impact on Politics, Economics, and Family Life.** Garden City, N.Y.: Doubleday, 1961.

Lichthein, George. **Marxism: An Historical and Critical Study.** New York: Harper Brothers, 1961.

--- **The Concept of Ideology and Other Essays.** New York: Harper Brothers, 1967.

--- **Imperialism.** New York: Harper Brothers, 1971.

Luckman, Thomas. **The Invisible Religion.** New York: Macmillan Co., 1967.

McBrien, Richard P. **Do We Need the Church?** New York and Evanston: Harper and Row Publishers, 1969.

Magdoff, H. **The Age of Imperialism. The Economics of U.S. Foreign Policy.** New York: Monthly Review Press, 1969.

Mannheim, Karl. **Ideology and Utopia.** New York: Harcourt, Brace, and World, 1936.

--- **Essays on the Sociology of Knowledge.** Edited by Paul Kecskemeti. New York: Oxford University Press, 1952.

--- **Essays on Sociology and Social Psychology.** Edited by Paul Kecskemeti. New York: Oxford University Press, 1953.

--- **Essays on the Sociology of Culture.** Edited by Ernest Manheim and Paul Kecskemeti. New York: Oxford University Press, 1956.

-- **From Karl Mannheim.** Edited by Kurt H. Wolff. New York: Oxford University Press, 1971.

Marcus, Herbert. **An Essay on Liberation.** Boston: Beacon Press, 1969.

Marx, Karl, and Engels, F. **On Religion.** New York: Schocken Books, 1964.

Merton, Robert K. **Social Theory and Social Structure.** Glencoe, Ill.: The Free Press, 1951.

Miguez-Bonino, Jose. **Doing Theology in a Revolutionary Situation.** Philadelphia: Fortress Press, 1975.

Miller, William Robert, ed. **The New Christianity.** New York: Delacorte Press, 1967.

Moberg, David O. **The Church as a Social Institution. (The Sociology of American Religion).** Englewood Cliffs, N.J.: Prentice-Hall, Inc., 1962.

Moltmann, Jurgen. **Religion, Revlution and the Future.** New York: Harper and Brothers, 1969.

Moodie, T. Dunbar. **The Rise of Afrikanerdom: Power, Apartheid and Afrikaner Civil Religion.** Berkeley: University of California Press, 1975.

Murdock, G.P. **Social Structure.** New York: Macmillan Company, 1940.

Newman, William M., ed. **The Social Meanings of Religion.** Chicago: Rand McNally College Publishing Company, 1974.

Niebuhr, Reinhold. **The Irony of American History.** New York: Charles Scribner's Sons, 1958.

--- **Pious and Secular America.** New York: Charles Scribner's Sons, 1958.

--- **Essays in Applied Christianity.** Selected and edited by D.B. Robertson. New York: World Publishing Co., 1959.

--- **Moral Man and Immoral Society.** New York and London: Charles Scribner's Sons, 1960.

--- **Faith and Politics.** Edited by Ronald H. Stone. New York: George Braziller, 1968.

Oden, Thomas. **Beyond Revolution.** Philadelphia: The Westminster Press, n.d.

Pascal, R., ed. **German Ideology.** New York: International Publishers, 1963.

Pope, Liston. **Millhands and Preachers.** New Haven: Yale University Press, 1942.

Porteous, Alvin C. **The Search for Christian Credibility. Explorations in Contemporary Belief.** Nashville and New York: Abingdon Press, 1971.

Redfield, Robert. **The Little Community: Peasant Society and Culture.** Chicago: Phoenix Books, 1969.

291

Roberts, J. Deotis. **Liberation and Reconciliation: A Black Theology.** Philadelphia: The Westminster Press, 1971.

Rodny, Walter. **How Europe Underdeveloped Africa.** Washington, D.C.: Howard University Press, 1974.

Roszak, Theodore. **The Making of a Counter Culture.** Garden City, N.Y.: Doubleday, 1969.

--- **Where the Wasteland Ends: Politics and Transcendence in Post-industrial Society.** Garden City, N.Y.: Doubleday, 1972.

Ruether, Rosemary. **Liberation Theology.** New York: Paulist Press, 1973.

Russell, Letty M. **Human Liberation in a Feminist Perspective-A Theology.** Philadelphia: The Westminster Press, 1974.

Snyder, Howard A. **The Problems of Wine Skins.** Downers Grove, Ill.: Inter Varsity Press, 1977.

Stark, Werner. **The Sociology of Knowledge: An Essay in Aid of a Deeper Understanding of the History of Ideas.** New York: Free Press, 1958.

Weber, Max. **Protestant Ethic and the Spirit of Capitalism.** Translated by Talcott Parson. New York: Charles Scribner's Sons, 1958.

Weber, Max. **The Sociology of Religion.** 4th ed. Boston: Beacon Press, 1963.

Wilkins, M. **The Emergence of Multinational Enterprise.** Cambridge, Mass.: Beacon Press, 1970.

Yinger, Milton J. **Religion in the Struggle for Power.** Durham, N.C.: Duke University Press, 1946.

--- **Sociology Looks at Religion.** New York: Macmillan Company, 1963.

--- **The Scientific Study of Religion.** New York: Macmillan Publishing Company, 1970.

Articles on Missions: Problems and Prospects

Allen, Daniel Von. "The Birth of Theology: Contextualization as the Dynamic Element in the Formation of New Testament Theology." **International Review of Mission** (1975): 38-55.

Arias, Mortimer. "Contextualization in Latin America." **Occasional Bulletin of Missionary Research Library** 2 (January 1978): 19-28.

Azariah, V.S. "Self Support: True or False?" **International Review of Mission** (1938): 361-371.

Baago, Kaj. "The Post Colonial Crisis of Missions." **International Review of Mission** (July 1966): 322-332.

Banks, Donald. "Causes of Friction Between Missionaries and Nationals." **Evangelical Missionary Quarterly** 12 (1976): 149-154.

Bates, Gerald E. "Mission and Cross Cultural Conflict." **Missiology** 5 (April 1977): 195-202.

Baum, Gregory. "The Jews, Faith and Ideology." **The Ecumenist** (July/August 1972): 71-77.

Bergquist, James A. "Christian Mission in Transition." Lecture presented at Overseas Ministries Study Center (OMSC), Ventnor, N.J., January 3, 1979.

Bronkema, Frederick. "A Look at **The Future of the Missionary Enterprise,** An IDOC International Documentation: Participation Project." **Occasional Bulletin of Missionary Research Library** (April 1977): 11-16.

Busia, K.A. "Has the Christian Faith Been Adequately Presented?" **International Review of Mission** (1961): 86-89.

Calkins, Harvey Reeves. "Foundation of Facts: The Ground of Self-Support." **International Review of Mission** (1923): 421-433.

Campbell, Richard. "Contextual Theology and Its Problems." **Study Encounter** 12 (1976): 11-25.

Capell, A. "One New Man: Success or Failure of Christian Mission." **International Review of Mission** (1961): 149-157.

Carman, John B., and Douglas, Ian H. "The Post-Colonial Crisis of Missions--Comments." **International Review of Mission** 55 (1966): 483-489.

Carr, Burgess. "The Mission of the Moratorium." **Occasional Bulletin of Missionary Research Library** 25 (March/April 1975).

Carvaldo, J.M. de. "Focus on Moratorium: The Dawning of Partnership." **AACC Bulletin** 9 (1975): 41-44.

Cassidy, Michael. "The Third Way." **International Review of Mission** (1974): 12-17.

Conn, Harvie. "Contextualization: Where Do We Begin?" **Issues for Christian Leaders** (January 1977).

Costas, Orlando. "Evangelism and the Gospel of Salvation." **International Review of Mission** 63 (1974).

Dayton, Edward R. "Current Trends in North American Protestant Missionaries Overseas." **Occasional Bulletin of Missionary Research Library** (April 1977): 2-7.

Diaz, Zwinglio. "Evangelism Among Europe's Masses." **International Review of Mission** (October 1977): 361-365.

Donalds, Kenneth G. "What's Wrong With Foreign Money for National Pastors?" **Evangelical Missionary Quarterly** 13 (1977): 19-25.

Droogers, André. "The Africanization of an Anthropologist's View." **Missiology** 5 (1977).

Efefe, Flonda. "Revolution in Theology." **AACC Bulletin** 5 (September-October 1975).

Empie, Paul C. "Dilemmas of World Confessional Grops With Respect to Engagement in Mission and Unity." **International Review of Mission** (1965): 157-170.

Evangelical Missionary Quarterly. Special Issue on Contextualization. 14 (January 1978).

Garcia, Samuel Ruiz. "The Incarnation of the Church in Indigenous Cultures." **Missiology** 1 (April 1973).

Garjardo, Joel. "Mutuality in Mission." **Occasional Bulletin Mission to the U.S.A.** (n.d.).

Carvie, A. E. "The Evangelical Faith and Other Religions." **International Review of Mission** (1933): 354-360.

Cascoyne, Cecil W. "Indigenous Christianity." **International Review of Mission** (1924): 722-732.

Gatu, John. "Missionary, Go Home!" **The Church Herald**, November 5, 1971.

George, Poikail J. "Racist Assumptions on the 19th Century Missionary Movement." **International Review of Mission** (1970): 271-284.

Glazik, Joseph. "The Meaning of the Place of Missiology Today." **International Review of Mission** 57 (October 1968): 459-467.

Goodsell, Fred Field. "Grand Strategy in World Mission." **International Review of Mission** (1946). 199-206.

Habergger, Howard J. "Moratorium: What is Behind the Call?" **The Mennonite**, November 18, 1975, p. 650-652.

Hayward, Victor E.W. "African Independent Church Movements." **International Review of Mission** (1963): 163-172.

Hopkins, Paul. "What is the Call for Moratorium and How Should We Respond?" **Concern** (November 1974): 13-15.

--- "Basic Duidelines for Determining (UPC) United Presbyterian Church Mission Participation in Africa. Program Agency, New York, n.d.

Jocz, Jakob. "Foreign Missions as a Theological Corrective." **International Review of Mission** 36 (1946): 256-262.

Johnston, George. "Should the Church Still Talk About Salvation?" **International Review of Mission** (April 1972): 46-60.

Kane, Herbert. "God and Caesar in Christian Mission." **Missiology** (October 1977): 411-425.

--- "Mission in Modern Milieu." **Evangelical Missions: Information Service** 4 (July 1978).

Kraft, Charles. "Can Anthropological Insight Assist Evangelical Theology?" **Christian Scholars Review** (1977): 165-202.

Latourette, K.S. "A Suggestion Towards a Reorientation of Mission Policy." **International Review of Mission** (1934): 405-413.

--- "Indigenous Christianity in the Light of History." **International Review of Mission** (1940): 430-440.

295

Latourette, K.S. "What Can We Expect in the World Mission?" **International Review of Mission** (1951): 141-148.

--- "The Light of History on Current Missionary Methods." **International Review of Mission** (1953): 137-143.

Loffler, Paul. "The Biblical Concept of Conversion." **Study Encounter** 1 (1965): 93-101.

Loram, T. "The 'Separatist Church Movement.'" **International Review of Mission** (1926): 476-482.

McGavran, D.A. "Christ, Christian America and Third World." **International Review of Mission** (1936): 116-129.

--- "New Methods for a New Age in Missions." **International Review of Mission** (1955): 394-403.

Macquarrie, J. "Christianity and Other Faiths." **Union Seminary Quarterly Review** (July/October 1965).

Makunike, Ezekiel C. "Evangelism and Cultural Context." **International Review of Mission** (1974): 57-64.

Margull, Jochen H. "Mission '70--More a Venture Than Ever." **International Review of Mission** (1971): 51-57.

Mbiti, J. "Church and State: A Neglected Element of Christianity." **Africa Theological Journal.** No. 5 (December 1972): 31-45.

Mediwaka, H.W. "Christianity and Nationalism." **International Review of Mission** (1924): 52-59.

Mey, Gerhard. "Theological Education in a Post-Moratorium World." **International Review of Mission** (1975): 187-192.

Morgan, E.R. "The Study of Church History in Relation to Christian Missions." **International Review of Mission** (1933):

Murray, J.S. "If Mission Help is Cut-off! What Should the Church Do?" **International Review of Mission** (1958): 417-427.

Nacpil, Emerito P. "Mission But Not Missionaries." **International Review of Mission** (1971): 356-362.

Oldham, J.H. "Christian Missions and African Labor." **International Review of Mission** (1920): 182-195.

Orchard, Ronald K. "The Future Role of Western Missionary Bodies in Christian World Mission." **International Review of Mission** 55 (1969): 258-269.

Pannell, William. "Evanelism and the Struggle for Power." **International Review of Mission** (1974): 201-212.

Parsons, Robert T. "The Missionary and the Cultures." **Internatio-nalReview of Mission** (1956). 161-168.

Ranson, Charles W. "The Christian World Mission in the Perspective of History--The End of an Era." **International Review of Mission** (1954): 381-389.

Ray, Eldon. "The Christian Missionary--Vanishing Species." **The Ecumenist** (July/August 1972): 77-80.

Rossman, Vern. "The Breaking of the Future: The Problem of Indigenization and Cultural Synthesis." **International Review of Mission** (1963): 129-143.

Setiloane, G.M. "The Missionary and His Task--at Edinburgh and Today." **International Review of Mission** (1970): 55-66.

Shenk, Wilbert. "Mission Agency and African Independent Churches." **International Review of Mission** (1974): 475-491.

Sider, Ronald J. "Evangelism, Salvation and Social Justice." **International Review of Mission** (1975): 252-267.

Thorne, John. "Focus on Moratorium: Becoming Prisoners of Hope." **AACC Bulletin** 9 (1975): 38-40.

Thorogood, Bernard. "Mature Relationships." **Council for World Missions** (London) (August 30, 1978).

Visser t'Hooft, W.A. "Evangelism in Neo-Pagan Situation." **International Review of Mission** 63 (January 1974): 81-86.

Webster, Douglas. "The Missionary Appeal Today." **International Review of Mission** (1958): 279-288.

Wilmore, Gayrand. "Black Theology: Its Significance for Christian Mission Today." **International Review of Mission** (1974): 211-231.

Winter, Ralph D. "The New Missions and the Mission of the Church." **International Review of Mission** (1971): 89-150.

Published Articles on Africa and Mission: Accommodation and Confrontation

Afigbo, A.E. "Christian Missions and Secular Authorities in South Eastern Nigeria From Colonial Times." **ODUMA** + (October 1973).

Anderson, G.H. "Christians in Dialogue with Men of Other Faiths." **Study Encounter** 3 (1967): 52-56.

Ayandele, E.A. "Traditional Rulers and Missionaries in Pre-Colonial West Africa." **TARIK** 3 (1969): 23-37.

Barrett, D. "AD 2000: 350 Million Christians in Africa." **International Review of Mission** (1974): 38-50.

Crane, W.H. "Indigenization in African Church." **International Review of Mission** 53 (1964): 408-422.

Curtin, Philip D. "Scientific Racism and British Theory of Empire." **Journal of the Historical Society of Nigeria** (December 1960): 40-51.

Echeruo, M.J.C. "The Relgious Culture of 19th Century Lagos." **West African Religion** 12 (1972): 16-25.

Egudu, R.N. "Nigerian Poets and Nigerian Traditional Religion." **West African Religion** 16 (1975): 1-6.

Ekechi, F.K. "Colonialism and Christianity in West Africa: The Igbo Case, 1900-1915." **Journal of African History** 12 (1969): 103-116.

--- "Traders, Missionaries and the Bombardment of Onitsha 1879-1880." **The Conch** 1-2 (1973): 61-81.

Ezeanya, S.N. "The Place of Supreme God in the Traditional Religion of the Igbo." **West African Religion** (May 1963).

--- "Christianity and African Traditional Religions." **West African Religion** 13/14 (September/December 1972): 32.

Flatt, Donald C. "The Cross-Cultural Interpretation of Religion in Africa." **Missiology** 1 (July 1973): 325-338.

Graw, E. "Missionary Policies as seen in the Work of Missions with the Evangelical Presbyterian Church in Ghana." In **Christianity in Tropical Africa**, Chapter 3. Edited by C.G. Baeta. London: Oxford University Press for the International Africa Institute, 1968.

Groves, C.P. "Missionary and Humanitarian Aspects of Imperialism 1876-1914." In **Colonialism in Africa 1870-1960,** vol. 1, pp. 462-496. Edited by L.H. Gann and P. Duignan. Cambridge: Cambridge University Press, 1966.

Horton, Robin. "African Conversion." **Africa** 41 (April 1971): 87-108.

Ifemesia, C.C. "The Civilizing Mission of 1841." **Journal of the Historical Society of Nigeria** 2 (1962): 291-310.

Ikenga-Metuh, Emefie E. "Igbo World View: A Premise for Christian and Traditional Religion Dialogue." **West African Religion.** Nos. 13 and 14 (September and December 1972).

Ilogu, Edmund. "The Biblical Idea of Partnership and Modern Missionary Task." **International Review of Mission** 44 (1955): 404-407.

--- "Problem of Indigenization in Nigeria." **International Review of Mission** 49 (1960): 167-182.

--- "Worship in Ibo Traditional Religion." **Numen: International Review for the History of Religion** 23 (1973): 229-238.

Isichei, Elizabeth. "Seven Varieties of Ambiguity: Some Patterns of Igbo Response to Christian Mission." **Journal of Religion in Africa** 3 (1970): 209-227.

Iwuagwu, A.O. "Chukwu: Towards a Definition of Igbo Traditional Religion." **West African Religion** 16 (1975): 26-34.

Kalu, O.U. "Peter Pan Syndrome: Church Aid and Selfhood in Africa." **Missiology** 3 (January 1975): 15-29.

--- "Traditionalization and Modern Evangelical Strategy in Nigeria." **West African Religion** 16 (1975): 23-31.

--- "Gods in Retreat: Models of Religious Change in Africa." **Journal of Religious Thought** 3 (1976): 20-31.

--- "Children in the Missionary Enterprise of the 19th Century." **The Calabar Historical Journal** (vol. 1, 1978).

Kiplagat, B.A. "Christianity and African Novelists." **International Review of Mission** 61 (1972): 130-143.

Luke, E.W. "The Quest for African Christian Theologies." **Ecumenical Review** 27 (July 1976): 258-269.

McKenzie, P.R. "Indigenization and Orthodoxy." **West African Religion** (July 1976): 55-60.

Mbiti, J. "Christianity and the Traditional Religion of Africa." **International Review of Mission** 59 (1970): 430-440.

Niles, D.T. "Christianity in a Non-Christian Environment." **The Student World** 47 (1954): 259-263.

--- "Some Binding Principles in Missionary Strategy." **The Student World** 48 (1955): 25-34.

Nwabara, S.N. "Christian Encounter with Indigenous Religion at Onitsha 1857-1885." **D'Etudes Africaines** 44 (1971): 589-601.

Olisa, M.S.O. "Taboos in Ibo Religion and Society." **West African Religion.** No. 11, NSUKKA (January 1972): 1-18.

Onyeidu, S.O. "Confession in the Traditional Religions of Africa." **West African Religion** 16 (1975).

Parratt, J.K. "Religious Change in Yoruba Society--A Test Case." **Journal of Religion in Africa** 2 (1969: 113-118.

Patterson, Patricia J., and Harris, Ruth M. "People in Mission: Towards Selfhood and Solidarity." **International Review of Mission** 64 (1975).

Paul, G. Hiebert. "Missions and Anthropology: A Love/Hate Relationship." **Missiology.**

Ponsi, Frank. "Contemporary Concepts of Mission." **Missiology** 6 (April 1978): 139-154.

Rossman, V. "The Breaking in of the Future: The Problem of Indigenization and Cultural Synthesis." **International Review of Mission** 52 (1963): 135.

Sawyer, H. "Christian Evangelistic Strategy in West Africa." **International Review of Mission** 54 (1965): 343-352.

Shelton, Austin J. "The Presence of the Withdrawn High-God in North Igbo Religious Belief and Worship." **Man** 65 (January 1965): 15-18.

Tasie, G.O.M. "Christian Awakening in West Africa 1914-1918: A Study in the Significance of Nature Agency." **West African Religion** 16 (1975): 32-42.

Turner, P. "The Wisdom of the Fathers and the Gospel of Christ: Some Notes on Christian Adaptation in Africa." **Journal of African Religion** 4 (1971): 45-68.

Udo, E.A. "The Missionary Scramble of Spheres of Influence in Eastern Nigeria 1900-1952." **Ikenga** 1/2 (1972): 22-36.

Wallace, Anthony F.C. "Revitalization Movements." Reprinted from **American Anthropologist** 58 (April 1956).

Walls, A.F. "Missionary Vocation and the Ministry: The First Generation." In **New Testament Christianity for Africa and the World,** pp. 144-150. Edited by M.E. Glasswell and Fashole Luke. London: SPCK, 1974.

Westermann, Diedrich. "The Value of the African's Past." **International Review of Mission** (1926): 418-437.

Wilson, Brian. "An Analysis of Sect Development." **American Sociological Review** 24 (1954): 3-15.

Dictionaries

Brauer, Jerald C., ed. **The Westminster Dictionary of Church History.** Philadelphia: Westminster Press, n.d.

Coxill, H. Wakelin, ed. **World Christian Handbook 1962 Edition.** London: World Dominion Press, 1962.

Dayton, Edward R., ed. **Mission Handbook: North American Protestant Ministries Overseas.** California: MARC Press, 1976.

Douglas, J.D., ed. **The New International Dictionary of Christian Church.** Grand Rapids, Mich.: Zondervan, 1974.

Faris, Robert E.L. **Handbook of Modern Sociology.** Chicago: Rand McNally & Co., 1964.

Gould, Julius, and Kolb, William, eds. **A Dictionary of the Social Sciences.** New York: The Free Press of Glencoe, 1964.

Hyams, Edward. **A Dictionary of Modern Revolution.** New York: Taplinger Publishing Co., 1973.

Martin, David, ed. **Sociology: Fifty Key Words.** Richmond, Va.: John Knox Press, 1970.

Neill, Stephen; Anderson, G.H.; and Goodwin, J., eds. **Concise Dictionary of the Christian World Mission.** Nashville and New York: Abingdon Press, 1971.

Weiner, Philip P., ed. **Dictionary of the History of Ideas.** Vols. 1-4. New York: Charles Scribner's Sons, 1973.

Encyclopedias

Dwight, Henry O.; Tupper, Allen H.; and Bliss, Edwin R., eds. **The Encyclopedia of Missions: Descriptive, Historical, Biographical, Statistical.** 2nd ed. New York and London: Funk & Wagnalls Co., 1904.

Edwards, Paul, ed. **The Encyclopedia of Philosophy.** Vols. 1-4. New York: The Macmillan Co. and The Free Press, 1967.

The Encyclopedia Americana. International Edition. Vols. 15-18. New York: Americana Co., 1975.

Encyclopedia Britannica. Vols. 12-14. London: William Benton Publishers, 1971.

Freitag, Anton, et al. **The Twentieth Century Atlas of the Christian World.** New York: Hawthorn Books, Inc., 1963.

International Encyclopedia of the Social Sciences. Vols. 8-9. New York: The Free Press, 1968.

Ph. D. Dissertations (Unpublished)

Hart, John William. "Topia and Utopia in Colombia and Peru: The Theory and Practice of Camilo Torres and Gustavo Gutierrez in Their Historical Context." Union Theological Seminary, New York, 1978.

Jensen, Maud Keisler. "The Missionary Motif in the Theology of Emil Brunner and Its Relation to Specific Doctrines." Graduate School, Drew University, 1978.

Njoya, Timothy. "The Dynamics of change in African Christianity." Princeton Theological Seminary, 1976.

Park, Seong Mo. "Reinhold Niebuhr's Perspective on Marxism." Graduate School, Drew University, 1976.

Poitras, E. Whitney. "H. Richard Niebuhr and the Christian Missionary Witness." Graduate School, Drew University, 1966.

Stonesby, Ella V. "The Sociology of Urban Protestantism According to Harlan Paul Douglass." Graduate School, Drew University, 1976.

Thompson, Litchfield O'Brien. "Recurring Ideological Themes in the Sociology of Black Nationalism." University of Oregon, 1975.

INDEX

312